D1035007

GV
1052   Smith
.U6   A social history
S6   of the bicycle, its
        early life and times
        in America
Date Due

OCT 9 73			
MAR 1 1 '74			
AUG 18 76			
MAY 2 '78			

0165   00 770293   01 4   (IC=1)
SMITH, ROBERT A.
A SOCIAL HISTORY OF\N AMERICA.
(B) [1972 GV1052.U6S6 $9.95

Onondaga Community College

Syracuse, New York

PRINTED IN U S A.

A SOCIAL HISTORY
OF THE

Its Early Life
and Times in America

by

ROBERT A. SMITH - *1918 -*

American Heritage Press

A Division of McGraw-Hill Book Company
New York   St. Louis   San Francisco   Düsseldorf
London   Mexico   Sydney   Toronto

Book design by Elaine Gongora

This book was set in Patina by University Graphics, Inc.,
printed by Halliday Lithographers, and bound by Book Press.

Copyright © 1972 by Robert A. Smith.
All rights reserved. Printed in the United States of America.
No part of this publication may be reproduced,
stored in a retrieval system, or transmitted, in any form
or by any means, electronic, mechanical, photocopying,
recording, or otherwise, without the prior
written permission of the publisher.

123456789HABP798765432

Library of Congress Cataloging in Publication Data

Smith, Robert A   date
  A social history of the bicycle.

  Bibliography: p.
  1. Cycling—United States—History. I. Title.
GV1052.U6S6   796.6   72-3733
ISBN 0-07-058457-5

This book is dedicated to
Pauline and Floyd Smith
as partial repayment

Contents

Preface

Ten years ago I was scanning microfilm copies of the *Minneapolis Tribune* in search of information regarding the iron-mining industry of the Mesabi Range. When I reached the decade of the 1890's I came upon material unique in my experience as a researcher—not just pages but entire sections of each newspaper were devoted to bicycle news. Curiosity overcame my dedication to mining and I began reading pages containing information about the bicycle, how it was constructed, experiments with different gear systems, the controversy over costuming, and the nationwide adulation of bicycle racers, or "cracks" as they were called.

As a youngster I had raised a cracking tenor to support my father's rendition of "Daisy, Daisy, give me your answer do . . ." and had heard casual comments to the effect that Americans had once been bicycle crazy. The references I encountered in the *Tribune* conjured up visions of young men, mustaches matching the handlebars of their machines, racing through the streets of sleepy villages and towns, scattering pedestrians, terrifying horses, and being pursued in turn by packs of yapping hounds. But at the time I was busy with other things, so I drew the blind on this brief glimpse of bygone America and went on with the work at hand.

Three years ago I raised the blind again and took a longer look at the Gay Nineties and the bicycle, prepared to maintain the frivolous attitude that generally characterizes our approach to the era of the Beef Trust Chorus, Diamond Jim Brady, and "Jawn L." Sullivan. And indeed, some facets of the bicycle mania of the 1890's seem rather inane to us today. The bitter conflicts over proper costume and over the moral aspects of cycling, the complaints of saloonkeepers who saw business lost in the name of good training, and the passion for testing both the machine and the human body in endurance contests make us smile.

Yet slowly my amusement was replaced by astonishment as I discovered the impact of the bicycle on American life, an influence far transcending its use for mere sport. Although far from definitive in treatment, this book tries to describe some of this influence and impact, especially in the areas of technological advances and alterations of the transportation system.

Americans transferred much of their love for the horse to the bicycle, they wrote poems in praise of the "steel steed," they petted and pampered it, they damned it when it balked and they adored it when it carried them swiftly through the countryside. As one man put it, for a time all America was divided into two classes of people—those who rode the bicycle and those who did not.

Look at the joy and exhilaration on the face of a child today who is riding his new bicycle for the first time. And then remember that as far as the bicycle was concerned, we were all children in the Gay Nineties.

Acknowledgments

It is obvious that few persons can write history without relying on the assistance of the many people whose profession it is to aid in resurrecting the past. To those generous people must be added still others who gave their time, the benefit of their knowledge, and their advice to help translate the idea from the mind to the manuscript.

It is a cliché that any work owes much to people who are anonymous for the most part, but it must be repeated with respect to this volume. To those individuals in the Library of Congress, the Minnesota Historical Society, the University of Minnesota Library, the Library of the University of California at Riverside, the Riverside Public Library, and the Library at California State College at San Fernando go my heartfelt thanks for the services rendered.

I wish also to express my gratitude to members of the library at California State College at San Bernardino, Miss Jeanette Bernthaler, Mrs. Frances Ekaitis, and Mr. John Tibbals. With them must be placed Mr. Wayne Wilbank of the Audio-Visual Department.

I am indebted to Mr. Andrew Stephenson of the Riverside Public Library for special assistance and to Mr. Donald Ward of the University of California at Riverside. Mr. Earle H. Simpson of Pasadena, California, supplied information on the Pasadena Cycleway, as did Mr. Dennis Alward of the Pasadena Public Library. Miss Elizabeth Haney of the Los Angeles County Library was helpful, and I am grateful to Mr. David Shapiro of the Title Insurance and Trust Company for making material available to me. Mr. Joseph L. Hart of the League of American Wheelmen generously provided me with information on cycling, past and present, as did the Bicycle Institute of America. In addition, the Bicycle Institute graciously granted the use of their pictorial material, including the cards that begin each chapter of this book.

To my friend and former colleague, Dean George McMichael of the California State College at Hayward, goes a particular expression of my appreciation for reading the manuscript and thereby saving me from many a literary *faux pas*. The book has benefited enormously from his suggestions and advice. I also want to thank Barbara Leish, who edited this volume and improved it considerably.

To Mrs. Penny Jones, who typed the final copy and unraveled the mysteries of the working manuscript, go my special thanks.

It goes without saying that none of the persons above are responsible for the errors in the book—those are mine alone.

CHAPTER 1

"Hurrah, Hurrah, for the Merry Wheel"

THE EARLY DEVELOPMENT OF THE BICYCLE

BICYCLE INSTITUTE OF AMERICA

SETTING THE PACE

When the English poet Thomas Gray sat in the churchyard at Stoke Poges, four miles south of Windsor, and searched for the opening lines of his famous "Elegy," it is doubtful whether he let his eyes wander to the stained-glass window above his head. Had he done so he would have seen, among the colored lozenges, a male figure astride an awkward contraption consisting of a saddle connecting two cumbersome wheels.

The window dates from 1642. Two and a half centuries later the machine the glazier had outlined was to be denounced as the invention of Satan himself, at best a snare for the weak and willful, at worst an engine for human destruction. On a Sunday morning in 1896 a Baltimore preacher thundered from his pulpit:

These bladder-wheeled bicycles are diabolical devices of the demon of darkness. They are contrivances to trap the feet of the unwary and skin the nose of the innocent. They are full of guile and deceit. When you think you have broken one to ride and subdued its wild and Satanic nature, behold it bucketh you off in the road and teareth a great hole in your pants. Look not on the bike when it bloweth upon its wheels, for at last it bucketh like a bronco and hurteth like thunder. Who has skinned legs? Who has a bloody nose? Who has ripped breeches? They that dally along with the bicycle.[1]

The preacher was not alone: the bicycle was once regarded as sheer evil by many of America's men of God. They assaulted the machine from pulpits, they swatted it with newspaper columns, and they swooped down on it with street corner sermons. It was altogether a strange attitude.

Not everyone agreed with the preachers. The *Detroit Tribune* called the perfection of the bicycle the greatest event of the nineteenth century. In Washington, D.C., the Bureau of the Census stated solemnly that "few articles ever used by man have created so great a revolution in social conditions as the bicycle."[2] And that judgment stood despite the fact that the Linotype machine, the incandescent electric lamp, the telephone, and a multitude of other inventions were all on the patent books.

One thing cannot be denied, however: The development and distribution of the safety bicycle inspired a most phenomenal outburst of enthusiasm from Americans. This fervor started with fanaticism at one end and stretched to mania on the other. Defenders around the turn of the century called it a scientific angel that carried the cyclist into the very presence of the Deity. The friends of the bicycle insisted it was the cure-all for what ailed the human race, those who sold the machine and its accessories cherished it as the mother lode, lovers extolled it as the best means to elude parental surveillance, and the police regarded it as a positive contribution to the job of law enforcement.

True, there were some whose businesses were threatened by the bicycle. Saloonkeepers actively disliked the new distraction, piano salesmen deplored its coming, keepers of livery stables hurled imprecations at it. Investors who owned stock in the street railway systems cursed the bicycle. But the men who established the cycle factories smiled as they watched the machines roll off the assembly lines and counted the profits.

The social, moral, and economic debate over the bicycle meant nothing to the turn-of-the-century American child who stood, wide-eyed with rapture, on a Christmas morning and admired the marvel of shining spokes and glistening enamel under the tree. The "bike" was truly an awe-inspiring thing, a machine that at once created childhood pride in the new owner and childhood envy in those unfortunate youngsters who remained earthbound—lesser mortals from that moment on. There the bicycle stood, gleaming, inviting, and ready to take its new master to unknown places for unimagined adventures.

The child to whom the cycle beckoned could not be aware that he was looking at the most recent model of an evolutionary technological process that had had its rude beginnings during the century before. Nor could he know that many problems of design and construction had had to be met and solved before he would be able to roll away down the street.

It's difficult to pinpoint exactly where and when it all began. Some researchers believe that suggestions of bicycles can be seen in the tombs of Egypt and among the frescoes of Pompeii. The origin is debatable, and if the ancestor of the bicycle existed in remote antiquity, the succeeding centuries were not kind to its memory. The only certainty is the uncertainty of knowing who first addressed himself to the task of developing a man-propelled, two-wheeled vehicle.

Nevertheless, somebody did. In 1665, twenty-three years after the Stoke Poges window was set in place, the English diarist John Evelyn visited friends near Epsom and found them making a "wheele for one to run races in." Early devotees of the "wheele for one to run races in" were grappling with problems of basic design: how many wheels, how should they be placed with reference to each other, how joined, and by what?

About one hundred years later a Frenchman, M. de Sivrac, came out with his own version of a bicycle, a vehicle with two wheels joined by a wooden frame resembling the body of a horse. This ungainly machine actually bore a saddle for the rider, was propelled by the feet, and was demonstrated before Marie Antoinette in the courtyard of the palace of Versailles. There is no evidence that the vehicle ever became popular with Parisians, and only the *aristos* wheeled along in the twilight of their era. The Bastille fell and so did Louis XVI before another Frenchman, the photography pioneer Nicéphore Niepce, came out with his own version of the bicycle at the beginning of the nineteenth century. He electrified strollers in the Luxembourg Gardens as he zipped by on the *célérifère* ("celeripede" or "fast feet" to the English)—just two wheels fastened together by a beam. The rider—better called a "runner"—straddled the beam, rested his hands on a crossbar, and propelled the machine by running along. In all, it was not a very promising affair, because it could not be steered properly and had to be pushed rather than pedaled. The French soon lost interest in Niepce's private amusement.

But at about the same time, eastward along the Rhine River, Baron Karl von Drais de Saverbrun, Master of the Woods and Forests to the Duke of Baden, was at work. The baron was trying to figure out a way to make his task easier, and the result was an improvement on the *célérifère* that came to be called a *draisine*. Old illustrations show that the baron's chief improvement was a fork for the front wheel, which permitted the machine to be steered by handlebars. The rider still perched on a saddle and propelled the machine by running, except downhill. Then he merely lifted his feet and enjoyed the thrill of a downward coast, probably the fastest speed achieved by a horseless human up to that time.

In 1816 Baron von Drais described his machine as having the following capabilities:

> 1. that on a well-maintained post-road it will travel uphill as fast as a man can walk; 2. on a plain, even after a heavy rain, it will go 6 to 7 miles an hour, which is as swift as a courier; 3. when roads are dry and firm it runs on a plain at the rate of 8 to 9 miles an hour which is equal to a horse's gallop; 4. on descent it equals a horse at full speed.[3]

In the last two advantages he hit upon one of the primary attractions of the machine, its speed, and pointed out the biggest drawback, the lack of good roads. In the years to come the mania for speed and good roads would grow fantastically.

Early nineteenth-century patent laws were honored largely in the breach: Baron von Drais's machine was copied by others in France and England, including Dennis Johnson, a London coachmaker, who added an adjustable saddle and an armrest to minimize the strain on the forearms. These refinements gave birth to the age of the hobbyhorse, or the "swift-walker." For a while the prevailing English name was the dandy horse, an apt bit of nomenclature since the machines were so expensive that few could afford them except the Regency bucks who clustered around King George IV. The streets of London were already too crowded and too rough to permit the new vehicles to be used to the best advantage. The country roads and lanes were better suited to it, and dandy horses could be seen in the evenings, rolling between Ipswich and Whitton. In terms of design the machine was a long way from the solutions of later years; but various men were already devoting themselves to the task of harnessing the power of the rider's legs to the wheels of the hobbyhorse.

By 1821 Louis Gompertz developed a machine that could be propelled by the action of both the feet and the arms—a four-cyclindered motor, so to speak. By 1830 the *draisine* had been so much improved that the French government purchased some for its rural postmen, but the rigors of the winter caused the trial to be suspended. Six years later Kirkpatrick McMillan of Courthill, Scotland, made himself a vehicle whose rear wheel was rotated by a system of cranks and levers; for the first time the man on the *draisine* could lift his feet entirely off the ground and still propel himself. Shortly thereafter Gavin Dalzell, a cooper from Lanark-shire, Scotland, constructed a similar vehicle. Both machines were made only for the use of their owners, and there was little basic improvement in the cumbersome design. For the most part, these and other precursors of the bicycle remained obscure novelties.

Americans were not unacquainted with these new means of motion. Soon after Baron von Drais offered his cure for the ills of walking, the *draisine* made its appearance in the United States. It was an immediate hit with young men, especially in New York City, where the swains frequented the hill from Chatham Street to City Hall Park. But, as in Europe, the vehicle was a passing fancy, and few men kept it up, no matter how challenging the hill or how admiring the maidenly glances. The *draisine* slid into its American oblivion in two or three years.

The big problem in cycle design—a problem that had been attacked by McMillan and Dalzell—was to get the rider's feet completely off the ground so they could be used more efficiently. Man was not going very far or very fast so long as he had to propel himself by stretching for the surface of the road with the tips of his toes to nudge the machine along. The solution finally came, although the identity of the person responsible for it is subject to dispute. Some contend that the first man to put cranks on the front wheel and pedals on the cranks was a French carriage maker named Ernest Michaux, who turned the trick in 1855. Many Frenchmen defended Michaux's claim to priority, and a generation later they erected a monument to his memory in Bar-le-Duc, France.

Monument or no monument, other historians maintain that the cranks were actually the invention of Pierre Lallement, who saw an early model near Nancy and perfected the crank-pedal arrangement later when he went to Paris to work for Michaux. The outcome, regardless of who invented it, was called the velocipede. It consisted of two iron-tired wooden wheels mounted one behind the other, a front fork and handle-bars to permit steering, pedals on the axle of the front wheel, and a saddle fastened to the wooden frame with a steel spring. The spring was not very effective in absorbing the bumps, and the machine deserved its popular name of boneshaker. Although not yet called a bicycle, to all intents and purposes it was one.

Lallement mastered the twin arts of keeping the machine upright and in motion, a feat once thought to be impossible, and allegedly rode his mount down Paris' Boulevard St. Martin in 1863. Two years later he demonstrated it at the Paris Exhibition, but Lallement seems to have thought so little of his invention that he failed to patent it. In 1866 he migrated to the United States to make his fortune.

Lallement arrived in Ansonia, Connecticut, bringing with him the parts of two disassembled boneshakers, and that fall he cycled down the shady streets and across the bridge leading to the nearby town of Birmingham. He did not know it, but he was on a collision course, destined to take the first of the many "headers" cyclists would suffer in the United States. Breezing along the country road, the Frenchman breasted the rise of a hill and flashed down the lane, dead on target with a wagon driven by two gentlemen who looked back in terror at the apparition descending upon them. Without brakes, another problem yet unsolved, Lallement swept down the incline, his pedals blurring in the sunlight because he had "lost" them, as the saying went. The wagoners whipped up their horse in hope of outrunning the onrushing boneshaker, but the speed that was later the boast of so many Americans proved too much for the animal. Thanks to Baron von Drais's steering mechanism, Lallement was able to swerve aside at the last moment, but in doing so his front wheel came crosswise and he sailed over his handlebars into an adjacent ditch.

Such near catastrophe did not deter Lallement, however. The next year he rode a boneshaker through the New Haven streets onto the village green, and tradition has it that he was arrested twice for frightening horses. Lallement was possibly the first, but certainly not the last, to run afoul of the law for terrifying horses.

The important thing was that the basic bicycle was at hand and the word was "Go!" In May, 1886, Lallement and James Carrol became business partners, but unfortunately neither had the capital to manufacture the machines, and the Frenchman eventually gave over the venture and went back to France and his old employer, Ernest Michaux.

When Lallement returned to Paris he left behind a mounting fever called the velocipede craze, although it is difficult for later generations to understand how people could get heated up over an unwieldy machine that weighed almost a hundred and fifty pounds. One man, rhapsodizing over the vehicle, said it was "so perfect in its propelling power, so easy to ride, so swift, that it seems impossible for history to repeat itself with regard to the present mania."[4] Schools of instruction sprang up all over the country. New York was alleged to have had five thousand riders, not just silly faddists but sober, substantial men like Charles Dana, publisher of the *New York Sun*. In Brooklyn the preacher Henry Ward Beecher shook back his long locks and predicted that soon a thousand velocipedes would bring his congregation to church. He comforted his hearers that such activity would not violate the commandment against profaning the Lord's Day, but as we have noted, other ministers were not so sure.

However, by 1869 the fever was beginning to subside, and the heavy velocipede began sinking into the same oblivion that had overtaken the *draisine*, urged into darkness by whispers of ruptures induced by cycling over rough roads. By 1870 few machines were to be found outside junk piles. There were still too many design problems to be cleared up before the bicycle could become popular. For instance, the wooden bodies and wheels were neither very light nor structurally dependable. So the inventors went back to work.

Most of the subsequent alterations of the vehicle were in the direction of creating the old high-wheeler called the "ordinary," which was the first machine popularly designated as a bicycle. In May, 1869, the English firm of Reynolds and May showed its "Phantom" model at the Crystal Palace in London, and for the first time the world saw a high-wheeler made of iron instead of wood and equipped with rubber tires. Although awkward-looking today, it was a picture of grace itself when compared with Lallement's machine.

The experimenting went on. Rubber-covered pedals replaced metal ones in 1871, thus permitting the cyclist to use the ball of his foot rather than the instep. Steel rims were also perfected, and Parisian designers began to increase the size of the front wheel and reduce the diameter of the rear one. By 1876 the ordinary was ready for the New World, and the New World was waiting.

Americans celebrated their centennial that summer with a gigantic display in Philadelphia, an exposition that set the style for succeeding celebrations in the nation. All the sunny summer long, thousands of people ate ice cream, goggled at the mighty Corliss Steam Engine, shook their heads in amazement over the monster cannon produced by the Krupp factories in Germany, and stood transfixed by the first ordinary put on public display in the country. The enthusiastic response to the ordinary began to create a market for the bicycle. A St. Louis man bought the exhibition model that had been demonstrated by John Keen in Philadelphia, and took it home to put on display as one of the new wonders of the world. The firm of Timms and Lawford of Baltimore began to import English bicycles.

As matters turned out, the most important individual who viewed the bicycle at the Philadelphia fair was Albert A. Pope, a former Civil War officer from Boston. Pope fell in love with the high-wheeler. The following year he inspected the cycle industry in England and came back convinced that the machine had a promising future. In 1877 he converted the Pope Manufacturing Company from shoes and small mechanical parts to an import house for bicycles, and he opened a riding school.

Then Pope did something of greater significance. He commissioned a mechanic named Atwell to build a bicycle, using the English models as designs. The result was a seventy-pound machine, costing $313, which was allegedly the first real bicycle made in America. It launched Pope's career as the father of the industry.

Years later Pope's photograph shows him to be the essence of a model tycoon, beard spade-trimmed and shot with gray, with the bold and confident look befitting a former soldier and a man who had the foresight to get in on the ground floor of the bicycle industry. In 1878 he began manufacturing the "Columbia" model ordinary. This, according to Charles E. Pratt, one of the earliest cyclists and an ardent admirer of Pope, represented the dawn of the bicycle age in the United States. However, there were still problems to be solved before cycling could become truly popular.

First of all, while Pope was occupying himself with organizing his company, holders of ancient bicycle patents dusted them off and entered the courts. These men had acquired their rights back in the days of the velocipede and had quietly collected royalties of from two dollars to thirty dollars on every machine constructed. If the ordinary ever became popular, these inventors stood to make a great amount of money without turning their hands. But Albert Pope and those who followed him were too shrewd to be held to ransom. They bought rights where they could and in other cases went to court. Generally they were successful at law and provided an example for the automobile industry, which underwent a similar round of patent suits before it really got into production. Finally the way was clear for Pope to begin the expanded production of ordinaries.

At this point a different question presented itself—how to get the general public to accept the cycle. Pratt, who wrote the first handbook for cyclers, *The American Bicycler*, in 1881 and who might be allowed a little bias, maintained that bicycle riders simply had no rights on the nation's streets and roads. With his eye fixed firmly on the main chance, Albert Pope rushed in and underwrote the legal expenses for much of the litigation that was necessary before the riders could take their "birotate chariots," a term Pratt coined, into parks and on the highways.

As a part of the publicity campaign Pope also carried his message of cycle-induced health and happiness to all who would listen or read, in the effort to promote the cycle as a machine for the improvement of humanity. This was done in the face of attacks from physicians who turned on the high-wheeled bicycle as they had once tried to destroy the velocipede. The bicycle was declared to be almost as dangerous as a fused mortar shell, and the physiological consequences of riding the device were pointed to with a rising note of alarm. In response Pope offered prizes to doctors who published the best articles defending bicycle riding as a positive aid to good health. He was not disappointed in the results.

But Pope and other bicycle manufacturers, such as A. H. Overman of the Victor Bicycle Company, were not willing to depend on doctors or medical publications alone. These men gave their patronage to specialized publications such as the *Bicycle World* and *The Wheel*. They paid for the distribution of cycling handbooks and gave away thousands of copies of Pratt's *American Bicycler*, which partially explains the latter's laudatory articles about Colonel Pope. With sixty thousand dollars, these businessmen did more. They secured the editorial services of S. S. McClure and underwrote the publication of a monthly magazine, *Wheelman* (later changed to *Outing*), one of the most important sporting publications ever published in the United States.

Of course, it would do these manufacturers little good to make bicycles or create a favorable climate of opinion if the machines could not be distributed efficiently. Albert Pope saw the merchandising aspect of cycling with considerable clarity. It was he who conceived the idea of a national network of bicycle agencies to retail the "Columbia" at a fixed price, regardless of whether the sale was made in Maine or California.

In creating the idea of independent agencies and a set price regardless of freight costs, Pope became the founder of marketing techniques that saw their grandest flowering in the sales of automobiles.

His work did not stop there. He was instrumental in founding one of the first of the many cycling clubs that sprang up throughout the nation. It was only fitting that Pope and his two brothers, Edward and Arthur, became the first officers of the group, organized in Boston. Soon other clubs blossomed all over the Eastern United States, then spread westward to San Francisco.

Exactly what kind of a machine was it that engendered so much praise and scorn, so much acrimony and sulfur-and-brimstone preaching? What sort of a device was Albert Pope promoting? The ordinary of precious memory weighed from thirty to sixty pounds and was made of tubular steel, mostly imported from England. It had a front wheel that varied in diameter from forty to sixty inches, behind which was a smaller "trailer wheel" to add stability. The two were connected by a curving frame on top of which was the saddle for the rider. The cranks and pedals were a part of the axle of the front wheel, as in a child's tricycle, and the rider sat virtually atop the pedals. This placement shifted the center of gravity so far forward that the rider was apt to take a header at the slightest lapse of attention or encounter with a small rock.

When a person purchased an ordinary it was literally fitted to him, since the diameter of the front wheel had to conform to the length of the cyclist's legs. If the front wheel was too small, the rider crouched over the handlebars like a jockey on a racing horse, and if the wheel was too large he could not reach the pedals. In spite of the reasonableness of such fittings, the passion for big front wheels seethed in the early days, no doubt because the absence of gearing on the bicycle made some cyclists prefer the larger diameter for the added speed. In fact, the short-legged secretary of one of the early clubs had his shoe soles built thicker so he could reach the pedals of a fifty-inch wheel.

Both wheels of the ordinary had steel rims and spokes, and each had a solid-rubber tire, the cost of which was sometimes equal to that of the rest of the machine. The tires were shrunk on the rims or sometimes held on by a wire or rope through the center. These tires were more comfortable than the iron tires of the boneshaker, but they still left much to be desired as far as comfort was concerned. Naturally the larger the diameter of the tire, the greater the ease in riding, but the bigger solids had an alarming tendency to twist off the rims when rounding corners, leaving the rider tangled in the bent tubing and writhing spokes of a machine that had cost him over a hundred dollars. At such times the unfortunate man was likely to forget the arguments advanced by one cyclist that red rubber tires looked best but gray rubber showed the dust less.

Truth to tell, it made little difference whether the tires were large or small, red rubber or gray, since the streets of the nation were not suitable for extended cycling. For that reason cyclists turned almost immediately to lobbying for the improvement of city streets and country roads. As might be expected, Colonel Pope was in the foreground, raising his voice before those political agencies that supervised the repair and maintenance of streets and highways.

Another obstacle in the infancy of American cycling was one of the most serious encountered. This was the multitude of horses, which until then had endured no real competition in the use of the streets and highways. It seems that horses instinctively recognized the enemy when they saw it come down the street, its spokes flashing in the sun, and frequently they tried to run away from the thing they neither knew nor wanted to understand. As a result, the horse-driving public was in a fury, and it lashed back with the law. Most of the suits that Pope fought so sedulously in the early days were against ordinances restricting cyclists in the name of the horse.

In 1883 Pratt suggested what may be considered one of the first sets of road signals ever devised in this country. The driver's upraised arm indicated that the oncoming cyclist should use caution in passing; the arm raised two or more times in a pumping motion meant the horse had the bit in his teeth and the cyclist should dismount immediately. But mounting and dismounting from an ordinary was not that easy, and if these road rules were satisfactory to Pratt, it is unlikely that most cyclists agreed. Getting on a bicycle meant running alongside the ordinary until it got up speed and then putting the left foot on the mounting bar that was welded to the frame. Hoping that momentum would continue to carry the bicycle forward, the cyclist next vaulted into the saddle and frantically tried to get his feet on the pedals, which all this time were turning with the front wheel. Altogether, this was not the kind of performance one liked to repeat every hundred yards or so. Consequently, the feud between those who rode bicycles and those who drove horses was not quickly resolved.

The fact was that cyclers thought the horse was passé. In *The American*

Bicycler Pratt quoted an unidentified author who stated that the horse had been a "blindly cherished obstacle" to human progress. Man, faced with the problem of moving the greatest distance in the least time and at the lowest cost, was mistakenly clinging to the horse when something better was at hand.

But the association between "horse" and "riding" was too strong to break entirely, and Pratt himself described the bicycle in terms distinctly equine. "It runs, it leaps, it rears and writhes," he wrote in 1883, "and shies and kicks; it is in infinite restless motion, like a bundle of sensitive nerves; it is beneath its rider like a thing of life, without the resistance and uncertainty of an uncontrolled will."[5] On another occasion he wrote that the machine was an "always bridled horse" that required no harness and was always ready to do its master's bidding.

Another American, after extolling the virtues of riding a bicycle, wrote, "No wonder, then, that the bicyclist should feel for his machine a tender sense of gratitude for the service it has done him, resembling in kind the sentiments an Arab feels for his horse. . . ." And with a perfectly straight face, *Wheelman* printed:

> Hurrah, hurrah, for the merry wheel,
> With tires of rubber and spokes of steel;
> We seem to fly on the airy steeds
> With eagle's flight in silence speed.[6]

The horsemen said "Bushwah!" to all this and continued their assault.

Obviously Colonel Pope—he was seldom called anything else—could not carry the full responsibility for defending the birotate chariot against the onslaught of irate teamsters and cab drivers who were spending a lot of time sawing the reins of runaways. It would take some kind of an organization to bring maximum effort to bear in behalf of cyclers. And this was at hand in the form of one of the most vigorous pressure groups in an era when pressure groups abounded. In 1880, while Pope and those who followed his lead were increasing their production of the ordinary, the League of American Wheelmen was organized to "promote the general interests of bicycling, to ascertain, defend, and protect the rights of wheelmen, and to encourage and facilitate touring." From the very beginning the league—or the LAW, as it was usually referred to—came on the stage breathing fire and with its fists clenched to do battle. Not the least of its functions was overseeing bicycle racing and exerting its influence in behalf of better roads.

Enrollment in the league was limited at first. The basic price of between

$100 and $150 represented about four months' pay for the average factory hand, and it can be taken as a sign of America's growing wealth that so many people could afford cycles at all. But the quality of membership was high, if one is to believe a writer named Edward Howland. He told Americans that the cycler was a man of exceptional quality and not the blithering idiot so many horsemen accused him of being. With obvious conviction, he wrote in *Harper's:*

> The wheelman being generally a man of enterprise, as he shows by the fact of becoming a bicycler, he is not a person to whom routine forms are an impassible barrier; and therefore the bicyclers collectively form inevitably a body of persons to whom the public can legitimately look with confidence, for the future, as men ready to examine the claims for consideration of the new, while not contemptuously disregarding the old; that is, a class, who infused with the best spirit of the times, can naturally be counted upon to make themselves felt as a power in the future, to be counted upon the side of the right in the work before us for the further development of the possibilities of life.[7]

Anyone who has the tenacity to wade through such befuddled prose will immediately get the idea that the author thought bicyclers were paragons, even though events would eventually prove that they were not.

Nevertheless, neither technology nor public relations had yet advanced to the point where they could bring about the widespread acceptance of the bicycle. The onset of the real bicycle craze in the United States, as well as the rest of the world, awaited the advancement called the "safety bicycle." It came quickly. The ordinary was not more than ten years old when its replacement rolled onto the streets. In the new version the diameter of the front wheel was reduced and the fork was slanted forward a little, a modification which moved the saddle farther back and reduced the possibility of headers. The "dwarf ordinary" appeared in 1883, but the real breakthrough came in 1884, when J. K. Starley made the "Rover" at the Coventry Machinists Company in England.

The "Rover" was an ugly and unwieldy machine, but it combined all the essential components of the safety bicycle and so started the Western world on its first mass adventure with speed. The vehicle had two wheels of approximately the same size and was propelled by an endless chain running over the pedal-driven sprocket and then over the gears at the axle of the rear wheel. The saddle was mounted near the center of the frame, and the steering mechanism was connected with the front fork by levers instead of acting on it directly.

In the United States the turning point came when A. H. Overman of Chicopee, Massachusetts, patented the Victor Bicycle in 1887, the first of a long series of models to roll off his assembly line. The Victor's two wheels were identical in size and were connected by a frame built on the system of the triangular truss, the so-called diamond frame. It, too, was propelled by an endless chain. The entire machine weighed fifty pounds.

Getting the rider closer to the ground minimized some of the consequences of sailing over the handlebars, but it did not eliminate the jarring that made the name "boneshaker" appropriate. The next important invention was the pneumatic tire. The solid tires of the ordinary had provoked incessant cries for some improvement that would eliminate the constant pounding cyclists got on the bad American streets. Some of this vibration could be reduced with springs of various kinds, but the air-filled tire was the real solution.

The credit for solving the problem goes to an Irish veterinary surgeon named John B. Dunlop, a name still known and respected in the tire industry. According to the story, Dunlop fitted a piece of rubber hose to his son's bicycle in 1889 and, by filling it with compressed air, invented the pneumatic tire. This fortunate idea was followed quickly by other inventions aimed at perfecting valves. However, cyclists were generally skeptical of punctures and blowouts, and therefore they tended to shy away from the pneumatics in the beginning. But all the advantages soon outweighed the misfortunes of punctures, and by 1891 the new tires controlled 40 per cent of the market. Two years later any cycle with solid rubber tires was a curiosity.

Only a few changes and additions remained, and for the most part they were made before the safety bicycle was ten years old. The perfection of ball bearings reduced wear, and the production of lighter steel tubing made the machines better. Last to be invented was the coaster brake. The final result of these improvements was a decade during which Americans went more than slightly mad about a fast machine (and not for the last time either).

This delirium was directly translated into an industrial boom during the otherwise chronic depression that began in 1891 and lasted until after 1898. While farm prices fell and unemployment grew, the bicycle firms of Pope, Overman, Spaulding, and others were booming to the accompanying "ding-a-ling" of bicycle bells and the shouted curses of wagonmen. While William Jennings Bryan threatened the cities of the land in his "Cross of Gold" speech, Americans took to the bicycle with such abandon and in such numbers as to force the police of New York City to put their patrolmen on wheels just to give them an even chance at the apprehension of criminals. The getaway car had yet to chug on the scene, but the getaway bicycle was already present.

It turned out to be a grand and glorious debauch in speed and freedom, the likes of which Americans had never seen.

CHAPTER 2

"The Sundries Cost More Than the Wheel"

THE BICYCLE INDUSTRY AND
THE BICYCLE CRAZE

RIDING TRICYCLE

The last half of the nineteenth century saw American industrialists make tremendous advances as they propelled the United States toward first rank in world production. Such effort was not wholly selfless or patriotic. There was a lot of money to be made, and the number of millionaires in the country increased along with industrial expansion.

However, the great majority of American factories were relatively small operations, whose existence was constantly threatened by entrepreneurs striving to consolidate both production and control in the form of organizations popularly known as "trusts."

In 1890, for example, the average American bicycle factory employed fifty people or fewer; one eighth hired over five hundred employees, and only four were "giants," with a thousand to fifteen hundred workers.

Soon after the safety bicycle appeared on the market, the larger plants showed the future direction of industrial technology and in so doing paved the way, as we noted in the previous chapter, for the automobile industry, commonly thought to be the ultimate in technological organization. Indeed, many automobile makers got their original training in bicycle plants. In 1891 *Scientific American*, describing the Overman Works in Chicopee, Massachusetts—where the Victor Bicycle was manufactured in an environment essentially like that used later in Detroit and Flint—called the plant "nothing but a huge machine." [1]

The Overman factory had many parts. There were special rooms for nickel-plating the showy parts of the bicycles. Then there was a room where bicycles were assembled and where the subdivision of labor had already been introduced. In still another room, machines made all the screws and bolts used to construct a bicycle. The Overman works had its own steam-power system, its own dropforging room, and its own electric-light plant for the one thousand lamps that illuminated the premises, one of the earliest examples of all-electric lighting. The plant also made its own rubber tires; if Armour and Swift were utilizing all of the hog but the squeal, Overman was close behind in utilizing full production techniques. By 1895 the Victor Bicycle was made entirely within the plant, a fact *Scientific American* called "almost unique."

The *Scientific American* article also described a system that was to become familiar to most Americans. This was the assembly line, a form of organization necessitated by what the magazine called "these days of high pressure." Production demands could be met only by the "utmost regard for system," not only in the assembling but in the arrangement of all the processes involved, "so that every motion of the mechanic or the machine counts in the production of the finished article and no energy was uselessly expended." One could hardly describe a modern automobile plant more accurately.

The bicycle industry also anticipated the production of automobiles in another way: Overman had its own cycle-testing track where a variety of surfaces were duplicated so the machine could be checked thoroughly before being shipped out. Not to be outdone by his rival, Albert Pope introduced his own testing techniques. Overman had a dynamometer for measuring the strain on the pedal crank and used the amassed information to design new and better parts, but Pope tested even further than that. He measured frames for stresses arising from vibrations, he crushed ball bearings to determine the amount of friction they could tolerate, and he stretched chains to the breaking point. Pope pioneered in other developments. In 1892 he also set up his own metallurgical laboratory for the purpose of developing lighter and stronger alloys to reduce weight. At the time, the laboratory was the only one of its kind outside the steel mills, and it was unique in testing for light metals. Before the bicycle craze had subsided, Pope Manufacturing led the way in improving automatic screw-making machines, turret lathes, dropforgings, and single-purpose machines for making pedals, spokes, and the like. And the technological advances continued. In 1896 a machine was introduced that stamped out blanks for wheel rims, which in turn were cut out by still another machine. Other machines hammered rivet heads on the sprocket chains.

American bicycle manufacturers at first were entirely dependent on English production for the steel tubing for the bicycle frame, and the mills of Birmingham spat out the miles of hollow pipe that the American makers absorbed. In fact, the American consul in that city reported in 1895 that the United States bicycle industry took the *entire* output of the mills, and that tube-making shops were springing up all over England to capitalize on the market. However, by 1896 American factories had begun producing seamless steel tubing, and improved American machines for making it began to replace English machines even in the factories of England itself.

In spite of all these production advances, the demand for bicycles had increased to the point that such plants as Overman's and Pope's could not meet their orders, and makers had to resort to subcontracting, another instance of anticipating the automobile industry. Watch factories began to make cyclometers, a knitting-needle factory got busy turning out spokes, and manufacturers of rubber hose turned themselves to the production of tires.

One practice it appears the cycle makers originated was planned obsolescence, which existed in the industry from the very beginning. In 1895 *The New York Times* took notice of the growing practice of American cyclists to purchase new models in the spring, sell them the following fall, and then wait for the new cycles that would be shown in January. Directly, the newspaper accused the industry of fostering this rotation by rendering the old machines stylistically out-of-date through the introduction of changes that bore little relationship to the performance of the bicycles. The paper's competitor, the *New York Journal*, in 1897 diverted its attention from the Cuban revolt long enough to agree that moving the sprocket back and forth, putting double crowns on the front fork, and increasing and decreasing the diameter of the tires served no useful purpose but to line the pockets of the manufacturers with money. In a cartoon printed the same year, a cowboy was pictured talking to a stranger in the main street of an obscure Western town.

Stranger: "This is a hustling community, isn't it?"
Cowboy: "I should say not. I'm going to move next week. Why, the people jist elected a man for mayor that rides last year's wheel." [2]

All these stylistic changes should not obscure the fact that concrete advances were made in the design of the bicycle. Dunlop's work with pneumatic tires in Belfast was continued in the United States. Late in 1890 an American paper called attention to tires that it said were made of canvas and "blown up like a football" and were to be seen only on English-made bicycles.[3] At first pneumatics were used only on racing cycles, and it was held that the tires conferred such unfair advantages that those who used them were given time or distance handicaps.

By 1892 pneumatics had become more common, and the influential *Outing* magazine accurately predicted they would "shove everything to the wall."[4] However, the editor observed that cyclists had a deplorable tendency to show off new tires by riding full tilt over the rough cobblestones of the streets, thus rupturing the side walls. Furthermore, no inventor had yet found a quick, efficient way to repair the tires, neither the wag who recommended putting chewing gum over the puncture and holding it with friction tape nor the riders who allegedly sealed a puncture by putting a few spoonfuls of sugar and beer into a tire and then pumping it up again.

The makers worked hard to solve the apparently insoluble and, in doing so, produced some oddities. One puncture-proof tire was filled with water instead of air; another was stuffed with small cork balls. But the best was the tire patented by Dr. Emil Christiansen of Leavenworth, Kansas. Dr. Christiansen's tire was inflated with air but was also distended by a series of internal springs that pushed rubber-tipped plungers against the outer circumference of the tire itself. If punctured, the air would escape, but the spring-loaded plungers would keep the tire distended and allow the cyclist to continue. Silly as it sounds, and unsuccessful as it was, this idea came close to duplicating the inner metal tire that later was to be found on some "puncture-proof" tires sold to motorists.

By the middle of the nineties the industry had yet to solve the puncture problem, but it had come about as far with the pneumatic as it could go. Both single-tube and double-tube tires were on the market; the purchaser could take his choice. The single-tube tire was the grandfather of the so-called tubeless tire of the present.

There was a tough contest over the sale of pneumatics. Several companies, including one still in the business, got together and licensed their tires in the effort to protect both sales and infringement on patents. Albert Pope, B. F. Goodrich, Boston Woven Hose and Rubber Company, the Hartford Rubber Works, and the Hadgman Company all underwrote a full-page advertisement that appeared in *Harper's Weekly*. It contained some doubtful logic:

> No honest cycler will ride infringing tires! Cycling produces Health, Health produces Honesty, Honesty impels Cyclists to ride licensed SINGLE TUBE TIRES![5]

Apparently this admonition did no good, because it was estimated that there were at least thirty different makes of pneumatic tires on the market in 1896. And the papers were filled with advice on how to care for the tricky things: Do not wash them with kerosene or the rubber will rot, keep them properly inflated, do not lose the "pretty little brass cap and chain from the valves." If all these precautions were observed the owner could expect to get one season's wear out of a set, or about five thousand miles.

The search for a durable air-filled tire was not the only quest during the heyday of the bicycle. The perfection of the saddle was also of major importance.

The inventiveness of Americans was lavished on seats of coiled wire, seats with springs, and seats with canvas-covered and padded surfaces, all leading up to the sort of thing that now graces most bicycles. *Harper's Weekly* carried an advertisement for the Sager Pneumatic Seat, which was recommended "by a physician for anatomical reasons," and H. M. Rosenblatt and Company showed models appropriately designed and descriptively named the "Florence A" and the "Jerome A." However, it was difficult to tell the difference.

Probably few bikemaniacs were as comfortably equipped as the lush Lillian Russell, Diamond Jim Brady's girl friend and the ornament of Delmonico's Restaurant. In late August, 1896, the New York press noted that Miss Russell was seen riding her bicycle, all happy and at ease, on her "plaster-cast, self-adjusted, nature-fitting saddle!" It was noted further that the special saddle had cost twenty-five dollars and, probably an exaggeration, that many women of the metropolis were using similar ones.

The secret to such a custom-fitted saddle was the way it was made. The cyclist took his or her own machine to the shop, where the cycle was locked in a frame, then the regular saddle removed and replaced by a special one. This last was a wooden seat covered with an inch-thick layer of modeling clay overlaid with a silk cloth to prevent soiling the clothes. The cyclist mounted and pedaled for fifteen minutes, during which time "every pecularity of pose and shape would be worked out on the clay."[6] In all likelihood the delicate nature of the process called for female attendants to be present when ladies were imprinting their "pecularities." Next a cast was made of the clay seat, a cast that became the form for a final saddle built of composite materials, felt padding, and a cover of pigskin or sealskin. Thus equipped, a cyclist was ready for the street or the highway.

As the bicycle became more popular and city streets became dueling grounds between horse-drawn vehicles, pedestrians, and cycles, all fighting for the right of way, many cyclists came to realize that brakes were desirable. The ordinary had had a small lever-type brake that used friction to slow the front wheel. Offhand it would seem that nobody would quibble over the necessity of having some kind of a device that would at least slow down the fastest thing outside a locomotive, if not stop it altogether. Yet there were riders who stoutly maintained that not only were brakes unnecessary, but they added useless weight to the cycle. As it turned out, brakes were an option on the early safety bicycles, and one had to pay extra for them.

The question arises then as to what a cyclist did in those days when he wanted to make a stop, and the answer is that he got off as quickly as he could. Dismounting was a regular part of the training in the riding schools. In this the men had a more difficult task than the women, who had the better of it with the open drop-frame that is still used in women's bicycles. The expert cyclist learned to dismount either to the right or the left and in some instance over the rear wheel—or that was the theory. One is left with the feeling that much dismounting was headfirst over the front wheel. Otherwise the rider was taught to backpedal, the favorite way of slowing the cycle on steep grades. In some emergencies the rider put the sole of his shoe against the front tire and braked with that.

One enterprising American patented a brake that seems to have been the prototype of the modern brake drum and brake shoe. His invention consisted of a steel, leather-lined drum that encircled the axle of the rear wheel. By means of a hand lever the lining of the drum was forced against the axle, and the resulting friction slowed the bicycle. The final solution, the coaster brake, came just as the bicycle craze was beginning to decline in 1898. For the first time cyclists had an effective brake, simple to operate and cheap to manufacture.

Anyone who has ridden a bicycle knows that it is really at its best going downhill, next best on flat surfaces, and just plain hell going uphill. The fixed gear ratio between sprocket and the rear wheel is all very good for ordinary riding but inadequate for most riders where any kind of an upgrade is encountered. Consequently experimentation on changing gear ratios began almost at the same time the safety bicycle was perfected, although few experiments amounted to much. For example, one device was a tricky pedal that would bend and so lengthen the foot crank on the downstroke, thus increasing the power. Frank Bigelow of Gloucester City, New Jersey, patented a gear system that had two different-sized sprockets mounted on either side of the frame; power was shifted from one sprocket to the other through the hollow shaft connecting the pedals. Another inventor came out with a gear consisting of a circular plate driven by pedals; power was taken off the plate by a roller which, in turn, transmitted its motion to the rear axle. Gears could be shifted by moving the roller in toward the center of the plate or out toward the edge. Pope came out with a sprocket that had its teeth set on a detachable rim; one could merely put on a larger or smaller set of teeth. None of these gearing experiments was successful, and modern times had to produce a satisfactory gear system.

All these were attempts to change the basic elements of the bicycle, but cycling also spawned a host of related gadgets. As more town and cities required warning devices on bicycles, a multitude of bicycle bells came into being: continuously sounding bells worked by the front wheel, a bell contained inside the handlebars and worked by a thumb lever, and whistles and sirens for warning all and sundry that the "scorcher" was on his way.

If warning signals were required for bicycles, so were lights, not so much to show the way for the cyclist as to warn pedestrians that something was coming at them. Lights were made mandatory by most towns, but there is reason to believe that many cyclists ignored the ordinances. For those who did want them, lanterns using kerosene or carbide were made for bicycles. And in 1896 *Scientific American* showed pictures of an electric bicycle lamp whose power was supplied by a small dynamo driven by the front wheel.

Other gadgets included a pair of "learner's wheels" that fastened just in front of the sprocket; a lock, patented by Yale and Towne Manufacturing, that held the front wheel at an angle and thus prevented a thief from riding away with the bicycle; and a rearview mirror for the bicycle, a device that sat atop an arch fastened to the handlebars. The mirror invention was shown with a small flag flying from the top.

Lest anyone think the business of making accessories for bicycles was a picayune matter, it was estimated in May, 1896, that Americans had invested $200,000,000 in sundries including repairs and only $300,000,000 in bicycles themselves. Altogether five hundred separate plants of varying sizes were manufacturing accessories for bicycles. Or as one paper put it:

> Hey diddle, diddle
> The bicycle riddle—
> The strangest part of the deal.
> Just keep your accounts
> And add the amounts
> The "sundries" cost more than the wheel.[7]

Most of the inventions already mentioned were practical, but bicycle enthusiasts evolved their own brand of mechanical fun. For example, in 1895 Evaristo Fernandez of New Orleans patented a water bicycle. It had wheels composed of shallow copper bowls fixed rim-to-rim to form a hollow sphere for flotation, the rearmost with finlike paddles around its circumference to provide propulsion. An illustration in *Scientific American* showed a man, presumably the inventor, mounted and riding the waves, but it is unlikely he ever really solved the problem of equilibrium.

If one man could invent a bicycle for water, another, or rather two others, could invent one for riding on ice. That is just what Samuel Young and Michael Powers did in Ontonagon, Michigan, in 1894. Not only did the machine have a runner where the front wheel would be normally and a chain-driven rear wheel with spikes for traction, it also had the added touch of a body shaped like that of a horse. Young and Powers were not alone; at least two other men took out patents for cycles to be used on ice.

In New York City, Mr. Estanislao Caballero do los Olivos patented a harness that fastened the cyclist's shoulders to the frame of the bicycle and, by giving him an anchor, added to the thrust he could get from his leg muscles. Ostensibly this would enable the rider to go faster, but no racing cyclist seems to have used the device.

A few experimented with bicycles designed to utilize the rails of the nation's railroad system; still others invented unicycles, where the rider sat inside a wheel that rolled over and under him and was propelled by a system of chains and pedals. One exciting invention was a machine that could be ridden along the top rail of the wooden fences that paralleled the boggy, rut-creased roads of the American countryside.

Possibly the crowning act of cyclomania was the Eiffel Tower Bicycle, which was seen in 1894 on the streets of New York. A standard bicycle frame had been extended until the rider sat ten feet or more above the ground, giving him a magnificent view into second-story windows, if nothing else. The bicycle was for an advertising scheme of Dunlop Tires and had no practical value. In fact it was downright dangerous, and *Scientific American* observed that the "adventurous spirit who has been seen riding this remarkable wheel is usually accompanied by a number of companions who serve as a sort of body guard and prevent vehicles and pedestrians from obstructing."[8]

However, for sheer workmanship at rock-bottom prices nobody rivaled fourteen-year-old Fred Dodson from Fishing Creek, Pennsylvania. Young Dodson made his own bicycle completely of wood including the tires and except for the sprocket and chain, and he offered to take orders for others at the fixed price of twenty-five cents each. Naturally the tires were puncture-proof. The young man was not the only one to experiment with wood, and at least one manufacturer marketed a bicycle made of hickory with a price of $125. It was thought that hickory would minimize the vibrations, a nice word for the gut-pounding one got riding cycles over the streets, but the machine did not catch on. Most Americans who bought bicycles purchased conventional ones made of steel tubing.

And they did buy them. There is no way to determine how many bicycles there were in the country in 1890, two years after Overman began to produce his safety bicycle. But twenty-seven American cycle manufacturers were hard at work trying to meet the demand, even at the high prices they were charging for the new machines. The sports-oriented *Outing* magazine concluded in April of 1891 that at least one hundred different patterns of safeties would be presented to the public that year, and at least half of these would sell for $135 each.

It is difficult to evaluate the relative purchasing power of the American dollar at different times in its history, but this much can be said: Any of the nearly two-thousand men employed in cycle plants in 1890 would have had to work nearly half a year at the prevailing wage to purchase one of the machines he helped assemble. Which points up that the bicycle in its infancy was expensive and certainly not available to the masses. A price cut was a necessity before there could be any craze. Two forces did finally bring about a drop in prices: public pressure and, more important, overproduction on the part of the manufacturers.

In the spring of 1893 complaints about the high price of bicycles were heard throughout the land. The *Minneapolis Tribune*, which had previously looked upon the entire bicycle hoopla as a fad, switched about and admitted that cycling was full of promise and that the only thing that prevented it from becoming a craze was the high cost of the machines. Not only did this prevent a lot of people from being able to buy them at all, but it drove away a group of potential customers who were too stubborn to lend themselves to what they considered "bank robbery" on the part of dealers and makers. Allegedly many had indicated they would purchase a new safety when the price got to be fair.

Responding to the charges, "Prowler" a columnist in *Outing* magazine, in May, 1893, defended the manufacturers. Obviously aware of his magazine's old and very close relationship with Albert Pope and A. H. Overman, "Prowler" said with some petulance that the average bicycle owner had little knowledge of what it cost to make and sell a bicycle and that a lot of nonsensical talk about lowering prices would actually put the price below the makers' costs. He went on to write that most people would be astonished to know how much capital was required to tool up for cycle production or to meet office expenses. Salaries for salesmen were another drain on profits, and advertising outlays were an absolute necessity in a sharply competitive industry. "Prowler" ended by flatly denying that cyclists were the victims of "wholesale robbery."

But he had his limitations as a prophet, because the summer of 1893 was not over before one cycle company touched off a storm by sharply reducing prices. The culprit responsible for this shakeup was the respectable Warwick Company, which announced that it would cut its prices from $150 to $85. In August "Prowler" denounced the new price as "below all reason," said it would demoralize the industry, and added that he regretted the price cut because it raised hopes in the minds of cyclists that all the concerns would lower their prices.

If there was demoralization in the industry it was gone by the fall of that year, and *Outing* predicted that cyclists who thought they were going to get a high-grade machine for $80 the next year were mistaken.

The following April, 1894, the demand for bicycles grew in spite of the financial panic that had struck the country the previous winter. Indeed, it was estimated that the cycling business would continue to expand, with projected sales of 250,000 for the season and 400,000 in 1895. No wonder enterprising men with an eye on the main chance rushed into the field, and small bicycle plants and subcontracting shops sprang up all over the nation.

Prices of bicycles did decline throughout the summer of 1895, to about one hundred dollars, and sales multiplied. The craze was on. In Chicago a "bicycle row" grew up on West Madison Street as store after store displayed their wares. The district was not only a place to buy a machine, but a social spot as well, since cyclists made it a habit to ride over in the evenings to pump up tires, get minor repair work done, and flirt with girls.

The number of academies or riding schools, where one was taught the proper way to ride a bicycle, increased in 1895 and 1896. These schools were operated by sales agencies and by manufacturers as well as by private people. The *New York Herald* said that there were twenty-five "first class" riding schools in the city in 1896, which probably means there were at least four times that many all told.

There were two kinds of school. Those in the first group were not particular; they admitted any person who could walk into the establishment and lay down his fifty cents for a half-hour lesson on the school's machine. At Snow's Academy in Minneapolis, trial lessons were a half dollar for thirty minutes; a full course of lessons for ten evenings cost five dollars, which could be applied to the purchase of a bicycle.

The second kind of academy was much more discriminating, took learners only by appointment, and kept out spectators who otherwise gathered to watch the discomfiture of the tyros. The Metropolitan Academy in New York not only had a special area of its riding hall set aside exclusively for women, but actually installed shower-baths for the fairer sex, the first institution of its kind to do so this side of the Atlantic.

Mass cycling meant mass instruction, and Albert Spaulding and his brothers claimed they operated the largest bicycle academy in the world at the original Madison Square Garden. They had started out using the roof garden, but when they were dispossessed by a vaudeville show they moved downstairs and started over again, in a spacious hall with fifty instructors. In announcing the school's new location, the operators said they hoped to be able to accommodate five hundred pupils by the middle of the summer. There is no evidence that their expectations were in error.

Much of the success of the New York riding schools was a result of their ability to attract the ladies' trade by scheduling matinee sessions. The Metropolitan Bicycle Company aped high society's Four Hundred by opening its riding academy with a formal tea. Such practices may have accounted for the fact that the Bidwell-Tinkham Bicycle Company's twenty instructors were credited with sixteen-hundred lessons in one week.

Chicago also had a rapid growth of cycling academies during the boom, and it was reported that they were busy seven hours of the day. The best schools gave a set of seven lessons, the first on a fixed "trainer" with cycle wheels set on rollers. From this the beginner advanced to a duplex (two cycles mounted side by side with a single steering wheel in front), then a tricycle, and finally the bicycle itself. Anticipating some automobile proving grounds, one academy had its floor altered to duplicate the hollows and other obstacles the fledgling cyclist would encounter in riding on real roads. Unhappily, they could not put in a wagon and a team of horses.

Instructors were recruited from the young men who had taken to the bicycle at an earlier time, and *The Wheel* hinted that they had their social shortcomings. The magazine insisted that a pupil could not be expected to learn to ride if the instructors continued to chew gum while they gave advice.

> Keep yer body straight (chew, chew). No, leanin' over ain't necessary (chew, chew). Keep a-pedalin', keep a-pedalin' (chew, chew). Ye ought to know by this time that you can't keep no balance if you bend first to one side and then t'other (chew, chew). There, you've tore your skirt (chew, chew.)[9]

Ultimately, the ladies got into the promotion of the cycle. The schools recruited stylishly clad young women, or "bicyclettes," to ride around New York City to publicize both the sport and the academy. Once enrolled, the bashful misses of the day could find female instructors, to avoid the gum-chewing men.

Although the schools seem to have had all the business they could handle, the fact remained that most cyclists taught themselves to ride, though not always with the best results. An example was Sergeant Wood-

it, stationed at the military academy at West Point, who spent t
months thinking it over and then bought a bicycle. It took the sergeant,
a man otherwise known for his courage, another month to get up the
spirit to try the cycle in the hall where the band practiced. After one
hour he emerged, threw the machine against the wall of the engine house,
and then took an ax to it. That night Sergeant Woodit slept soundly,
for he had indeed "mastered the bicycle."

Booming as the bicycle business was in 1895, there were hints at still
lower prices in the offing. The *Indianapolis Journal* presented information that something extra special would happen to cycling in 1896: the
price of a first-rate machine would drop from one hundred dollars to
thirty dollars, driven down by the productive capacity of the "combine"
that was then being formed to make 400,000 bicycles. More ominously,
no less a person than Albert G. Spaulding, one of the nation's leading
bicycle makers, told the country that the wheel-making business was
bound to be overdone.

The makers could not be blamed for paying little attention to Spaulding's prediction. After all, they merely had to pick up the want ads to
gauge the mounting fever of the cyclists. People apparently would trade
anything for a bicycle. A horse and buggy, a new sidesaddle, a "fine old
violin," room and board, a set of the *Encyclopaedia Britannica*, cigars,
and a "collection of Angora cats" were all advertised for trade in the
newspapers. In Buffalo a notice offered a "folding bed, a child's white
crib, or writing desk for ladies' bicycle."

As the craze spread like an epidemic, some individuals purchased
bicycles, then rented them to those who did not want to own their own.
Rental places, or "wheeleries," flourished around the country. One
owner-operator said that almost every Sunday his cycles were rented
out. Even the weekday business was good, because women dropped by
to rent a bicycle just to take a ride in the park.

There was room in the boom for everybody. Gangs of swindlers
moved around the country selling bicycles on installments to unsuspecting purchasers. Such a troop, calling itself "The American League of
Cycle Associations," passed through Syracuse, New York, taking advantage of an implied relationship with a prominent racing league to collect
down payments on bicycles. Unhappily, the fine print in the contract
made the purchaser a stockholder in the company. Many a gullible buyer
not only failed to get his cycle but found himself legally liable for the

company's unpaid debts. In one or two unfortunate cases preachers, among the gullible buyers, were haled into court, to their personal dismay and financial loss.

In the Midwest, cycle makers generally ignored Albert Spaulding simply because so many orders had gone unfilled the previous year, 1894. Unfortunately, this optimism did not take into account the fact that many small shops were in production, or that thousands of agents had rushed into the business, ostensibly to get their slice of the huge profits that beckoned for 1896. Hardware stores had always competed with legitimate cycle-sales agents, but the boom of 1895 saw drugstores, clothing stores, cigar stores, and even saloons rush into the act. Even so, the future still looked rosy, because hopeful estimates put the number of Americans cycling at about four million, and surely a fourth of them could be persuaded to buy a new bicycle the next year, particularly if one changed the models a little. Also contributing to the optimism was an increased demand for women's bicycles. But a hint of the future was evident in May, 1896, when the agents, feeling the pinch, began to extend their store hours later into the night.

Despite the stiff competition, bicycles still cost about one hundred dollars, and this caused the wag to comment that six things were required to have a happy home: "A good bicycle, and Money, Money, Money, Money, Money." It was the high costs that led the *New York Herald* in August, 1896, to accuse the cycle manufacturers of profiteering. Banner headlines charged "Huge Profits in Making Bicycles!" The paper concluded that the hundred-dollar "crack" wheel really cost only $30.31.

"Entirely untrue," "misleading," shouted the influential cycling magazine, *The Wheel*. There were no "cycle barons" in the industry, and only two companies out of two hundred would "show up a million dollars or more." Further, the bicycle the *Herald* had dissected was not a "crack" wheel but a machine that was liable to break down and could be sold for one hundred dollars only to the "crack-brained." *The Wheel* then launched into a familiar description of the woes of cycle making:

> The bicycle is very much like the newspaper. The man who assembles . . . [it] is the least important part of the business. There is invested capital, there is brains in the office and on the road, there is advertising, there are bicycle shows, there are racing teams to support, there are repairs on tires which are sent back, repairs on wheels which break down or are broken down, and there are a hundred and one leakages which would not be found or tolerated in any other business. The agent has to

give away oil; sometimes he has to present a lamp to a fractious customer; he has to keep men to pump up tires, to rub down wheels and to give all manner of petty attention to his customers, otherwise they will go down the street to the other man. It is a taxatious and expensive business.

The business of making wheels requires talent and delicacy; the business of selling wheels requires wide-angled commercial foresight and energy, as well as an experience peculiar to the bicycle trade itself. One must go through the bicycle trade in order to master it.[10]

Of course, none of this was proof that the *Herald* had been wrong when it had suggested that the sale of a bicycle for one hundred dollars would give its makers a profit of about 200 per cent.

One thing that can be gleaned from *The Wheel*'s comments is that competition in selling was on the upswing, for despite some failures, there were still over five hundred shops making bicycles in the United States. Such competition made it imperative that makers keep the sport of cycling before the American public as much as they could. Aside from the steady flow of advertisements in newspapers, magazines, and trade journals, the big publicity splurge in the industry was the annual bicycle show. Here again the industry anticipated automobile makers, and the techniques and showmanship evolved in the big exhibitions accustomed the public to the lavish displays that later were sponsored by the automobile industry.

The first cycle show in the United States was held in 1883 in Springfield, Massachusetts, at which event eighteen makers exhibited their highwheelers to a small crowd of fans. Three years later Boston was the site of the second show, held in conjunction with the meeting of the League of American Wheelmen. There was an interval of five years before the next bicycle show in 1891 at Philadelphia, where the new safeties were demonstrated. But the eight hundred dollars in admissions that rolled in made the managers resolve to hold another show the following year. By 1894 big exhibitions were being held annually in Chicago and at Madison Square Garden in New York City, where some of the larger manufacturers became so enraged at the limited space allotted them that they rented additional facilities elsewhere in the city and held their own shows. One observer even went so far as to applaud the shows for their democratizing influence because one rubbed elbows with mechanics and laborers, something that never happened at the horse and dog shows.

It was in 1895 that the exhibits grew up. Burning with cycling fever, Americans came to stare at the newest improvements: aluminum wire saddles, lighter tubing for the frame, narrowed handlebars with cork grips, and a cycle with a bamboo frame. Before they were unveiled at the exhibition, the new models for the year had been concealed carefully from the public eye. As a consequence, trade had come to a momentary standstill because dealers were reluctant to put in orders for any model until its appeal had been tested at the shows. It seems obvious that the automobile industry adopted its own atmosphere of mystery and secrecy from the cycle industry.

The 1896 shows in Chicago and New York exceeded previous demonstrations by enormous lengths. In Chicago, over 225 exhibitors showed their new models and rubbed their hands as they looked at the crowds surging through the aisles. One hundred thousand people attended the week-long show and not only gaped at the new cycles but collected souvenirs and catalogues distributed by the different makers. Pins, buttons, canes, spoons, knives, watch charms to hang on watch chains that were made to look like miniature bicycle chains—all were swept up by a crowd seemingly motivated by the sheer desire to accumulate anything and everything that had to do with cycling.

Each maker had its own brand of come-on. Over in one corner the Fowler Bicycle Company composed and printed an eight-page daily newspaper in a packing crate. Each exhibit was plugged by a special pitchman, and daring "bloomer girls" raised their voices as counterpoints to the booming of Sycamore Ike, a gigantic Indian of undetermined tribal affiliation.

The pandemonium of the sales pitch was accentuated by the sheer exuberance of the cyclers. The next-to-last evening of the show, January 11, 1896, was club night, and the bicycle organizations of the Windy City converged on the auditorium preceded by bagpipers, trombone players, and club yells. All of which caused some old-time cyclers to insinuate that the cycle shows were attracting a low class of people.

Four hundred exhibitors later that month flocked to Madison Square Garden on Fourth Avenue. Albert Spaulding opened the show, while D'Arquin's Military Band played appropriate music. To the "Ohs!" and "Ahs!" of a generation not yet accustomed to electricity, the Garden's chief electrician threw the switch that lit up the gigantic bicycle over the entrance. It was twenty feet long and thirteen feet high and composed of over two thousand small electric lights that simulated a bicycle in motion. Then, while New York society paraded in evening wear—just as they did at the horse show—the rest of the crowd scrambled to look at the new models and get souvenirs.

The New York reporters duly noted that socially prominent Pierre Lorillard, Jr., of the tobacco family, drifted through the crowd carrying a sheaf of cycle catalogues. Oliver H. P. Belmont, who gave his attention to banking, and Mrs. Belmont, who gave hers to the cause of woman suffrage, put in appearances, as did the younger J. P. Morgan, who actually bought a bicycle. These were the upper crust, but equally important were the thousand or more bicycle agents from twenty states who were wined and dined by the manufacturers. When the show closed on Saturday night, Albert Spaulding reversed his dire prediction of the previous year and said that business looked good. In light of the 120,000 people who had attended the exhibit, New York was accurately described as being "bicycle crazy."

During the summer of 1896, the National Board of Trade of the Bicycle Manufacturers, known as the Cycle Board of Trade, bound its members to keep their cycles out of shows not sanctioned by the trade. In 1897, although there were signs that the market was saturated and prices had begun to drop, cycle shows were again held in Chicago and New York, and enthusiasm seems to have remained fairly high. In New York that year the fans were out on souvenir night, and one young bicyclette paraded the aisles with thirty-eight buttons and badges on her shirtfront, or enough to "stop a bullet," according to one newspaper reporter. Mr. and Mrs. Reginald De Koven, he fresh from directing another smash operetta and she from writing an article on cycling, strolled through the lanes of booths, as did the socialite William De Peyster. The manly beard of Colonel Pope could be seen over everybody's head as he smiled benignly at the 2,000 agents who flocked to the exhibit and the 100,000 sightseers who kept them company. Among those demonstrating cycling equipment was the pride of Minnesota, Pudge Heffelfinger, former football captain at Old Eli. How many people were attracted to his patented bicycle shoes was not recorded.

In 1898, however, the market for cycles fell, prices collapsed, and the Cycle Board of Trade quit the shows, which continued to be sponsored by desperate local cycle agents. By late summer the cycle shows were passé.

Of course, the cycle makers developed techniques other than exhibits to get their products before the public. At the height of the boom (1895–

96) the Chester Bicycle Company of Indiana, one of those newcomers that mushroomed in the business, came up with the "low overhead" argument. Chester claimed it could sell hundred-dollar bicycles for eighty-five dollars because it did not subsidize a racing team, did not advertise widely, and did not pay big commissions to agents or high salaries to company officers. While others raced, the company stayed at work and passed the savings on to customers who bought the Chester Bicycle. According to the company, ordinarily ten dollars of the cost of every bicycle went to support a racing team.

But Chester was the exception, and the cycle makers anticipated automobile manufacturers by several decades in their awareness of the advertising potential of racing. The Remington Arms Company proudly announced in 1895 that the winner of the Irvington-Milburn Road Race had used one of its bicycles. With customary modesty, the company attributed his victory to the fact that he was riding one of Remington's "scientifically constructed" bicycles. The Waltham Manufacturing Company boasted that the famous racer Walter Sanger rode one of their bicycles, but they neglected to mention that Sanger was paid by Waltham.

Other advertising ploys were tried. The Davis Sewing Machine Company, makers of the Dayton Bicycle, fell back on classical history and the story of Diogenes, the Greek cynic philosopher, who walked through the streets in daylight with a lantern, searching for "an honest man." The Davis version showed an attractive maiden shining her lantern on "An Honest Wheel." The company proudly announced, "Miss Diogenes has found it!" Albert Pope, a fighter all the way, inaugurated a contest to determine how much return he was getting for his advertising dollars by offering a new Columbia Bicycle to the person who clipped and sent in the greatest number of ads from the newspapers. The Boston Woven Hose Company displayed a buxom young lady in daring décolletage being wafted along on the new "Vim" tire, a connection not readily apparent unless it was that both the lady and the "Vim" were equally pneumatic.

All this advertising was to lure the customer into the dealer's shop and set him up for the coup de grâce in the form of the purchase of a new machine. But selling a new model was a difficult business as long as the prices stayed above a hundred dollars. Therefore, encouragement had to be given in the form of installment sales. It appears that the down-payment idea began around 1892. The initial amount paid was substantial, frequently from 75 to 90 per cent, while the remainder had to be paid off quickly. There is no way of knowing how widespread installment buying of bicycles became, but a good guess is that more and more Americans made installment purchases as prices began to fall. In July, 1895, the *Minneapolis Tribune* reported that a "great many" bicycles had been sold on the installment plan, and that the buyers were keeping up on their payments, a fact that the paper attributed to the growing tendency of a "better class of people" to turn to cycling.

In addition to the inducement of deferred payments and giveaways, the dealers found they had other things to consider when it came to merchandising. For example, what was the most effective environment for selling cycles to the women who formed 25 to 30 per cent of the market?

Dealers were warned that women would not come into dirty hardware stores or smelly implement houses to purchase cycles, and that salesmen would have to spruce up the premises, which is exactly what an enter-prising dealer did in Southern California. He not only painted his shop in the pink and blue colors of the new March Bicycle, but he also pro-vided a changing room for women who wanted to switch into cycling clothes before trying out a machine. However, he was a little concerned over the effeminacy of the new colors; and to counteract this, he publicly announced that since the March had changed to pink and blue, it had won more professional races in California than any other bicycle.

A small problem was created for dealers by the practice of planned obsolescence. To get the public to buy the new models every year, a dealer frequently had to take the old one in trade and then had to sell the used machines. And in 1895, buying a secondhand bicycle was no less tricky than buying a used car now. The *Minneapolis Tribune* said that the average American knew almost as much about buying a used bicycle as he did about buying a horse—nothing! Whereupon the paper pro-ceeded to give some advice on how to buy a used machine. It warned the prospective purchaser to beware of any wheel that did not show the "blush of maiden modesty unmarred," and to be especially suspicious of dealers who admitted the cycle had only been used a few times and then showed the future owner clean tires and shining nickel. Instead of being dazzled by these, the customer should inspect the saddle, a good place to spot signs of wear. Above all, the purchaser should keep in mind that the plainer the bicycle the better, because accessories were just things to get out of order.

Spurred by tight competition at home, the American makers decided to expand overseas, an invasion that caused a polite Gallic shudder to run through the frame of one Henri Desgranges, a journalist of Paris, France. Desgranges wrote that "American bicycles bear the stamp of their national individuality and show particular regard for comfort and practical usefulness and an undeniable tendency toward a uniform type of machine." No full-blooded American could quarrel with that statement. But Desgranges went on to say, "Some parts may hurt our esthetic feelings, and we would almost call them rather heavy. . . . Let us keep for ourselves those adorable little [French] machines, which one must needs love with their charms, and particularly with their virtues of invincible attractiveness."[11] Vive la France!

The Frenchman was right to have been apprehensive, because in 1896 and 1897 American makers poured bicycles into Europe. Once, Americans had been happy behind tariffs of 50 per cent on English cycles, but the industry petitioned Congress to lift the tax in 1898, hoping that retaliatory European tariffs would also fall.

The flood of American machines sent overseas was an indication that the home market was becoming saturated, the very thing that Spaulding had predicted. In 1897 the home market broke, and what the papers called an "ironclad" agreement among the big manufacturers collapsed. It was at this point that Albert Pope reduced the price of the popular Columbia, a competitive blow that hit the smaller firms like a bombshell, partly because the larger firms followed Pope's lead. One paper saw the reduction as the opening step toward driving the smaller makers off the market entirely. "It means that Colonel Pope is tired of the tactics of the small dealers and makers. Men that list their wheel at a fair figure, then take whatever price is offered provided it leaves a profit, however small."[12] If the purpose of the price war was to drive out the small concerns, then it succeeded extremely well. Before the trade stabilized, 131 bicycle firms went to the wall, approximately 35 per cent of all the makers in the country.

The trade war swept on. Late in the spring Wanamaker's in New York began to close out its 1897 models to make room for the 1898 machines—seven months before they came out—and offered some cycles at $27.50. In three days the store in New York and Wanamaker's in Philadelphia sold 617 bicycles, and in another two-day spurt the customers grabbed up 535. Not to be outdone, A. G. Spaulding and Brothers offered used 1894 bicycles for as low as $15, and credit sales for as little as $1.50 a week. The big Siegel-Cooper department store in Manhattan leaped into the competition with the Elkhart Bicycle, which had originally been priced at $100 but which it would sell for $22. Either somebody was taking big losses or the *Herald's* charges of exorbitant profits were true.

The Alpine Company of Cincinnati advertised for dealers with a pitch that sounds uncommonly familiar to one who reads the want ads today. Taking a page in a national magazine, the company shouted, "Agent's Outfit Free, No Capital Needed! Weekly Sales Pay Big Money! We make a high grade Bicycle as low as $24.00. Fully Guaranteed. Shipped anywhere on approval, *direct from our factory.*"[13] Pope held the reduced price of the Columbia to seventy-five dollars, but even he had to concede to the competition by selling the Hartford model at thirty dollars.

As both customers and sellers sought agreement, the rash of installment buying increased. Three references and a steady job were all that was needed, but one could hazard the guess that these requirements were frequently ignored. Credit buyers, however, had to pay full price, while cash purchasers in 1897 got a discount.

As bicycle prices plummeted in the summer of 1897, dealers made frantic efforts to cut their losses by unloading high-priced cycles at a 40 per cent discount on the grounds that they were "shopworn," a tactic that was the antecedent of the sale of "demonstrators" and "executive cars" by automobile companies. And when it came to trade-ins, those who had really paid high prices for machines in 1896 could expect nothing for them a year later. Those who had bought the 1897 models immediately after the winter shows, only to see the price fall in June, also suffered. One such purchaser, a Mrs. Daniel Peckham, bought a new model in April for one hundred dollars, of which seventy-seven dollars was the down payment. Before she could pay off the balance, the price fell below the seventy-seven dollars she had paid down, and she indignantly refused to pay the balance. The court ordered her to fulfill the contract.

In the fall of 1897 the industry sat back to lick its wounds and think about future strategy while *Harper's Weekly* explained the collapse to the public. The magazine said that the collapse had started in 1896, when production caught up with demand and passed it. The fall of prices was staved off for a time by cutting prices on 1896 bicycles in stock while maintaining the prices of 1897 models. However, the journal contended that not more than a score of makers had made profits in 1896.

Particularly burdensome, so *Harper's* believed, was the guarantee, which had constituted the nightmare of the makers since it had been introduced. "There is opportunity for so much dishonesty in this regard that little short of highway robbery has been practiced by unscrupulous purchasers when anything went wrong with the wheel."[14] The manufacturers bluntly stated that making good on guarantees was costing them too much—shades of the automobile manufacturers' warranties of the late 1960's—and by 1896 they were saying they would have to raise the price of bicycles 25 per cent to cover the cost of repairs. Some makers contended that the guarantee problem arose from the manufacturing of cheap machines in 1896. These shoddy products of fly-by-night enterprises were foisted on the unsuspecting public as first-class wheels.

Rumor had had it early in the summer of 1896 that reputable bicycle makers were going to try to get state laws passed that would protect purchasers by compelling the maker to identify his product properly. He would have to give the buyer a *detailed* statement as to the materials used in making the cycle, the quality of workmanship involved, and the grade of the machine. If the man wanted to buy a cheap bicycle he could do so, but the big boys wanted no cheap competitors for the high-grade machines. Had such a law been passed, it would have marked a milestone in quality control and "truth in selling."

In 1898 the makers did move to cover themselves, not only reducing the period of the guarantee to sixty days but also wording it in such a way as to make it almost worthless. For example, during the sixty-day period the makers would repair all parts that had proved defective, but only if the machine were sent back to the factory, with the owner paying the freight charges. It might not be too costly to send a front axle back to Pope's Hartford Plant, but what if the frame was out of line? It would be similar to having to send a Ford back to the River Rouge Plant. (The tire makers accomplished the same end by inserting in their guarantee the escape clause that guarantees would be fulfilled "at our option.")

On one point the *Harper's* analysis erred. One thing was certain, the magazine said, and that was that there would be no combination in the industry. All the talk about creating a bicycle trust was just so much nonsense, because the plants were scattered too widely for effective administrative unification. Admittedly there was the Cycle Board of Trade, which had been organized in 1894 to oversee the business. But it had not been able to hold the makers together during either the boom period or the price war of 1897. Therefore, said *Harper's*, the rumor that a trust had been conceived in Toledo was just so much talk. Furthermore, the Cycle Board of Trade was said to be much upset at the rumor that Albert Spaulding was trying to put some kind of combination together, and presumably the board would throw many obstacles in his path.

But some plans were in fact being made in the industry. After all, it was the period for "trust," to use the term popularly applied to the gigantic business combinations that controlled both manufacturing and marketing, so why not create a bicycle trust? Early in June, 1899, Spaulding was joined by Pope, who agreed to bring his two bicycle factories and one rubber plant into the trust. In a secret meeting held at the Waldorf-Astoria Hotel, the American Bicycle Company was created. In time it would absorb thirty-six other companies and forty-one factories, control the lion's share of bicycle patents, and control 75 per cent of the bicycle trade.

In 1900 *Outing* magazine took notice of the formation of the trust. The editor expressed the nostalgic fear that some of the old and familiar model names would pass from the land, and that the Victor, the Columbia, the Warwick, and the Waverley would be seen no more. Where would a fellow go to get his favorite tires—Kangaroos, or "Won't Slips" with their pebble treads, or Dreadnoughts, or Corkers? To the fans, the future did not look very bright. But the American Bicycle Company, like the General Motors Company, was too shrewd to lose all that love and faith. It said it would keep most of the prominent names even though they would all be made by the same company.

The future was unhappy for the ABC. Almost immediately an internal struggle for control developed. By mid-July, 1899, the powerful U.S. Rubber Company had demanded that two of its own competitors be expelled from the trust. Since these two firms were also owned by big bicycle makers, the latter threatened to withdraw their cycle companies also, thus weakening the trust's capacity not only to own the various companies but also to control all the processes that went into making a bicycle. The American Bicycle Company had the same objectives as all the other trusts, the general elimination of competition.

In June, 1902, *The New York Times* carried a little notice to the effect that Albert Pope and John D. Rockefeller had gotten control of the American Bicycle Company. Ten months later it was announced that the company was going into the hands of receivers after having defaulted on its bonds. It was further revealed that its stock was heavily watered, which is another way of saying that the company was overcapitalized. The big bicycle boom was truly dead.

The prospects had been grim for a while. By 1898 *Outing*, for the first time in ten years, devoted less than a full page to its bicycling column and then only to announce that the makers were moving the announcement of the new models forward from January to October and November. This was an obvious attempt to put off further decline by pushing obsolescence for all it was worth. One year later the magazine admitted that the cycling craze was dead.

In the show at Madison Square Garden in January, 1899, which for the first time was called the "Annual Cycle and *Automobile* Exhibition," the machine that was to replace the bicycle in the affections of most Americans was demonstrated. The automobile had come to stay, and no less a person than Colonel Albert Pope showed an electric runabout from his Columbia Bicycle Works. Pope had assisted at the birth of the American bicycle; he was there to officiate at its first interment.

In January, 1900, *Outing* printed a section on the automobile, and two months later it admitted that this was the machine of the future. By way of farewell, the publication observed that people had tended to see the bicycle as a "clever machine making its way alone into popular favor rather than a single part in a great and widespread move in transportation which it was in point of time at least privileged to lead."[15]

Then *Outing* turned to other things, leaving behind the faint odor of kerosene and machine oil, saddle soap and new rubber tires.

Bizarre and Beautiful Beginnings

Stained-glass window from church at Stoke Poges

Above: *draisine.*
Below: lionizing the *Célérifère.*

Above: celeripede, 1816
Below: Julien's "Everlasting Treadmill"

CULVER PICTURES, INC.

New Developments

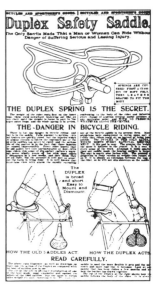

Top, left: Lewis' improved
velocipede—1869
Bottom, left: Michelin ponders
the pneumatic tire
Top, right: springing the saddle
Bottom, right: the Lallement
velocipede—1866

TOP, LEFT, AND BOTTOM, RIGHT: CULVER PICTURES, INC.

Riding Ahead

Below: Columbia Bicycle poster
Right: A. B. Ayres with his bicycle
Bottom, right: tricycle of 1884

COLUMBIA TRICYCLES.

Stanch, Reliable, Light, Easy - Running, Finest Materials, Skilful Workmanship, Beautifully Finished, Every Part Interchangeable. So adjustable that the same machine can be ridden by any size of rider. Price, $160. With Columbia Power-Gear, which enables the rider to instantly increase the leverage, and easily ride up steep grades and over rough places, $180.

Send stamp for Illustrated (36 p.) Catalogue.

THE POPE MFG. CO.,
597 Washington St., · · BOSTON, MASS.

ABOVE: CHICAGO HISTORICAL SOCIETY
TOP, RIGHT: NEW YORK STATE HISTORICAL ASSOCIATION, COOPERSTOWN
BOTTOM, RIGHT: BICYCLE INSTITUTE OF AMERICA

Moving Over

Match against Time or Wood beats Blood and Bone

The horse and bicycle conflict

TOP: NEW YORK PUBLIC LIBRARY PICTURE COLLECTION. BOTTOM: CULVER PICTURES, INC.

Cause and Effect

Pioneering bicycle manufacturers Albert G. Spaulding (left) and Col. A. A. Pope. Because of them the street scene changed.

TOP, RIGHT, AND BOTTOM: BROWN BROTHERS

Reprise

The velocipede of 1827 attracts attention.

NEW YORK PUBLIC LIBRARY PICTURE COLLECTION

CHAPTER 3

"*From 'Farmer's Rest' to 'Bicycler's Retreat'*"

THE ECONOMIC EFFECTS OF THE BICYCLE

BICYCLE INSTITUTE OF AMERICA

EASY RIDING

In the early summer of 1896 the *Detroit Tribune* commented on the influence of the bicycle:

> It would not be at all strange if history came to the conclusion that the perfection of the bicycle was the greatest incident in the nineteenth century. When we think of the effect upon the race of endowing practically all of the people with the means of greatly accelerated locomotion, the imagination knows no bounds. The effect, while it may not become readily apparent to us of the day, is likely to appear something tremendous to the future observer of events. We would be hardy to suggest a transformation and an expansion of humanity such as followed the invention of the printing press or the mariner's compass, but you can't tell. The bicycle influences a vast number of people, and it influences them by no means lightly or superficially. Less momentous and less universal circumstances than the wheel have strongly affected racial characteristics.[1]

From the vantage point of the late twentieth century it is possible to see that the paper had been carried away in its evaluation of the bicycle. However, there can be little argument that the coming of the bicycle influenced thousands of Americans. Even leaving aside people who made their living from manufacturing and selling the cycle and its accessories, the contrivance affected the well-being of Americans more sharply and more swiftly than some of the more famous technological advances then being made.

Every kind of transportation problem was eagerly scanned to see whether or not the bicycle could be adapted to its needs. For example, it was argued that the bicycle would be particularly valuable to anyone whose work demanded constant movement, and that doctors and ministers would find bicycles useful. However, at first many ministers and doctors believed that to ride one of the machines was not just a threat to the immortal soul and a menace to physical health, but an affront to personal dignity as well. Ultimately both groups took to the cycle in numbers, especially in the cities and larger towns where paved streets made riding easier.

It was also discovered that those who had to inspect the web of telephone lines that had begun to wrap American cities in wire cocoons could use the bicycle, and the New York and New Jersey Telephone Company announced in 1895 that it would put both inspectors and linemen on cycles where feasible. The superintendent of schools in New York City made his visitations on a bicycle. In Chicago the postmaster ran an experiment testing the horse and buggy, the bicycle, and the foot messenger in the delivery of special mail. The bicycle won easily, and a year later Chicago had 115 postmen on bikes at a savings of five thousand dollars a year in transportation costs.

In fact, Chicago proved to be a very fertile field for experimentation with the early birotate chariot. A physician named John T. Hinckley felt that the ambulance service was too slow for emergency cases, and with good reason. At the time, hospitals did not keep horse-drawn ambulances on the premises, and emergency calls were delayed while the hospital contacted the livery stable where the ambulance was housed. Dr. Hinckley designed and constructed a bicycle ambulance, consisting of two tandem cycles fastened side by side with a framework that also supported a canvas-covered box in which the patient lay on a stretcher. The machine was more than a passing fancy: ridden by two qualified physicians, it delivered over one hundred patients to the hospital in just a few months. Appropriately enough, the first customers brought in on the new speedsters were eight cyclists banged up or exhausted from Chicago's annual Fourth of July road race. The cycle ambulance was able to make a three-mile run through city traffic in sixteen minutes, a respectable rate of fifteen miles per hour, which a horse-drawn ambulance could not match. Although other doctors and other hospitals were reported interested in the cycle ambulance, its use never seems to have become widespread.

If postmen could cover their rounds more efficiently and the injured could be sped to the operating table faster, it stood to reason that the policemen of the city could also use the bicycle profitably. Besides, if criminals used the bicycle, what would enable the police to apprehend the culprits? Another bicycle, of course.

Actually the first bicycle policemen were propably traffic police employed by the Boston Park Commission to keep order in the city parks. It followed that as long as cycling was confined to park paths, few officers would be needed for traffic control. But once the use of cycles expanded beyond the confines of parks and onto the streets of the cities, a somewhat larger force became necessary. By 1894 the number of bicycle policemen had been increased in Philadelphia, Brooklyn (at that time not yet a part of New York City), Cincinnati, and Chicago. A Brooklyn police captain said that bicycle policemen had to be special types who could be trusted not to drink beer or play cards when they were supposed to be on patrol, because their work ordinarily would take them too far away from their supervisors. Since these Brooklyn cycle officers—"fly cops" as they were sometimes called—were used first to patrol the Coney Island Cycle Path, which ran through neighborhoods of painted frame residences, it is improbable that the officers were often diverted from curbing "the restless scorcher in his mad flight to the sea" and keeping a fatherly eye on all that went on along the path.

Not to be outdone, in December, 1895, New York City put on two bicycle policemen to patrol asphalted Eighth Avenue and Riverside Drive, the two streets most frequented by cyclists. Before the month was out, New York's Police Commissioner Andrews was experimenting with four bicycle policemen. They were proving their worth in outlying parts of the city and were beginning to develop the same tactics as modern motorcycle policemen and patrol cars. They undoubtedly learned by experience that to ride up behind another cyclist and dismount was only to invite the suspect to pedal away while the officer lost time and distance. Therefore, the cycle policeman was trained to catch up with the suspect and then cut in ahead of him, forcing him to stop. In one instance, when a cyclist proved uncooperative, the officer simply ran down both machine and rider. There were even a few instances where policemen had commandeered private bicycles—shades of "Follow that car!"—and had ridden their quarry to the ground.

In January New York's Chief Conlin told reporters that he was happy with the way the bicycle officers had helped control traffic, especially cycles, and he recommended that the city commissioners extend the same service to most of the improved city streets. He added that police patrols would be valuable in the outlying parts of the city, where the open spaces and greater distances made the work of patrolmen most difficult. He further proposed that the roundsmen, the inspectors in the district, be put on cycles to improve their work. The commissioners adopted most of the chief's recommendations.

In November, 1896, the Pittsburgh police force announced that after preliminary testing it was apparent that one cycle-mounted policeman was worth two on foot. In the Midwest, however, there was more skepticism about policemen on bicycles. The police chief of Davenport, Iowa, tried to persuade his board of aldermen to let him try a few bicycle patrolmen, a request that inspired the local newspaper to say:

> The spectacle of the staid, sober, heavyweight policemen of this city break-
> ing their necks and the injunction against profane swearing while learning
> to master their vicious steeds will be a show that will stand almost any
> admission the city may please to charge for it. The treasury reserve will
> be raised away above the low water mark by hiring a hall and giving this
> exhibition under a reasonable scale of prices.[2]

Yet most of the larger towns and cities in the United States saw the advantages of cycle policemen and put a few on the force.

The impact of the bicycle on the economic well-being of Americans was great. True, some of its affects were adverse; the bicycle was not an economic boon for everyone. Among those who complained of its impact were saloonkeepers, who maintained that the consumption of strong waters was declining and all because of the cycling craze. Many a man could take in enough whiskey to swim in and still make it home on foot, but not on a bicycle. The machine was a born wobbler. The minute the front wheel got the tiniest whiff from the jug of John Barleycorn, it started looking for the nearest lamppost. This did not result from the contrary nature of the beast, observed the *LAW Bulletin*, but because "the bicycle is, by its very inherent nature, a teetollaler. It is great on curves, but is no good *on rye-tangles*. Next to having sound lungs, a bicycle must have a clear brain and an easy conscience."[3] The fact remains that thousands who took their cycling seriously avoided the saloons. Frances E. Willard, a leader of the temperance movement, said the bicycle exerted a more powerful influence for temperance than the W.C.T.U. Other parts of the economy suffered from the advent of the bicycle, especially those sectors connected with horses. Before the coming of the cycle, all Americans who could afford to do so invested in a horse and buggy, and all "adequate" houses had a small barn or carriage house at the rear of the lot. Here the family horse was housed. The harness, redolent of saddle soap and neat's-foot oil, hung on a rack. Above was the loft where hay was stored and the dime-novel adventures of Mustang Sam were perused in an atmosphere reeking with the smoke of corn-silk cigarettes and potential catastrophe from accidental arson.

The carriage house outlasted both horse and bicycle, ultimately becoming the garage, but the bicycle struck the horse a savage blow from which the animal never recovered. The motor car simply delivered the head shot to a beast already critically wounded. In 1895, the *New York Sun* noticed something liverymen and horse sellers already knew, that the sale of horses had fallen. The paper said that the price of good-quality horses had reached an all-time low and that the business of horse raising had ceased to be profitable except for breeding racing thoroughbreds and others in "fashionable demand."

Inevitably, the demand for buggies and carriages declined at the same time. The failing demand for horses also depressed the income of blacksmiths, not to mention the business of livery stables. It is a double commentary on both the importance of the horse in nineteenth-century America and the powerful impact of the bicycle and the electric trolley that in 1895 the two new forms of transportation displaced an estimated 240,000 horses in seven American cities alone. In Chicago 75,000 horses fell victims of advancing technology; Philadelphia lost 50,000; New York City, whose transportation was already further advanced, lost 40,000.

The horse dealers tried to whistle away the disaster. One was quoted as saying, "The passion for bicycle riding is too violent to last, and in the course of one or two years the horse will resume its place in the interests and affections of men and women."[4] The drop in the sale of horses was of major proportions to those financially involved. New York City alone had bought about thirty thousand horses annually for pulling the trolley cars that antedated electric cars, and these had averaged about $125 each in value. A third of a million dollars is not pin money, especially in a day when wages were low and the purchasing power of the dollar was considerably greater than at present. "'Get a horse!" was the despairing plea of the breeders long before it became a cry of derision aimed at automobiles stuck in the mud.

The bicycle did, of course, have certain shortcomings compared to horses. Out on the North Fork of Wyoming's Cheyenne River, R. B. Mosely watched the experiments conducted with bicycles at Ft. Missoula to the north and then made his decision. The quarter horses on his ranch were retired to the corral to eat their heads off at his expense, and the cowboys were mounted on bicycles. Neither the attitude of the steers nor the punchers' comments have been handed down to posterity, but it was generally held that R. B.'s experiment was not an unqualified success. It was true, of course, that a bicycle could not ram its foot in a prairie dog's hole and throw its rider, but the cycle did leave something to be desired as a cow pony. With more courage than sense, one puncher tied the end of his lariat to the bicycle's saddle and quickly threw a loop over a steer's horns. For his trouble he was jerked into the adjoining county, where he was joined by another who had the guts to try to turn a stampede by getting out in front of it on his bicycle. In this endeavor the second man "met with poor success" and was last seen heading over a hill, letting as much daylight as possible between himself and the herd. In the countryside roundabout, R. B. Mosely was known as a "crank and a dreamer of dreams."[5]

Still others were disheartened by the bicycle craze. Theater owners complained that 1896 was the poorest season they could remember, not because of the economic depression the nation was undergoing, but because people were saving their money to buy bicycles rather than spending it in the theaters. Once they had a bicycle they still did not go to the shows but cycled out to the country to spend their time. In fact, in Chicago so many people had taken to the bicycle on Sundays that the theaters had to cancel Sunday performances.

Jewelers and watchmakers grumbled that Americans no longer saved their money to buy watches for children who reached their majority or older people who reached the age of retirement. In 1896 young people were clamoring for bicycles for their birthdays, not watches. Even candy manufacturers and cigar makers joined in the complaint. Candy was not good for a man who was training to ride his "century," as a hundred-mile ride was called, and cigars were likewise *verboten*. Instead of idling the Sunday afternoon, smoking a cigar and drinking a schooner or two of beer, the young bloods were out on their bicycles, scorching through the streets and breathing nothing but clean air. And this hurt the tobacco business. By the summer of 1896, the consumption of cigars was decreasing at a rate of a million a day, and the annual consumption had fallen off seven hundred million a year since the craze had begun!

The chain reaction went on. Tailors complained that so many men were spending so much time in cheap bicycle suits, they did not wear out their good clothes fast enough. As a result, the hand-tailoring business fell off considerably. In his report to his fellow unionists of the United Brotherhood of Tailors, Secretary Joseph Goldberg said that eight thousand of New York's twenty thousand tailors were out of work as a direct result of the popularity of cycling.

In the same vein, a hat was hardly the sort of thing one wore while cycling, so bicyclemaniacs took to the cap, with a resulting decline in the making and selling of hats. Shoemakers suffered, not only because the lighter bicycle shoes became popular and lasted longer, but because more people were cycling rather than walking, thus making their shoes last longer and require fewer repairs.

Even the publishing business declined. Irving Putnam of G. P. Putnam's Sons told a *New York Times* reporter that the bicycle had cut into the profits of publishing houses. Cyclists were simply not reading as much as they had formerly, or if they were, they were concentrating on the new road books published by the League of American Wheelmen. Putnam, himself a cyclist, suggested that the entire thing was a fad whose effect would be temporary. Charles Scribner's Sons and Dodd, Mead and Company agreed with Putnam that profits had been affected. But *Harper's* said "No," probably because the magazine contained enough cycling news to be popular with fans.

For those who made a livelihood selling pianos, there was equal financial trouble. In 1895, after a reporter from the *Minneapolis Tribune* had said he could hardly see the connection between the bicycle boom and the depression in the piano business, an irate Chicago dealer shot back:

> Well, if you were a dealer in pianos you would quickly discover it. For instance, I have sold many pianos to young married couples. Sometimes they have bought them on the installment plan. Sometimes they have saved enough to buy the instrument outright. . . . This has been a good source of business to the piano dealer. Now, what has happened since the bicycle came into popular favor? Why the young people that otherwise would save up for a piano save up for two bicycles. That is a fact. Other piano dealers will tell you the same. Two bicycles can be purchased at the cost of one piano and perhaps they furnish amusement and perhaps they don't. . . . It looks as if the piano dealers' only chance will be in a piano and bicycle combined.[6]

Barbers suffered. The barbershop, that male holy of holies filled with the odor of bay rum and the pale pink of the *Police Gazette*, was quieter than ordinary, and customers' shaving mugs stood unused in the racks. The barbers sat in their ornate chairs and complained that men no longer spent Saturday afternoons getting prepared to take their ladies to the theater. Instead they were out cycling, not caring whether or not they were clean-shaven. As a New York tonsorial artist put it, "If a man skips a shave today, we can't sell him two shaves tomorrow."

In Indianapolis the Plumbers' Union passed stern resolutions against the use of the bicycle by its members, on the grounds that the machine enabled them to get their jobs done too quickly.

The complaints by people who claimed they were losing business as a result of the bicycle craze weren't exaggerations. The *New York Journal of Commerce* estimated that the onset of the cycle mania had brought about an annual loss of $112,500,000 to other trades, and said somberly: "What is gain for the bicycle makers is a clear loss to other businessmen."[7]

But the moans of the losers were drowned out by the happy cries of those who made money from the bicycle. Repair shops, whether run by manufacturers or by independent mechanics, sprang up in the cities and towns and seem to have done rather well. The repairmen especially liked the big road races held in the early nineties, because any time one hundred to five hundred men started out through the city streets, the inevitable result of such a mob pedaling madly over the cobblestones was a rash of accidents. Sometimes over a third of the racers suffered some damage to their cycles; with ball bearings retailing at a dollar each, there was a profit to be made. Always, the repairs were costly; to mend a split frame cost $3.50 in New York, a relative cost equivalent to that of a major overhaul on one of today's automobiles. In fact, one newspaper predicted that "if you take your machine to the repair shop it is a sure sign you will not buy a new suit of clothes."[8]

Elsewhere subsidiary businesses sprang up. In New York City, the "House-to-House Cleaning Company" cleaned and repaired the family's bicycles at home for a preset fee, a service that was quickly taken up by an enterprising repairman in Washington, D.C. Other bicycle dealers introduced messenger service and parcel delivery for those who wanted to pay a modest sum.

Among those who profited indirectly from the bicycle craze were the keepers of the hotels and inns that dotted the American countryside, especially in the Northeastern states. The rural inn, which once had catered to stagecoach passengers, had fallen on evil days as a result of the triumph of the steam locomotive. Taverns located along the highways had become empty shells. And conditions stayed that way until the cycling craze came along and thousands of Americans took to the country roads on touring vacations. At first rural folk did not like the bicycle, an antipathy that allegedly resulted from thousands of frightened horses; but eventually the proprietors of inns learned to love the wheel. From the very beginning the wheelmen used their organized power to lever whatever concessions they could from hotel proprietors. As far back as 1884, in the heyday of the ordinary, the League of American Wheelmen had arranged with proprietors to give reduced prices to bona fide members of the organization. In return for this favor, the league published the names of such hotels in the official bulletin, and cyclists were encouraged to patronize only those establishments that had made formal arrangements with the LAW.

As long as the highwheeler dominated the scene, such pressure amounted to little because there were relatively few cyclists. But by 1895 the number had increased to thousands, and hotels were actively competing for the business of the touring cyclist. The manager of the St. Louis Hotel, in the lake-resort area of Minneapolis, informed the *Minneapolis Tribune* that he was working hard to get his establishment in shape for cycling guests by May 10 and that he would go out of his way to cater to the tastes of wheelmen, whether in matters of cuisine or the adequate storage of their expensive bicycles. In New York, where the winters are less frigid than in Minnesota, the proprietor of the Getty House at Tarrytown offered a free bottle of wine to the first cyclist to show up for New Year's Day.

Even the farmers along the roads for the most part came to be happy with the turn of events. Before Merrick Road from New York to Jamaica, Long Island, was converted from a plank road to macadam, farmers in the area had cursed "them derned bicycle fellers," who had forced them to use devious routes in taking their produce to market. But how things had changed by the summer of 1895! As the number of cyclists heading for the countryside grew, farmers saw the economic possibilities. Watering troughs for horses were removed to make room for bicycle racks. The Farmer's Rest tavern changed its name to Bicycler's Retreat, all in a bold bid for the business that packed the roads on weekends and holidays. Along Merrick Road the farmers were selling flowers, fruit, and freshly caught fish to the city folk, and—to demonstrate the possibilities for profit from the craze—for a half mile on either side of the tire-repair shops, the repairmen allegedly had sprinkled carpet tacks.

The exodus of cyclists from the city did not end with the turning of the leaves. The mild weather on Election Day, 1896, saw "tens of thousands" of bicyclers pack Merrick Road, taking advantage of the holiday. They started in the early morning and did not let up until late at night, descending on the countryside like the locusts commanded by Moses. They ate up all the food in the inns, and the waggish *New York Journal* remarked that one could not find even a "Raines Law Sandwich" in the entire distance between the city and Jamaica. The Raines Law prohibited the sale of alcohol except in those establishments that also served food. The response of the gin mills was to keep a sandwich prominently displayed on the bar as evidence that it was complying with the law. Under ordinary circumstances the concoction was never sold and never eaten, being simply a part of the decor. But the cyclists were hungry.

And thirsty, too. One of the wheelers on Merrick Road was the secretary of the Liberty Wheelmen of Brooklyn, one D. A. Sammis. It seems that Sammis was unhappy because the Raines Law also closed the saloons on Sunday, on which day cycling gave him a powerful thirst. He sat for a long time squinting at his bicycle until it dawned on him that the tubing of the frame was hollow. For the next two weeks he worked, urged on by the harrowing vision of another cycling Sunday without a snifter. The result of this inspiration was a small faucet at the bottom of the central tube of the diamond frame, a capped filler hole at the top, and a cup. The *New York Tribune* said it best.

> The hollow post will contain more than a pint of whiskey, and he believes that the result of his mental faculties will prove an invaluable boon to all wheelmen who use stimulants. After the post has been filled, there is a little steel cap which screws on and makes it airtight. Sammis gave his improved wheel, as he calls it, a trial a few nights ago, and was wonderfully pleased with the results. The Liberty Club, it is said, will adopt the idea. In this connection it might not be amiss to state that the center post of the latest bicycles is nearly twice as large as heretofore.[9]

Sammis's invention notwithstanding, a large number of Sunday cyclers returned to the city without getting a bite to eat or a drop of spirits. No doubt the hunger and frustration was partly responsible for the many accidents that occurred on the roads. It was reported that repairmen could make a fortune in one day fixing broken machines.

Under the circumstances, it was no wonder the *New York Journal* said that farmers who had lived on unproductive farms prior to the cycling rage were happy about the outcome. In the country, shaded tables of food and drink awaited the cyclists' coming, and entire farm families were hard at work "making money hand over fist." The paper claimed that farmers were beginning to take a leaf from the booklet of the captains of industry and charge all the market would bear.

But while farmers and rural folk were counting their profits, the enterprising city boys were also hard at work. At 101 Street and Riverside Drive in New York a steep hill led up to Grant's Tomb. At the foot of this incline two young men with strong legs and heavy bicycles stationed themselves during the summer of 1895. They waited for an overly ambitious bicyclienne to come along and try to make the climb on her own. At the precise point of physical collapse, one of the young men would ride up. His polite inquiry of, "May I be of help, Miss?" usually elicited a gasp of consent. Tossing the lady a strap, one end of which was fastened to his belt, the young entrepreneur literally towed the exhausted one up the hill. After the young lady had endured this routine more than once and had gained some confidence, the young man simply put his hand—wearing a glove, naturally—on her back "just above the waistband of her bloomers" and shoved her up the hill. A small fee was, of course, expected.

Other ways to make a living out of the craze occurred to those who were inventive. D. A. Sammis of tubing fame was merely a man desperately thirsty, but there was a young man in Indianapolis who took advantage of the Sunday closing laws to become a real entrepreneur. He patrolled the cycling paths wearing a coat especially made to hold many small bottles filled with liquor. But this bicycle saloon was arrested, giving the cause of free enterprise another setback.

For those who did not want to make an honest living from the cycle business there were always opportunities to make a dishonest one. The more bicycles being ridden, the more there were to steal. In Minneapolis a man named Baker was arrested for stealing several cycles. He repainted them after filing off the serial numbers, and in some cases he even went so far as to disassemble several bicycles, mix up the parts, and then put them back together again. Unfortunately for Baker, he was arrested before his work really came to fruition, a sudden termination that probably was brought about because the culprit had a police record. He had previously stolen five hundred dollars' worth of buggies from a local firm, and the men in blue were watching him.

A year after Baker was apprehended, a team of bicycle thieves worked the Midwest with skill and profit. They moved into a town, pinched as many bicycles as they thought prudent, and then shipped them on down the line. After accumulating a stock-in-trade, they calmly got on the train, caught up with their stolen goods, sold them, and then repeated the entire process. It is likely this team was the same one that the *Minneapolis Tribune* called the "Denver Ring," which was broken up in November, 1895. In the Mile-High City the police arrested W. L. Bonner and J. S. Holmes, alias Stratton, alias Fuller, and in so doing recovered four bicycles, which the thieves had disassembled for shipment to Minneapolis as household goods. When the police broke in, Bonner was sitting on the floor taking a cycle apart. He submitted without a struggle, but Holmes, alias Stratton, alias Fuller, plucked a line from the dime novels of the time and told the arresting officers to "Shoot and——!"[10] A real pistol persuaded him to acknowledge the error of his ways.

Of course this was big-time stuff and not on the order of the petty thievery that sprang up all over the nation, if stealing a cycle that cost $125 can be called petty theft. In the late summer of 1895 New York City was titillated by a bloomer-clad woman thief who calmly picked out a bicycle, mounted it, and rode away. There is some likelihood that bystanders were mesmerized by her costume, but the *American Wheelman* scored it as a victory for the gallantry of the American male, since no man would be so boorish as to stop a lady if she wanted to steal a bicycle.

Simply appropriating a bicycle seems to have been easy enough, however. Some thieves lurked outside stores waiting for trusting souls to leave their bicycles untended. Others acted as potential bicycle purchasers, taking trial runs from which they never returned. Stealing rented bicycles became so common that one New York judge said it would soon take all his time just to preside over such cases. Then there was the thief who would accost a lady cyclist with the offer to repair some nonexistent flaw in the operation of her machine. Under the guise of road testing it, he would calmly ride off, leaving a sadder but wiser bicyclette behind in the roadway.

The result of all this pilfering was an outburst of indignation and an upswing in production at the Yale and Towne Lock Company and in human ingenuity. One disgruntled Midwesterner reverted to the day of the horse and chained his bicycle to a heavy weight, an imitation of the portable horse block. Such tactics may have sufficed in rural areas, but they would not work in New York City or Boston. So once more private enterprise leaped to the fore. The increase in cycling thefts was accompanied by the rise of "protective agencies," which insured bicycles and tried to recover them if they were stolen. The Wheelman's Protective Company in New York City warned, "Remember, thieves are riding better every day!" The company boasted that it had recovered 40 per cent of the bicycles registered with it and pointed out that any wheel that bore the numbered tag of the company was usually given a wide berth by thieves.

Seeing a tidy profit to be turned in the business of protecting cycles, the National Bicycle Protective Company advertised that for $2.50 a year it would guard against theft, and for an extra $1.50 it would also insure the bicycle against damages. This kind of collision insurance was to become a standard feature for automobiles. In the event a bicycle was stolen, the owner was to notify the company within two days. If the cycle were not recovered within thirty days, the company promised to replace the machine with one of the same make and style, although it did not specify that the replacement would be of the same age. It was alleged that the company was very slow in filling the claims, taking as long as three months to make good, and even then the replacements were sometimes inferior to the stolen machine.

The protective idea spread. The Wheelman's Protective Company struck back at competitors by calling on the public to "Patronize the Pioneer Protectors!" and cutting its rates to two dollars for the first year and one dollar for every year thereafter. For publicity's sake it sent Charles Rockwell of New York on a cross-country bicycle ride to advertise the company's services.

Business must have been pretty good, because the League of American Wheelmen, never averse to picking up a dollar where it could, got into the protection business. It issued its own plate testifying that the owner was a member of the league and offered a reward of twenty-five dollars for the arrest of anyone who stole a member's bicycle. It was fondly believed that the reward acted as a deterrent.

In spite of precautions and arrests, a ring of bicycle thieves worked the Midwest again in the summer of 1896. They were based in Chicago, where an estimated 200,000 bicycles constituted the mother herd just waiting to be raided. The cycle rustlers disposed of their hot merchandise in Cincinnati, St. Louis, and Indianapolis. In ten days the ring got away with sixty-three bicycles. Two bicycle policemen riding around in plain clothes failed to stem the outgoing tide.

In New York City the pilfering also continued, protection societies and police notwithstanding. James Quinlan broke into a bicycle shop on Fulton Street and purloined three bicycles, for doing which the judge sent him to Ossining Prison for nine years. Since this was an average of three years for each bicycle, it is plain that bicycle theft was not regarded as petty thievery. The LAW had been demanding that the judges come down hard on cycle thieves, but even the wheelmen had suggested only one year in jail.

If one chose not to steal bicycles, one might use the bicycle to steal. In Hempstead, Long Island, a cycle burglar was able to make five raids in one evening, an increase of about 50 per cent in efficiency. And a juvenile apprentice in the trade found his bicycle lamp very useful in making sure that he took only things of value from the houses he entered.

But breaking and entering was small coin, and two men in Buffalo, Illinois, decided to try for something bigger. Just as in the olden days when the James boys rode into Northfield, Minnesota, the pair pedaled down the main street of the sleepy little town, leaned their bicycles against the front of the bank, and proceeded to rob it of ten thousand dollars. They escaped on their machines and disappeared into the bottom lands of the Sangamon River.

Six months later, on a smoky Indian Summer day, two men walked into the bank in Sherburne, Minnesota. They were appropriately dressed in cycling clothes and used drawn pistols to reinforce their demands for the money. They departed with the swag and raced toward the nearby Iowa line, trying to put as much distance as they could between themselves and the two men they had left dead on the floor of the bank. A pursuit followed that anticipated Mack Sennett, save for the fact that it was in deadly earnest. One of the bandits was cornered near Elmore, Iowa; but he killed a deputy and managed to escape again. However, five miles out in Iowa countryside, heavy with unpicked corn, the old bugaboo caught up with the bandit—he had a puncture. No longer mounted, the robber ran into an adjacent field and shot himself to death rather than surrender. A day later his colleague was run to the ground near Lake Mills and surrendered. At the time of his capture the culprit was armed with three revolvers and two Bowie knives, whose combined weight may explain why he had not escaped.

If one did not steal bicycles for a living or use them in the perpetration of crimes, one could always prey upon those who rode bicycles. As cyclists got farther and farther afield, and especially after night riding became a fad, petty thieves and holdup men took to haunting the country roads. A young cyclist from Paterson, New Jersey, was "boldly and brutally" robbed by four men while riding to Passaic. Out near Freeport, Long Island, a night-riding party of six was rolling merrily along when the leader parted company with his cycle, having run full tilt into a log laid across the road in the best style of the Wild West. Nothing came of it, since the size of the party scared off the bandit.

As such muggings increased, *The New York Times* reported that cyclists were beginning to talk about carrying guns when they rode out into the country. One dressmaker reported that he was stitching revolver pockets into the cycling habits of women. In 1898, Sears, Roebuck and Company, always on the alert, advertised a collapsible "bicycle rifle" that could be carried in a leather holster and be fired as either a pistol or a rifle. When folded it measured only sixteen inches long and weighed less than two pounds. If one wanted an all-purpose weapon, this looked like the thing.

In 1896, William Randolph Hearst's *New York Journal* took time out from its newspaper war with Pulitzer's *World* to observe that tramps had been molesting cyclists for at least three years, and that so many riders had taken to carrying revolvers for protection that the arms industry had enjoyed an unanticipated boom. In the interest of under-standing the situation, it must be said that the United States had been in the throes of a major economic decline since the winter of 1893, and the nation was overrun with men whose only crime was to be jobless. They could not be expected to be overly sympathetic to a bunch of gay blades who could afford to pay half a year's salary for a bicycle.

Anyway, to separate a cyclist from his cash was to do him a favor and save him from physical debilitation. If the cyclist had no money he would be unable to repair his cycle when it broke down, and perforce he would have to stop riding. Once he got off the bicycle he would no longer be exposed to "kyphosis bicyclistarum," terrible "bicycle hump" of the "scorchers."

CHAPTER 4

"A Scientific Angel"

THE DEBATE OVER HEALTH, RELIGION, MORALS, AND MANNERS

BICYCLE INSTITUTE OF AMERICA

ROLLING CIGARETTE

When President Dwight Eisenhower in 1955 suffered a serious heart attack, the people waited anxiously for the prognosis. During that time they were treated to a series of statements by the attending physician, a noted heart specialist who extolled the virtues of bicycle riding as a way to good health. At the time there were relatively few people in the country who took exception to Dr. Paul Dudley White's dictum that pedaling around the streets was a good form of moderate exercise for those whose lives were otherwise sedentary.

It is doubtful that Dr. White knew, or cared, that at the onset of the bicycle craze in the United States there was considerable discussion among physicians and laymen regarding the harmful effects of riding the new-fangled machines. Bad riding posture and ill-fitted saddles were accused of producing "irritation" and "congestion," which led in turn to "chronic disease," whatever that meant. A few physicians contended that excessive cycling created a heavy thirst, which was relieved by drinking beer, which in turn made for kidney stones. One physician warned that cycling might bring on insanity. Elsewhere the rumor circulated that to take children cycling would be to risk damage to their nervous systems.

However, the passage of a decade brought an amazing about-face. By 1893 physicians were lining up to praise the virtues of cycling as a cure for almost any ailment. Carried away by enthusiasm, one proponent pointed out that cycling aided both respiration and digestion and by so doing attacked anemia and nervous prostration; it also was beneficial in cases of asthma, was effective in combating the influence of tuberculosis, and was magnificent against headaches, insomnia, and neuralgia. Indeed it would seem that riding the bicycle had all the beneficial results that could be expected from taking a bottle of Dr. Hostetter's Bitters or an equal amount of Lydia Pinkham's Compound for Women.

A Frenchman, Henri Desgranges, previously quoted as extolling the grace of French cycles, wrote in 1895 that cycling had its interesting moral side in the sense that a sound mind in a sound body was moral.

> Quite a large number of our young men, who formerly were addicted to stupid habits, and the seeking of nonsensical distractions and vulgar pleasures, are now vigorous, healthy, energetic, and for the sake of this extraordinary machine submit themselves to an ascetic rule of life, and, induced by taste and passion, acquire habits of temperance, the imperative desire of quiet and regular living, and, most important of all, the steady exercise of self control, by resisting their appetites and doing, without hesitation, all that is required for effectual training.[1]

Of course some precautions had to be taken. In the early days Charles Pratt warned against riding too much either on a full stomach or an empty one. To those bewildered about just how to attain a gastronomic balance, he recommended a pretrip breakfast of either a little bread and butter, a cup of coffee and a roll, or a glass of milk. No stirrup-cup, however, because alcohol "unsteadied the nerves," and nerves showed an alarming tendency to be unsteady anyway when one mounted the old highwheelers.

The cyclist was also advised to breath through his nose lest he draw the cold, dust-laden air into his lungs, and to wear woolen underwear, avoid drafts, and be sure to change clothing at the end of his run. *Bicycle World* told its readers in 1892 to stick to the shady side of the road, stay clear of ice water, and avoid alcohol when the temperature went over 90 degrees. No wonder saloonkeepers complained.

Here and there a voice advised that young people whose skeletal structure was not mature should be prevented from slumping over the handlebars. From England came the solemn warning of Sir B. W. Richardson, a prominent physician, to the effect that the nervous system might suffer as a result of having to be constantly on the alert.

But then he relieved the fears he had conjured up by saying that cycling could not cause hernia or enlarged veins. He did suggest that riders who suffered from "twitching muscles" at the end of the ride should take things easier, especially if they were middle-aged.

Eventually most American physicians who went on record recommended the sport. They urged moderation in cycling, proper breathing, and proper posture, but generally they approved. As for the effects on human hearts, most of the doctors were of the opinion that cycling would not harm sound hearts and might actually improve those that were unsound, a distant strain antedating Dr. White's advice.

Cycling was definitely recommended as a means of improving circulation, strengthening the lungs, and building good muscle tone. No doubt many corpulent members of a generation that was famous for its girth took to the cycle for weight control, but with very unsatisfactory results, if Joseph Grimes of Cleveland was an example. Mr. Grimes, who was twenty-eight years old and a veteran cyclist of three years, took a six-month bicycle tour of Europe to help keep his weight down. Unfortunately, the trip did little for his sixty-one-inch chest, sixty-three-inch waist, and sixty-eight-inch hips. At six feet, four inches, he weighed 540 pounds! Mr. Grimes may have been a poor recommendation for cycling as a reducer of weight, but the fact that he could even find a bicycle to ride was a glowing testimonial to the durability of the American product.

The most vigorous debates over the influence of the bicycle on health came when women began to ride the machine. As long as the tricycle was the only thing available to her, a woman could sit between the two rear wheels and travel sedately down the street with a minimum of effort and a maximum of ankle coverage. However, with the advent of the safety bicycle the debate erupted, with some people stoutly maintaining that cycling was not for women. A patent-medicine company hinted that riding had harmful effects on the "weaker sex," then advised those women who rode the machine, and thus ran the danger of "heating the blood" and bringing on "certain complaints," to take Payne's Celery Tonic.

In March, 1896, Miss Marguerite Lindley told a Brooklyn audience that riding a bicycle was destructive of "feminine symmetry and poise, a disturber of internal organs and an irritant of external tissues."[2] What she meant was that cycling had a tendency to develop some parts of the body at the expense of others, notably the legs against the trunk and arms.

However, such warnings against women's cycling were the exception rather than the rule. By 1896 moderate cycling was even being recommended for expectant mothers. Not only was it healthy, but the morning air tended to dissipate the "blues."

A New York medical man told an audience that cycling had come along just in time to rehabilitate the American woman. Until then, he contended, women were in bad shape because their "nervous force was wearing out," and as one and all knew, the decline of every nation had begun with the debilitation of the nervous systems of its women. Before the safety bicycle, American women had been inclined to be morbid and stay indoors, where they had gotten into the habit of worrying and "fussing" about themselves when there was no need of it. Now, said the doctor, the bicycle would get them out into the clean air, where they could be in touch with other people and forget about themselves.[3]

Dr. A. L. Benedict, in a letter to the *Century Magazine* published in July, 1897, especially recommended riding for spinsters. For those who had not reached the "calm" of middle age and who were "passing through a period of mental fermentation and physical irritability of varying degree according to their social sphere, temperament, and habits," there came the mourning for the lost gaiety of younger days, not to mention mislaid opportunities. The spinster who was dependent on the bounty of a relative became the "prey of mental yearning and dissatisfaction and it is little wonder that actual disease follows." According to the doctor, first some special form of "neuralgia" might set in, then the supply of "nerve power" to the stomach became so deficient that "serious dyspepsia" resulted, followed by hypochondria and the stampede to Lydia Pinkham's Pills or Payne's Celery Tonic. For such sufferers the bicycle was a blessing because it brought the exhilaration of motion, made Nature accessible, and provided for some social companionship. Altogether it gave a "much-needed mental and nerve tonic" to those women who made up the army of "Aunties" in the latter part of the nineteenth century.[4]

In Chicago, Dr. Weller Van Hook recommended cycling for women because it would encourage them to discard the "murderous corset" and use their God-given muscles instead. Twenty-eight other doctors agreed with Dr. Van Hook. The corset business, whose devices had long been *de rigueur* for fashionable women, fought back. In 1895 the *Chicago Tribune* carried an advertisement for the "WB Bicycle Corset for Women." The American Lady Corset Company offered one hundred dollars of free bicycle accident insurance with every garment purchased. In Chicago, "sandwich men" on bicycles carried signs with the appeal that "Pretty Women Who Ride Should Wear Smith's Corsets."

Although doctors were generally agreed in recommending cycling as an adjunct to good health, a few did get carried away, or at least strayed a little. In Omaha a doctor advised cyclers to chew gum when they went on spins through the countryside; this would help them satisfy their thirst and prevent them from drinking from rural wells, which might be tainted with typhoid. There is no reason to doubt the importance of warning against drinking from strange wells, especially in an area almost devoid of the simplest sanitary engineering, but it took a Frenchman to come up with a new form of "gout," a pedal deformation he contended was brought on by cycling. "Prowler," in his column for *Outing* magazine in September, 1891, pooh-poohed the entire idea and said the disturbance came from having garters that were too tight. He advised cyclists to wear tights to avoid cutting off the circulation to the feet, although he admitted that the garments were not attractive.

As cycling became more and more popular it did cause some maladies that were not attributable to improperly fitted clothing. A New York doctor solemnly informed the readers of Gotham that there was such a thing as "bicycle walk." Not only did it exist, but the affliction was on the increase. The doctor described it as a walk that duplicated the motions of the feet and legs in pedaling a bicycle. This meant that when walking the cyclemaniac did not swing his foot forward, but lifted it off the ground in a rising, circular motion, as if he were riding the pedal. The "bicycle walk" was to be found among professional bicycle racers, who were also afflicted with a rolling of the shoulders and the head that came from the exertions of sprint racing.

More serious was the malady known as "bicycler's heart." One Dr. Petit said that overstrain from riding up hills, meeting head winds, and becoming excessively fatigued would injure the heart, but others suggested that "bicycle heart" was only another name for the enlargement that had long been known as "athlete's heart," no more, no less. Many famous professional cyclists were afflicted, but none seemed to be the worse for it.

"Bicycle heart" was less serious to the physician than the condition called "kyphosis bicyclistarum," otherwise called the "bicycle hump" by the unlearned. The first mention of this deformity came from the British Isles, where it was solemnly intoned that "dorsal curvature posteriorally which used to be uncommon in boys under fourteen was more frequently met with than in previous years."[5] This unhappy state of affairs was brought on by the practice of "scorching," or seeing to it that all other bicyclers were left behind on the road. By lowering the handlebars and raising the seat the cyclist reduced wind resistance while increasing the efficiency of his legs. The resulting posture was described in doggerel.

> He spun upon his waiting wheel,
> His vertebrae threw out of joint,
> And onward pedalled looking like,
> A great interrogation point.[6]

Another source described this curvature as a malady that caused young men to look as if they were the victims of stomach cramps or as if they were trying to "refresh their olefactory organs" by sniffing the rubber of their front tires. "Ye gods!" *Outing* snorted, "Why is it that these ignorant youths can not see the absurdity of their laughter-provoking attitudes."[7]

Sometimes the consequences of "bicycle hump" were terrible to the extreme. The *Milwaukee Telegraph* called attention to the story of the young Iowa couple who humped over their handlebars and were rewarded with an infant with the posture of a drawn bow. "Sit straight, confound you! Sit straight!" was the paper's admonition. This last was the most common advice given to riders of the steel steeds. On Staten Island a cyclist formed the Westfield Non-scorching Sit-Erect Bicycle Club.

Despite the concern, Professor Albert Abrams told his students at San Francisco's Cooper Medical College that the bicycle hump was a chimera. No one could point to a single case of spinal deformity arising from bicycle riding, and furthermore, if speed was the primary objective, the hump was the most efficient posture.

Other purported physiological ailments arose from using different sets of muscles or using the same muscles differently when cycling. For example, a Buffalo physician discovered the affliction known as "bicycle hands." It seemed to affect the left hand more than the right, because the left hand was seldom as strong as the right one. The first symptom of "bicycle hands" was a slight numbness of the thumb and fingers, although the doctor labeled the malady as "insidious" and said it might not be felt at first. Nevertheless, it was lurking in the musculature of the hand, and unless the unwary took immediate notice, he might suddenly discover that he could no longer hold anything in his hands. The doctor predicted that the affected member might become permanently useless. It was suggested that the only thing to do was to change the position of the handlebars just as soon as the hands began to feel numb.

Fortunately there is little evidence that "bicycle hands" was widespread or that it had serious consequences. Nevertheless in Chicago a budding inventor named Weeks turned his attention to the problem and produced a pair of pneumatic handle grips to alleviate the pain and discomfort. Mr. Weeks perfected two small, airtight sacks that could be laced to the handlebars and then filled with air to minimize the jar on the palms. It was predicted that the new grips would be used by the thousands, but this was wishful thinking on the inventor's part.

Having identified "bicycle hands," the doctors went a step further and found "bicycle wrists." This ailment manifested itself by sore and swollen wrists that came partly from the tight grip on the handlebars, but even more from the practice of backpedaling. Before brakes became common, backpedaling was the primary way of stopping the bicycle, and as the rider pedaled backwards he naturally pulled up on the handlebars. Alternately pushing down while riding and pulling up while backpedaling placed an unusual strain on the wrists.

The list of bicycle-caused maladies continued to grow. With a perfectly straight editorial face the *Minneapolis Tribune* reported an outbreak of "bicycle gums," brought on by excessive cycling. Allegedly the disease came about because a cyclist who rode fast and far heated up his system. But the faster and farther he rode the more he panted for air, and it was that cold air drawn in over the superheated gums that did the trick. This caused a "congestion" of blood, which led in turn to the loosening of the teeth and their eventual loss altogether. The only remedy mentioned was a closed mouth.

The next affliction to be diagnosed was "bicycle eye." Dr. J. D. Berry of Boston identified the disturbance for the public and described it for the *Boston Transcript*. Lecturing ever so slightly on physiology, the medical man explained that the muscles—*recti* to the professional— that lay below the eye and pushed it upward were the weakest of all the muscles controlling eye movement. When a cyclist went scorching down a thoroughfare he was laying himself wide open to "bicycle eye," because with his head lowered he then had to raise his eyes to see ahead. The equivalent of this action would be walking around for a prolonged time with the eyes rotated back into the head, looking as straight up as possible. Anyone who tries this will discover that after a short time the lower *recti* do indeed become fatigued, and prolonging the activity will only add to the discomfort.

Actually "bicycle eye" was more properly known as "bicycle face," also described in verse.

> The latest feature discovered by cranks
> On the faces of ladies fair,
> Is known in the great cycle-istic ranks
> Of the world, as the "bicycle stare".
> The stares, so 'tis said, on the face of the beauty
> Would frighten a mule from the path of duty.[8]

A Midwest paper divided "bicycle face" into three distinct parts. First, there was the "wide and widely expectant expression of the eyes." Then strain lines appeared around the mouth; and finally there was a "general focussing of all the features toward the center, a sort of physiognomic implosion." How or why did it happen? Let the paper speak for itself.

> Scientists took hold of the matter, and advanced theories about it. One learned man said that the bicycle face was the result of a constant strain to preserve equilibrium. Up popped another scientist who stated that the preserving of equilibrium was purely an instinct, involving no strain, and that if the first man knew a bicycle from a rickshaw he'd realize it. Thereupon the first scientist said that the second had a bicycle brain, and hundreds took sides in the discussion. A prominent bicycle academy instructor here is positive that he has solved the secret. The three component parts of the expression he ascribes to the following causes:
> The phenomenon of the wild eyes is acquired while learning the art. It is caused by a painful uncertainty whether to look for the arrival of the floor from the front, behind, or one side, and, once fixed upon the countenance can never be removed.
> The strained lines about the mouth are due to anxiety lest the tire should explode. Variations of the lines are traceable to the general use of chewing gum.
> The general focus of the features is indicative of extreme attention directed to a spot about two yards ahead of the wheel. This attention arises from a suspicion that there is probably a stone, a bit of glass, an upturned tack, barrel hoop or other dangerous article lying in wait there. It is temporarily lost when the obstacle is struck and the bicyclist's face makes furrows in the ground, but reappears with increased intensity after every such experience.[9]

Elsewhere a *New York Herald* reporter who attended the meeting of the League of American Wheelmen in Asbury Park, New Jersey, found "bicycle face" everywhere he looked. He compared the cyclists with their projecting jaws and bent necks to fish hawks questing for prey, but added that the strained looks on the cyclers' faces were beatific compared to the hunted expressions developed by pedestrians as a result of dodging scorchers all day long. Another paper noted that a man had grown a full beard just to hide his "bicycle face."

Fortunately, as far as "bicycle face" went, things took a turn for the better, brought on no doubt by improved skill and better roads. In 1896, the *Boston Globe* noted that the countenances of cycling men and women had relaxed and become more natural.

> The stare of the eyes has become softened; the once contorted features have become composed; the chin has returned to its modest place beneath the nose, instead of being thrust to the front like a bowsprit. Of the cyclists who swarm along the boulevards today, not one in ten bears the scowling and inhuman features that last year were to be seen on every hand.[10]

As if "bicycle eye" and "bicycle hand" and "bicycle wrist" and "bicycle face" were not enough, another expert discovered an unnamed malady that might have been named "bicycle twitch" or the "bicycle jerks." This disease was said to afflict women primarily and was evidenced by a sudden nervous twitch of the head to the rear, accompanied by downcast eyes. "The basis of it is the burning question: Are my bloomers on straight? This ailment has not yet become very general."[11]

Yet despite these bicycle-caused afflictions, most doctors agreed that cycling was good for human health.

Along with the debate over cycling and health, there was also a controversy concerning the effects of cycling on the practice of religion in the nation. In 1896 not the least of the institutions that had been affected by the cycle was the American church, especially in the small towns and villages where formerly there had been little to do on Sundays except go to listen to the preacher.

The bicycle changed all that, and God's House, as an institution, was in deep trouble. "The churches," wrote J. B. Bishop, editorial writer for the *New York Evening Post*, "are fast losing their young people and efforts to call them back by appeals to their sense of Christian duty"[12] were falling on deaf ears. Nor were the threats of eternal damnation having any better effect. A generation later, ministers condemned the motor car for having a deleterious influence on churchgoing because it became popular to take a Sunday drive, but long before such recreation became an institution in American life the bicycle had set the example. It was the first big-scale assault of American technology on institutionalized religion.

In the late nineteenth century the working week for most people was six days long, and recreation had to fall on Sunday. But the Sabbath had been set aside for the Lord's use, and a people strongly Calvinistic in orientation had developed strict ideas on what was allowable on Sundays. In most cases families attended church in the morning, went back home to a heavy, starch-filled meal at noon, and then sat around in a state of semistupefaction for the remainder of the day. Children were not supposed to play noisy games, and generally nobody was supposed to engage in anything but the most sedate activity.

And then the bicycle came and the Sabbath was defiled—so some believed—by crowds of cyclists slipping single file through the streets and along the roads. The worst thing was that they were riding during those hours when they should have been in church. That became the issue.

The attack against the cycle as a threat to institutionalized religion really did not reach its peak until the safety bicycle made the sport a public affair. But as the number of cyclists increased, filling the streets and roads on Sunday mornings, the outcry against the wheel mounted. Evangelists across the nation preached against the practice of cycling on the Lord's Day and followed with dire prophecies about the lack of future for those who failed to fulfill their religious responsibilities. A New Haven clergyman drew a terrifying picture of a long line of cyclists, all without brakes, rolling helplessly downhill to a "place where there is no mud on the streets because of the high temperatures."[13] A colleague said *all* bicycle riders were in danger of going to hell and virtually certain to do so if they rode on the Sabbath. His sentiments were echoed around the country.

In Chicago some members of the congregation of the Hope Baptist Church attacked the Reverend J. H. Messenger because he rode a bicycle on his pastoral calls. Rather than fight, the minister resigned, although the young people were on his side. In 1896, the Presbyterian Assembly of New York approved a resolution condemning cycling on Sundays. The New England Sabbath Protective League appealed to young people to avoid bicycle meets held on Sunday, events that were roundly condemned as both desecration and secularization of God's Day. In Chicago, the Reverend David Beeton contended that Sunday bicycle meets, parades, and races poisoned the very "lifeblood of American civilization."[14]

But the more bicycles the American public purchased, the more did the churches and their spokesmen tend to backpedal—at least in the cities. In the summer of 1895 the Baptist Young People's Union met in Baltimore and conducted a Sunday bicycle parade! All very decently done, of course, with lead cycles flying the flag of Maryland and the blue and white flag of the Baptists.

In Chicago, the same year that saw the Hope Baptist Church force its minister to resign, Jenkin Lloyd Jones preached that the bicycle was a good thing, spiritually and morally. Jones had created something of a sensation earlier by allowing cyclists in his congregation to check their bicycles in the church basement. Now he took an even more liberal position on Sunday cycling by saying that while the sport reduced church attendance, he felt that taking a ride through the countryside might put one in closer communion with God than just sitting in the sanctuary. Jones did issue the warning that a young man who "dons his jockey-cap, humps himself like a kangaroo and pumps away for dear life, apparently with no purpose in view except to see how quickly he can roll over fifty miles," was endangering his immortal soul. Evidently the Lord loved a cycler but abominated a scorcher. The Reverend Mr. Jones then warned his congregation that "from this time on, if it is the church or the wheel one needs no prophetic eye to see which will win in thousands of lives. All Souls Church of Chicago would fain avert the conflict by becoming the 'church of the wheel.'"[15] With such subversion in mind, Jones invited people to ride their cycles to Sunday services, saying the church would provide somebody to care for the machines.

Other ministers likewise rushed to the defense of the bicycle. In New York City the Reverend John Shaw, completely unabashed by his church's condemnation of Sunday cycling, told his Presbyterians that cycling contributed to the spiritual good of the community. Not content with defying the Assembly, he put forth the astounding theological observation that religious agnosticism frequently had its origins in dyspepsia, for which the cycle was a sovereign cure. The Reverend Mr. Shaw proceeded to thank God for the bicycle and said he would canonize the inventor if he knew the man's name.

As a matter of fact, the Presbyterian clergyman was merely echoing a colleague, Madison Peters, who had said the year before that cycling would defeat a sour stomach. However, Peters was less permissive and added that under the lights of Central Park "Jezebel spreads her nets and Delilah shears the locks of Samson."[16]

Aside from condemnation of Jezebels, a chorus of approbation rose from many pulpits. One minister was downright rhapsodical when he described cycling. "How tranquil and happy! How self-poised and self-reliant, how harmonious with nature and art, the cyclist seems as he passes along the highway, street and boulevard, like a bird on the wings of the wind."[17] In New Jersey, the Reverend John Scudder told a congregation that included two hundred attentive wheelmen that the bicycle was a "revolutionist," the advance agent of heaven, since "it enables us to fly in this life before we get the traditional angelic wings."[18] He also proposed that a Saturday half-holiday be established that could be used for recreation and so preserve the sanctity of Sunday. Very likely this is one of the few times such a radical proposal came from the pulpit.

In some respects the apotheosis of the bicycle came when the Reverend E. S. Upford told his congregation in Brooklyn's Tabernacle Baptist Church that the machine was a "scientific angel, which seems to bear you on its unwearied pinions."[19] He compared the earliest attempts to perfect the cycle with man's primitive state after having been driven from the Garden of Eden. The modern safety bicycle was symbolic of mankind's perfection and regeneration through Christ. The good man ended his sermon by calling on his congregation to be more like the bicycle—willing to serve mankind. No wonder Brooklyn was a cycle hotbed.

There were those who argued that if the cyclists would not come to the church, the church should go to them. In the summer of 1896 a party of clergymen went along the Merrick Road and held open-air religious services in groves of trees, but few cyclists stopped to participate. Then in Brooklyn a few cycle-riding laymen discussed the building of a portable, lightweight church that could be set up here and there around the countryside, wherever the cyclists were riding at the time. The best location would be near the end of a twenty-mile run, because at that point the cyclists would be stopping to rest. A portable building was regarded with favor because cyclers did not always ride the same route on successive Sundays; they liked a change of scenery.

Tongue-in-cheek, the New York Tribune offered some suggestions of its own. Why not have a bicycle as the bishop's seat, dress the choirboys in knickerbockers and sweaters, and have the stained-glass windows show pedals, brakes, and saddles? The opening hymn could be an adaptation of Cardinal Newman's famous work.

> Wheel, Kindly Light, along life's cycle path,
> Wheel Thou me on!
> The road is rough, I have discerned Thy Wrath,
> But wheel me on![20]

Obviously, concluded the paper, the congregation should be watched over by a preacher with wheels—in his head. With such a reception as that, the portable cycling church never got off the drawing board.

If surrender was the course chosen by the effete big-city parishes, the churches in small towns, the traditional strongholds of Jehovah, fought back. The Methodist Church of Camden, New Jersey, voted to expel any member who rode a bicycle on Sunday, although it must be said that the decision to do so split the congregation right down the middle. The losers publicly said that they would not abide by the vote. The issue seems to have been raised because members of the church had watched cyclists pour across the Schuylkill River from Philadelphia—somewhere around ten thousand such invaders every Sunday. Not only did jangling bells and blaring horns disrupt services, but out on Whitehorse Pike men sold beer openly over the tailgates of their wagons. Townships that had been "dry" for a quarter of a century were invaded by beer wagons, and roadhouses ran wide open. The church struck back. Seven hundred members, so we are told, of the Epworth League were enlisted against Sunday cycling. Solemnly the young people stood, raised their right hands and swore, "I promise that I will not ride my wheel on the Sabbath, only as it will honor my Master, and as I believe he would like to have me do. I also promise to exert all possible influence to discourage others in the use of the Sunday wheel."[21]

They had help. The Dunkards met in annual session in Covington, Kentucky, and voted overwhelmingly to excommunicate all members who had their teeth filled with gold or who rode bicycles, a strange juxtaposition of sins.

Even more than riding on Sundays, the issue of bicycling by women continued to occupy center stage during the nineties. The health issue may have been resolved; the moral issue had not been, and the ladies had to beat back the idea that a good woman did not ride the bicycle at all. The Women's Rescue League, a militant feminist organization that demanded that all bachelors be forced to marry, concluded that "bicycling by young women has helped more than any other media to swell the ranks of reckless girls, who finally drift into the standing army of outcast women of the United States."[22] In Chicago, the *Tribune* shook its head and called the pronouncement an hysterical outburst by an organization that was suffering from a "perverted moral sense coupled with dense ignorance."[23] As late as 1897, a New York lady named Charlotte Smith, who was the president of the Women's Rescue League, was doing all she could to condemn the bicycle as a cause of immorality among females. Although she got nowhere, she fought at every step. During the meeting of the state legislature in January, 1897, she prowled the halls in Albany trying to find a sponsor for her bills to outlaw cycling by women. Since the powerful lobby of the League of American Wheelmen was then encamped in the city, it is not surprising that she was unsuccessful in finding a representative gullible enough—or mean enough—to put his name to such a bill. The American woman might stop cycling, but if she did it would be of her own volition.

In fact, for women cyclers emancipation was the theme. Madelyne Bridges wrote a poem for *Outing* entitled "Wheels and Wheels," in which she described the freedom conferred by the bicycle.

The maiden with her wheel of old
    Sat by the fire to spin,
While lightly through her careful hold
    The flax slid out and in.

Today her distaff, rock and reel
    Far out of sight are hurled
And now the maiden with her wheel
    Goes spinning round the world.[24]

More and more women came to regard the cycle as a freedom machine. Until the 1890's they had confined themselves to demanding the right to vote and timidly advocating some dress reform. But on a bicycle the American woman was another being, free and her own mistress. She wore the kind of clothes she wanted, men's opinions notwithstanding, and she began to reach for even more freedom.

This was the "new woman," to give her the name she and others used. And she had her defenders outside the ranks of cycledom. In Chicago, the Reverend Carlos Martyn advised the Epworth League to be serene about the "new woman," since she was just the old in a new environment. Riding a bicycle would not destroy the home, he said, nor would it eradicate motherhood or grace or delicacy. He told his audience of young people that "it would be just as sweet and just as pleasant to make love to a woman wearing bloomers as to one who does not."[25] Obviously the preacher was referring to simple courtship here. The Reverend Mr. Martyn went on to declare that Americans were living in a period when life was larger and freer in every respect, and just as horizons had broadened for males, so they should for females. There seemed to be no limit to the man's radicalism, because he capped his speech by telling the youngsters of the league that women should also have the right to vote!

The *Minneapolis Tribune* added, "Cycling is fast bringing about this change of feeling regarding woman and her capabilities. A woman awheel is an independent creature, free to go whither she will. This, before the advent of the bicycle, was denied her."[26]

There were exceptions to this outbreak of support for feminine freedom, however. Louisville, Kentucky, papers were charged with carrying out a deliberate campaign to discourage women's cycling by printing pictures of outlandish bicycle garb for ladies, coupled with reports that tended to ridicule the ability of females to control the cycle. Some show managers of the "living pictures," the burlesque tableaus so popular in the nineties, included wheelwomen in hope that no lady would ride a machine that lent itself to such unseemly display. One Florida city would not permit women to ride the cycles on city streets until 1897.

Much of this had to do with propriety. From the moment the ladies took to the bicycle, the age addressed itself solemnly to the question of cycling manners. For example, should a gentleman cycling down a path in Central Park greet a young bicyclette when they encountered each other? And just when was it proper for a young lady to request assistance from a passing male? Trivial as such matters may seem today, they were weighty problems indeed for a period still cowering under the grim visage of the chaperon.

Harper's Weekly, after noticing that cyclists were having trouble working out proper rules of conduct, offered advice called "Etiquette for the Road." As a blanket statement, the magazine said that the people of "real or acquired refinement" who already knew how to comport themselves in the drawing room were unlikely to conduct themselves with less dignity on a bicycle. For example, while it was entirely proper for a strange gentleman to help a lady in distress when he encountered her on the path, a real lady would immediately take her bicycle to the nearest repair shop if one were handy, and not stand along the road waiting for a helpful male to pass.

As for greeting strangers, the article was adamant. "There is no more reason for a man cyclist touching his hat to a passing woman cyclist with whom he is not acquainted, than for a man riding, driving or walking. Different situations do not alter the laws of good manners." The same article went on to say that the "want of manners becomes discernible upon the road even more quickly than in the drawing room and rude and unpolished people will ride the wheel just as they will drive and ride horses or travel in public conveyances."[27]

The situation was altered, of course, if the cyclists knew each other. When a couple rode together, the woman was always to be accorded primacy by being allowed to ride in front, although such an arrangement would destroy the companionship for which the bicycle was being praised. In addition, the lady least capable of maintaining the pace during club runs should always be allowed to ride at the front of the column lest she lose out and be left behind.

The *Minneapolis Tribune* also listed some "do's and don't's" for lady cyclists, including, "Don't ride without gloves, don't wear flaming colors in the hat, don't ride a tandem on Sunday afternoon except with a male escort." The paper held that two women on a tandem were "an invitation to every rude man to make insulting remarks of a personal nature."[28]

A metropolitan paper, the *Riverside Daily Enterprise*, printed an article in June, 1896, called "Wheels for Widows," in which it solemnly stated that it was no longer necessary for widows in mourning to stop cycling or to give their bicycles away because an enterprising firm had provided a cycle approved for mourning etiquette. It was absolutely funereal, enameled in the blackest of ebony finishes and without any nickel or shining steel to suggest that the widow was less than completely bereaved. Consequently, those who "cared" could be seen wheeling through the streets of New York City, all mourning black on a cycle of somber hue. Happily, the women for whom such nonsense might have an appeal were seldom the kind who would ride cycles. The younger "new woman" was not anxious to accept silly ideas on etiquette, which she tended to look at as patronizing. She was likely to insist on equal treatment.

Equal opportunity sometimes meant equal shots at eligible males, and one did not have to be a touring cyclist to catch a husband. A short spin down a country lane under the "cycle moon" was often more likely to elicit masculine approval than wobbling around after having cycled twenty miles. The *New York Herald* assured the hopeful bride-to-be that a bicycle was a better matchmaker than a mother, and that the tinkling of a bicycle's bell frequently turned into the pealing of wedding bells. An alderman in Stamford, Connecticut, opposed bicycle lights because they would interfere with the privacy of young cyclers who were courting.

It was also believed that the tandem bicycle was a very important aid to achieving a state of wedded bliss—once the couple had solved the vexing problem of which seat the young lady should occupy. Generally it was held that the lady should always ride in front, where she could view the scenery without having a broad masculine back obscuring the countryside. At the same time, shifting the heavier burden of pedaling to her escort on the rear seat would give her the precedence due her sex. However, the front seat had its drawbacks. For example, it was the steering seat of the tandem and ladies were not given credit for being able to navigate in traffic. Equally worthy of consideration was that if the man rode in front he could act as a windbreaker, thus adding to the comfort of the lady on days when the wind was brisk and the temperature cool. Finally the manufacturers put an end to the debate by putting the lady's drop frame in front.

Once the seating problem was solved, the young people then got to the romantic part. The *Riverside Daily Enterprise* offered the opinion that a young man who pedaled his girl up a steep hill on a tandem was bound to give the impression of being strong and a fit object for matrimony. Not the least important was that such a performance would be a good indication that the prospective bridegroom had a good heart and would be around many years to provide for his wife and family. There was at least one drawback to the tandem, however, and that was the prevailing price of $150. But any young man who laid out that much money was probably serious about his intentions.

Since the bicycle was frequently compared with the horse, and the horse was inseparable from chivalry, it is not surprising that a certain mystique grew up around the cycle where romance was concerned.

> O, the knights of olden time
> Were brave and strong and true,
> And they loved their faithful steeds,
> My wheel, as I love you.

And swiftly forth they rode,
Some knightly deed to do
   To win their ladies' praise,
And for her hand to sue.

Knight of the wheel am I,
My lady's eyes are blue.
I kneel to kiss her hand;
She whispers, "I'll be true."[29]

The reader is left to wonder just what happened after this declaration, but the odds are that the rapturous lovers traded in his bicycle for a tandem and wheeled off together to the Land of Cockaigne.

It turned out that the bicycle not only encouraged romance but actually helped when it came time to get married. If parental displeasure barred the way, there was always the bicycle for elopement. In June, 1896, the traditional month for such affairs, Minnie Levinson and Bray Martin ran away from their parents in New Brunswick, New Jersey, and made it to the parson before anyone caught up with them. Another eloping couple wired their respective parents that they were married and would be home after a brief wedding trip "if our wheels remain intact." In Narrowsburg, New York, a young lady ran away from her farmer father on a tandem bicycle, thus making her dad's life doubly miserable because her mother had opposed his buying the girl a bicycle on the grounds that the machine would corrupt the young lady.

As a matter of fact sometimes married people used the machine for escape. In Newburgh, New York, a middle-aged farmer named Terwilliger bought a new bicycle for his twenty-two-year-old wife, the apple of his randy eye. The faithless one paid him back by donning her bloomer costume and pedaling away with a boarder. Terwilliger was fit to be tied, because not only had she taken the new hundred-dollar bicycle with her, but she had run off with a man even older than he!

In other words, the cycle might help tie the knot of matrimony or loosen it, depending on the way things went. Magdalena Zimpelman of Brooklyn claimed her husband was renting a tandem and taking another woman riding, and on this assumption she gave her spouse a sound beating and then divorced him. Mr. Zimpelman nursed his contusions and pleaded not guilty to the charge.

Sometimes the cause for the marital split was the bicycle itself. For example, a married woman in Detroit called in a lawyer to help her escape from a marriage that had previously fulfilled the description of having been made in heaven. In this case the serpent in the garden was a tandem bicycle that husband and wife had purchased. At first, the weeping wife told her lawyer, she had been extremely pleased at the purchase, seeing it as evidence of her husband's desire to be near her, but then he had changed. He developed a stubbornness she had never seen before, and they disagreed on everything important, such as where they should ride, when they should go, and how they should get there. She had had enough, and she wanted a divorce forthwith, since she would rather give up her husband than the tandem!

The unhappy Detroit wife was living in Loveland compared to Ann Strong. In an article in the *Minneapolis Tribune* Miss Strong ripped at the very foundations of American society, urged on by her infatuation with the cycle.

> I can't see but that a wheel is just as good company as most husbands two years old. I would as lief talk to one inanimate object as another; and I'd a great deal rather talk to one that can't answer than one that won't. I'd rather imagine a sympathetic response in a bright and shining handlebar than know it doesn't exist in a frowning man, who yawns or starts when I ask him a question.
>
> As for health, I am certain that a great many old maids will hail the advent of the bicycle as a rare substitute for the prescription so many doctors administer; "If you would only marry and have a family to care for your health would be all right." Compare a wheel with a family in this respect. You can make your wheel tidy over night, and it never kicks off its shoes the very last minute, and never smears itself with molasses. When you are ready you can start. No little elbows are stuck in your ribs; there is no wiggling; screams at the cars or at the candy stores. You glide along, silently, smoothly, swiftly. There is exhileration and nerve tonic in the very spice of danger, the need to look sharp, the chance of adventure.
>
> When it comes to a question of health there is certainly no comparison between wheel-riding and matrimony.
>
> Another great superiority of the bicycle lies in the fact that you can always get rid of it when you wish. You can roll it in and stand it up in a corner, and there it stays. It will neither follow you around or insist on receiving attention at inconvenient moments. When it gets shabby or old you can dispose of it and get you a new one without shocking the entire community.[30]

The newspaper said that the above statement would make men "real mad," and they were not kidding.

If Ann Strong had had a husband, it is probable that his favorite bit of bicycle verse went,

> Where once I heard her voice in song I hear it now insist,
> That "Holding tight to handlebars will strain the stoutest wrist."
> Where once she played a light guitar she now proclaims in ire
> That only "Dingbat tires are good" and sneers at single tires.
>
> Where once she spoke in charming ways of her way to build a cake
> She orates on the graceful ease she coasts without a brake.
> Of spokes and bloomers, sprockets, chains, of pedals and the like
> My better half will talk for hours since she has bought a bike.[31]

For this anonymous one and Ann Strong, however, the best poem on the bicycle was surely the one that appeared in a Western newspaper.

> I clasped the waist of fair Lenore,
> I praised her matchless worth,
> And asked her if she loved me more
> Than all else on the earth.
>
> She nestled closer to my side,
> I thrilled from head to heel
> As she in whispered words replied,
> "Yes dear—except my wheel."[32]

Regardless of one's position, doctor, preacher, parent, or lovesick swain, one had to admit that the birotate chariot had helped change things in America.

BICYCLE INSTITUTE OF AMERICA

"Of course woman's comfort and pleasure in the exercise greatly depends on her being properly and conveniently clothed for it. . . . Thoughtful people . . . believe that the bicycle will accomplish more for woman's sensible dress than all the reform movements that have ever been waged. It is not at all necessary to have a special gown when learning to ride. . . ." (*Demarest's Family Magazine,* 1895)

Bicycles and Fashion/Ladies...

CULVER PICTURES, INC. BUTTON: BICYCLE INSTITUTE OF AMERICA

BLOOMERS
INFLATED FREE
OF CHARGE
HIGH ADMIRAL
CIGARETTE

Preening on pedals—1890's style. Miss Lillian Russell (top, left); the other two belles of the boulevard are unknown.

TOP, LEFT, AND RIGHT: CULVER PICTURES, INC.
BOTTOM: BICYCLE INSTITUTE OF AMERICA

CULVER PICTURES, INC.

Mrs. Marie Reideselle (right) won the *New York Herald*'s prize for the best bicycle costume for ladies —1893.

THE LEAN ONE—"My doctor recommended bicycling to increase my weight."
THE STOUT ONE—"And my doctor recommended it to me to reduce mine."

Cartoon of 1896

CULVER PICTURES, INC.

Women's emancipation—1896. Riverside Drive between the hours of 8 and 10 A.M.

Bicycles and Fashion/... and Gentlemen

"Ball=Bearing"

Bicycle Shoes

are made to fit and wear. They touch and support the foot at every point. Many styles—high or low-cut. Corrugated soles. Pratt Fasteners secure laces without tying.

PRICE—Black, $3.00; Tan, $3.50; Ladies' Covert Cloth Knee Boot, $4.50 to $8.00. *Sold by dealers everywhere.* If yours does not keep them, shoes will be sent postpaid on receipt of price.

Look for Trade-Mark stamped on heel.

C. H. FARGO & CO. (Makers), CHICAGO.

No. 972

TRADE-MARK ON HEEL.

TOP, LEFT: BICYCLE INSTITUTE OF AMERICA
BOTTOM, LEFT: CHICAGO HISTORICAL SOCIETY
RIGHT: NEW YORK PUBLIC LIBRARY PICTURE COLLECTION

Bicycles and Fashion/... and Gentlemen

MUSEUM OF THE CITY OF NEW YORK

The self-made man's costume:
this gentleman won first prize for his sew-it-yourself outfit—1893.

Bicycles and Fashion/His and Hers

Clara: It is ever so much nicer at the seashore than
     it used to be.
Maude: How so?
Clara: The surroundings are so much more manly.
                    Cartoon: Life, Sept. 10, 1896

TOP, LEFT AND BOTTOM: CULVER PICTURES, INC.

Puck cover, May 20, 1896:
"The Biggest People on the Road!"

CHAPTER 5

"Sing a Song of Bloomers Out for a Ride"

THE CLOTHING REVOLUTION

BICYCLE INSTITUTE OF AMERICA

COASTING

From the first moment a man mounted the *célérifère* and waddled off down the road, he became something greater than the common run of human beings. With the advent of the ordinary, cyclists set about in earnest distinguishing themselves from people who were earthbound. One thing that separated cyclers from other Americans was that bicycle riders elected to wear distinctive clothing. At first many cyclists were members of a club, and each club had its own uniform. The Boston cycling club, for instance, included this description of its official uniform in its rules:

The uniform shall be dark seal-brown in color, and shall consist of a jacket, shirt, breeches, and stockings, and a cap; the latter to have the club monogram in silver on the front or left-hand side. (The cap will be furnished to each member without charge, on admission to the club; the silver monogram remaining the club property, and to be returned to the secretary whenever any members resign.)

The jacket to be of the short reefer patterns, made to button close around the neck at will.

The shirt to be of brown flannel, with turn-down collar, and two or more breast pockets, to be worn with a black-silk necktie.

The breeches to be of the same material as the jacket, and to button round the leg just below the knee.

The stocking to be of brown wool. Yellow gaiters may be worn on cold or wet journeys.

Fine cotton corduroy as the material for the uniform, and moderately thick boots with elastic-spring sides, are recommended.[1]

Charles Pratt, first president of the League of American Wheelmen and cycling's elder statesman, laid down the prescribed dress for wheelmen in *The American Bicycler*. Pratt did not insist that all uniforms be identical, and indeed, it was a foregone conclusion that cyclists would want to look a little different. Consequently, he made some broad recommendations that the costume, whether uniform or not, should be simple, light, and free for action, and should be in drab colors that would not show the dust so much. When one remembers that early cycling was done mostly over unpaved roads that seldom saw the sprinkling cart, it is easy to appreciate this last bit of advice.

For the most part uniforms were severely utilitarian. The dull colors of brown and gray concealed the dust, the short-tailed coat did not interfere with the seat in the saddle, and the long-visored cap was much better than a hat, which tended to blow off at the moment the cyclist was about to win an impromptu race.

It was the short trousers that represented the most radical departure in men's clothes. Although his ancestors had worn knee breeches, and although riding breeches had long been common (or at least long breeches tucked into boots), the ordinary American male scoffed at short pants. Never mind that long trousers got soiled by a mixture of axle grease and dust, never mind that the cuffs got entangled with the spokes of the front wheel and flipped cyclists over the handlebars, short pants just did not look right to men. Be at ease, wrote Pratt. Knickerbockers were best, and cyclists should keep in mind that the "smile of the supercilious was not a thing to be afraid of, if a man chooses to wear a cap and knickerbockers through the streets he may be dressed according to 'his work', he will not mind the gaze of the very proper and provincial nobodies."[2]

So most male cyclists followed Pratt's advice. The newly organized Pennsylvania Bicycle Club chose black cheviot suiting, the high-standing collar worn by the cadets at West Point, a black cap with silver cord trimming the visor, and white shirts piped in black. The breast pocket bore the club's monogram. Other groups added epaulets, while some deserted the short jacket for the heavy sweater.

In 1895 *Overland Magazine* rhapsodized over the appearance of a properly dressed cyclist. Such a rider looked

> as trim as a horseman. His body lightly enclosed in a woolen sweater of good quality and pattern and wearing a loose fitting coat trimmed with braid, knickerbockers not too shaggy, and heavy woolen stockings that fit well, a pair of low shoes and a cap to match the color of his coat. Strong riding gloves are sure to add to the beauty of this costume. A belt is sometimes worn and gives a sort of military look to the wearer.[3]

As a matter of fact, the male cyclist never got over the idea that he was a cavalryman.

For the most part, club uniforms disappeared toward the mid-nineties, when cycling became a sport for the general public and not a matter for the select. By 1896 the bright facings that distinguished these uniforms were vanishing, colored stockings with diamond inserts were going by the board, sweaters were seen only on fast riders and professional racers, and most people who rode bicycles were shifting toward the double-breasted coat.

"Cycling costumes" or suits for men began to appear in the clothing stores. Sears, Roebuck and Company advertised that it had made arrangements with one of the foremost manufacturers of men's bicycle suits to send a suit COD to the purchaser for only one dollar down, with an additional 3 per cent off for cash sent immediately. A complete outfit of sack coat, trousers, and wool "cassimere" cap could be bought for as little as $4.95. If a sedate outfit had little appeal, the prospective buyer was encouraged to buy the cycling pants separately for about $1.50 and add a heavy wool "bike" sweater in maroon or navy with dashing stripes on collar and cuffs, the last costing the same as the pants.

As for footwear, Sears sold ordinary bicycle shoes, but the "crack" might want to put something fancy on his feet, lest he be afflicted with "bicycle foot." If so, he could go to "Ball-Bearing Bicycle Shoes," which were constructed to give the foot the greatest freedom and proper support for cycling. These were exceedingly fancy and cost from three dollars to four dollars in 1896, or about the price of a complete outfit at Sears. (Ladies boots were much more expensive, since more leather was involved; ladies' trimmed knee boots were from $4.50 to $8.00, a handsome sum for the times.) In 1897 the shoe industry came out with "Best-Bike Shoes," "Ridemphast," and "Pedalshoe," the last sold exclusively by Siegel-Cooper's in New York City.

In fact, men's cycling styles began to be manipulated. In November, 1895, *The New York Times* duly noted that knickerbockers would be worn fuller at the knee in 1897 and that cycle shoes would be sturdier. Despite this, "Prowler," *Outing*'s cycling columnist, noted peevishly that the appearance of cyclers in Central Park was distinctly shabby. They wore nondescript costumes, exposed their shirt sleeves, and did not tuck in their sweaters, all of which offended the editor to the point where he had given up all hope of trying to get those "monkeys on wheels" to see themselves as others saw them.

"Prowler" did not stop giving advice on costume, however—especially on the effects of costume on health. He advised his male readers that a rubber band around the wrist prevented the cold wind from blowing up the sleeves and chilling the cyclist who braved the autumnal blasts. He also warned cyclists to beware of knickerbockers that were too tight below the knee, a maladjustment that brought on a severe pain at the kneecaps that once had been diagnosed as rheumatism.

It was not just "Prowler" who was concerned with the effects of costume on health. The *New York Herald* ran an article to the effect that cycling in golf stockings would induce varicose veins, then added that such stockings were only for "dear boys who simply make cute little trips to some twilighted bower where they sip tea and let the ladies admire them, but anybody who is going to pedal five or ten miles on a country road would soon learn that they were no good."[4] For those who were not "dear boys," the paper recommended a harness-suspender system that would hold up stockings but not interfere with circulation. Sears Roebuck, living up to its own publicity as the cheapest supply house on earth, sold stocking supporters for twenty-five cents a pair. The harness may not have worked too well, but the price was beyond criticism.

One problem occupied the attention of the cycling male when touring became popular. Long touring, the kind that took two or three weeks, raised the question of proper clothing, since it was generally felt that the cycling outfit of short coat and pants was not suitable for wear on off-cycle occasions.

According to *Outlook Magazine*, the solution was a bicycle touring case. *Outlook* described the dusty cyclist who slipped away to a changing room at the end of his day's ride and reappeared shortly clad in blue serge, clean linen, and patent leather shoes, all carried in his case. These cases were made to fit the diamond frame of the bicycle and were slung from the crossbar between the cyclist's legs. The magazine advised tourists to plan trips well ahead of departure, secure letters of introduction to people in towns where the stops would be made, and be sure to take an adequate supply of clothing. In addition to cycling gear, one was advised to take a sack suit to change to at the end of a day, several changes of underwear, clean dress "pumps," and a light camera.

A cyclist who took along only the clothing recommended by *Outlook* was virtually naked compared to the cyclist who took the outfit recommended by *Scribner's Magazine* in 1895. For a two-weeks tour, during which one might pedal six hundred miles or so, the male cyclist would need three light outing shirts, three suits of "gauze" underwear, a dark flannel bicycle suit, laced tan gaiters, lightweight rubber coat, comb, clothes brush, toothbrush, soap and towels, writing pad and pencil, maps, and matches. He would also require another suit for making calls, although it was admitted that this would make for extra weight. With such an outlay recommended for men, it was not surprising that a woman on tour was a comparative rarity.

The changes in men's costume introduced by the bicycle faded into insignificance when compared with the alterations in women's dress that rolled across the nation in the wake of the birotate chariot. In the 1850's dress reformers like Amelia Bloomer had striven with might, main, and determination to change clothing styles for women. But these efforts generally fizzled out before masculine scorn. Mrs. Bloomer's stovepipe pantaloons, peeking out below the hem of the skirt, seemed to have no other function than to encourage the lecherous leers of bystanding males. No matter that the ordinary American male was quick to peek at somebody else's woman, he wanted none to look at his.

The result was that very little dress reform occurred in the years immediately following the Civil War. Advertisements in magazines and newspapers show the American woman gliding toward the end of the century still clad in yards and yards of heavy material that swept the floor, gathering dust and dirt. Furthermore, she was burdened with whalebone-and-canvas corsets that pinched out the "hour-glass figure" so beloved at the time. These corsets also constricted her breathing, made her subject to fainting spells, and jeopardized both mother and child during pregnancy.

The issue of proper cycling wear for women came up very early in the history of the machine. In 1885, Mrs. Charles Bates, wife of the president of the LAW, addressed herself to the subject in *Outing*. Mrs. Bates blasted those who recommended that women wear knickerbockers under their skirts when they went cycling. When one realizes that the cycle she was talking about was the inoffensive tricycle, one gets some idea of the tempest then being raised in the teapot. Mrs. Bates contended knickers were awkward, unnecessary, and unfeminine. Also, they slowed down the sale of tricycles because women believed that for the sake of modesty they had to buy knickers before they could buy a cycle. Not so! cried Mrs. Bates. Any ordinary dress could be worn, although good sense called for restricting the number of underskirts to as few as possible. Mrs. Bates also advocated the wearing of a suit of woolen underwear as added protection against the cold, an indication of just how little she was conceding to immodesty. In fact, she strongly warned against wearing anything outré lest it give cycling bad publicity.

Mrs. Bates could have spared herself any anxiety concerning woman's cycle costuming, because as long as the ordinary was the only two-wheeler and only the tricycle was available to women, there would be little change and less agitation. However, the appearance of the safety bicycle launched a long assault on dress styles. Even after the bicycle declined in popularity, it left a lasting mark on American women. The most enduring monuments to the bicycle are visible ankles and calves, and uncorseted figures.

In 1891, "Prowler" described a vision of American loveliness he had seen in Central Park. The soft gray dress, the absence of tight lacing, the white straw hat with a red band, the sailor collar and the tan gloves "completed as pretty an outfit on as pretty a girl as ever I saw on a bicycle."[5]

A year later *Outing* included a few columns for women cyclists, written by Grace Denison. In addition to discussing how to maintain the cycle properly, Miss Denison gave advice on costumes for cycling. She recommended a blouse, lightly boned but without corseting, a serge skirt, low shoes with spats to keep the gravel out, and a walking hat, somewhat like a small Homburg, with a few unobtrusive quills. Make sure, she warned, that a few small lead weights were sewed in the front hem of the skirt in "case the wind should rise while you are taking your constitutional."[6] Those who wanted something less heavy could wear skirts with inside facings of leather.

By the time the cycling season got under way in June of 1892, Miss Denison was having her cycling skirts shortened by two inches in the rear lest they get tangled in the spokes of the wheel or caught on the high pedal when the rider mounted. She also argued that long skirts impeded movement and "pumped cold air against the abdomen."[7]

Grace Denison's column did not last the year. An example of her enthusiastic prose might explain why.

> Young men and old men, trimly clad, fitly trained, bright-eyed and merry, wait for the coming of the "ladies" and of whom, oh, happy day, I may be one. Hurry for the time is up: see, they are forming into line, *place aux dames!* In this civilized age we are expected to take the lead, eh, my sisters? How proud they are to have us! How happy we are to do! On to the halfway house, where tea and song await us; back under the very young moon. And tomorrow for tired bones to rest![8]

The following year found the bicycle even more popular with women, and dress reformers used it to encourage what came to be called "rational dress." It is difficult to determine when the cyclers' real offensive against the long skirt first started. Newspapers said it began with Mrs. Meta Boardman of 204 East 18th Street, New York, who first wore knickerbockers during the spring of 1893. Her costume created a sensation, partly because Mrs. Boardman was described as a "very plump woman" who looked like a "fat boy who was blessed with neat ankles and feet."[9] A year later the newspapers said nearly a hundred New York women were riding in "trousers," but mostly under cover of darkness.

Even staid Boston had its dress reformers. Mrs. Hattie Fowler and Miss Christine Brown did their utmost to publicize divided skirts and trousers (or "bifurcated garments," to use one of their names). Mrs. Fowler "braved the eyes of all Boston" in a skirt split *halfway* to the knee, but Miss Brown took the palm with long, baggy pants like those worn by Turkish soldiers. Those voluminous envelopes struck Miss Brown midway between ankle and knee and caused a ripple of consternation to roll across the city.

Generally, women defended the new style by saying that the long skirts, corsets, and heavy materials demanded by fashion not only endangered their health but had "recklessly cursed the unborn." Some women maintained that if they did not seize the opportunity to change to "rational dress," they had no right to ask for other privileges that had long been denied them. On the other hand, most men were prepared to enjoy the sight of a neatly turned feminine ankle, but they became slightly apprehensive when the dress reformers maintained that the time was ripe for more radical changes.

Most of the ladies were reasonably sensible, but here and there was a real radical such as Mrs. Ida Stewart, the wife of a New Jersey tugboat captain, who frequented the waterfront saloons of New York City. Clad in trousers instead of long skirts, she stood up at the bar with her husband and drank beer with the best of them. When Mrs. Stewart was arrested for disorderly conduct, she told the police magistrate that she liked pants, and anyway, it was nobody's business what she wore in public. The *New York Herald* did not record the disposition of her case nor the comments of her spouse.

The worst, or the best, depending on one's point of view, was yet to come. On Decoration Day of 1894, the dress designers opened the cycling season with the latest style, the bloomer costume. Bloomers, for generations that do not know them, were short, very full pants fastened at the knee, similar to the knickerbockers worn by men. They seem wholly appropriate to present-day Americans, but to a generation that had definite ideas about women who showed their legs, the bloomer costume was an eye-popper.

A New England editor described the ensemble like this:

> The bloomer dress is a pair of trousers, very baggy at the knees, abnormally full about the pistol pockets and considerably loose where you strike a match. The garment is cut decolette in the south end, and the bottoms are tied up around the ankles or knees to keep the mice out. You can't put it on over your head, the way you do your corsets, but you sit on the floor and put it on just as you do your stockings—one foot in each compartment. You can easily tell which is the right side to have in front by the button on the neckband.[10]

One such outfit was described in the *Riverside Daily Enterprise* as a blazer worn with a waist of black surah that had a bow of the same material at the throat. Below were "Turkish trousers," very full and fastened just below the knees, with black gaiters covering the ankles. A cap with a black leather visor and gray doeskin gloves completed the costume.

The bloomer costume was a hit. In the summer of 1895, *Cycling Magazine* said that a "fluttering roly-poly avalanche" of knickerbockers had descended on cycling America—a flood that the journal incorrectly blamed on the fact that the depression of 1894 had caused the girls to sell their own bicycles, put on their gym bloomers, and hop on their brothers' wheels. The magazine quoted a rider who had saved "stacks" of money since she had taken to bloomers, money that had formerly been spent on bicycle skirts. In fact, it was alleged that the revolution in women's clothes was eliminating many cycle accessories, such as skirt guards for women. Furthermore, as evidence that the revolution had not run its course, it was said that many women thought bloomers were too baggy and had begun to shorten and tighten them until the trousers were becoming "high-water pants," or, as one paper put it, "silly knickerbockers of scant cut."

By 1895 bloomers had become so common that they no longer had the attractions of the outré. In fact bloomers were the opposite of the cigarette smoked by the *fin de siècle* girl who remarked plaintively, "I wish this nasty thing was proper; then I could throw it away."

As a matter of fact, Nebraska *State Journal* ran a bit of doggerel detailing almost complete male capitulation.

> Now bloomers add not beauty to the female form divine,
> But these new fashioned women will advance;
> If emancipation notions ever strike that wife of mine,
> She is welcome to my Sunday broadcloth pants.
> She can have my broadcloth breeches, she can have my coat and vest,
> She can have my laundered linen, and all that;
> She can have my stand-up collars, new necktie and the rest,
> But darned if she can have my stovepipe hat.*

*I must wear something![11]

The implied prediction was fairly accurate; photographs and pictures show a distinct tendency for women's cycling costumes to adopt masculine lines, collars, ties, coats, vests, and hats.

That same year, 1895, a cyclist named Ellen Osborn touched on an aspect of costuming that was becoming a subject of hot debate: What would happen if a bicyclienne decided to wear her abbreviated costume when she was not on a bicycle? Was it proper to walk through the streets clad in bloomers or knickers and, if so, under what circumstances? Miss Osborn related that the previous winter "obviously bifurcated unmasculine specimens of the genus homo were observed skating in Central Park" and allowed that bloomers would be suitable for walking trips and shooting tramps in the country.[12]

In June, 1895, four schoolmarms, members of the profession that had long been the pillars of the feminine working force, kicked up their all-too-visible heels. At Humbolt School in Chicago, Miss Gyda Stephenson showed up in knickers to teach her pupils. Miss Stephenson rode her bicycle to school and saw no reason why she could not wear the same costume while she fulfilled her responsibilities. Her action generated heated debate. Some colleagues attacked knickers as improper in the schoolroom, while others argued they were just improper. However, the majority of the teachers are said to have applauded. Miss Stephenson herself stated that she did not belong to any special dress-reform movement, and that she wore bloomers only because they were the most sensible attire for one who cycled. As a parting shot she took the position that what she wore to class was none of the school board's business. In this she was partly supported by her principal, Professor Will J. Bartolf, who said he admired Miss Stephenson's pluck and independence and was happy to see a woman resort to her own judgment where health and comfort were concerned.

The Chicago teacher was upheld by higher authority when a member of the city board told reporters that the group had no right to dictate on matters of dress except in cases where the costume was definitely "immoral," which bloomers were not. But limited victory in big Chicago was not duplicated in little Flushing, Long Island. Two weeks after Gyda Stephenson delivered her blow for feminine freedom, three lady schoolteachers at College Point School were forbidden by the local school board even to ride their bicycles to class. The Misses Fairbrother, Van Nostrand, and Bleiderlinder objected to the ruling, but their female principal said that she would enforce the decision even though she, herself, had no objections. Dr. A. W. Reimer, a member of the board, cleared his throat and revealed the true reason for the prohibition against riding bicycles to school.

> It is not the proper thing for ladies to ride the bicycle. They wear skirts, of course, but if we don't stop them now they will want to be in style with the New York women and wear bloomers. Then how would our schoolrooms look with the lady teachers parading about among the girls and boys wearing bloomers. They might as well wear men's trousers. I suppose it will come to that, but we are determined to stop our teachers in time, before they go that far.[13]

There was some adult education left to do.

According to Isaac Newton, there is a reaction for every action, and the reaction against the shift to bloomers was vehement. In Missouri a young bicyclist, dressed in the height of fashion, mounted her machine and rode off to visit her grandparents, who responded sharply to the immorality of the bloomer ensemble. According to the papers, the young lady was greeted with no kiss of kinship, but her grandparents tore off her bloomers, put her in a dress, smashed her bicycle, and then sent her home. They knew how to handle wantons in Missouri!

In New York City reporters cornered Ward McAllister, who coined the term "The Four Hundred" for high society and subsequently became its arbiter, and asked him if he thought women should ride bicycles. The effete McAllister drawled that the question was purely academic since they *were* riding, but he added that the bloomer costumes "utterly destroyed the symmetry of their figures."[14] However, this was before the bloomer costume became popular at Newport, and in all likelihood a trimmer like McAllister changed his tune.

Some criticism was stronger. In Chicago's Lincoln Park, Mrs. McClom was pedaling down the path, proud of her new bloomer outfit, when Emmanuel Engstrom "hooted" at her. She had Engstrom arrested, but when the boorish fellow was hauled before the judge, he denied that he had hooted a single hoot. However, he did confess that he had laughed a great deal. The magistrate did not believe him and laid on a fine.

Fining Emmanuel Engstrom was one thing, but what did a judge do to the street gamins who helped make life miserable for the bloomer girl?

> Sing a song of bloomers out for a ride,
> With four and twenty bad boys running at her side,
> While the maid was coasting the boys began to sing,
> "Get on to her shape, you know," and all that sort of thing.[15]

Running down four and twenty bad boys was a lot harder than bringing in Engstrom.

The bloomer costume created a brouhaha in Chicago that transcended a little inordinate laughter. On July 17, 1895, the managers of the pavilion in Jackson Park held an invitational dance at which cycling costume was required for both ladies and gentlemen. When the band struck up its opening waltz that night, a hundred couples stood along the fringes of the floor waiting for some courageous pair to open the festivities. It was a critical moment, because if "rational dress" could not divorce itself somewhat from the bicycle, it was doomed to become simply another uniform. But the issue was saved, and while applause drowned out the music, Miss Minnie Burlett and H. Montgomery Fuller glided out onto the floor.

The managers of the park pavilion knew from the first waltz that they had a profitable thing on their hands and immediately scheduled another dance for the following week. But their advertisement for this dance had a different ring to it. Eddie Marcus and "Baby" Bliss were the two men cyclists who were to lead the grand march to open the second "bloomer dance." "Baby" weighed 485 pounds, making him certainly one of the most imposing figures ever to don knickerbockers. Although the dance was held, the censors had been alerted. On August 11, Chicago's men in blue appeared in Jackson Park and barred all cycling costumes from the floor at the request of the sponsoring cycle club. One bloomer-ette was quoted as saying, "Dis here club is gettin' too swell for cyclists. Dey'll be ridin' in coaches and four next."

Maybe it was that "lady" who prompted the ruling of the Chicago police, backed by the aldermen, that any woman who would wear bloomers while dancing in public was to be treated as a common prosti-tute. As a result, the dances were closed.

Even males, ordinarily in the cheering section, were sometimes critical. A reporter who visited the annual racing meet held in conjunction with the convention of the LAW wrote that the bloomer girl "was not the wildly beautiful creature many of the writers, especially the bicycle enthusiasts, would have one believe." Then he piled insult upon gaucherie by saying, "She does not stand the glare of sunshine well. Closer in-spection of the sort they have down here as can be had when she is riding a wheel wipes out a lot of romance. The bloomer cycle girl is, almost without exception, a woman rather beyond middle age."[16]

In Norwich, New York, a group of young men were alleged to have banded themselves into an "Anti-bloomer Brigade." Each member was supposed to take the following oath: "I hereby agree to refrain from associating with any young ladies who adopt bloomer cycling costumes and pledge myself to use all honorable means to render such costumes unpopular in the community where I reside."[17] They might just as well have saved their breath, assuming such an oath was taken seriously.

Norwich got some moral support from Riverhead, Long Island, so much so that one would almost think the people of Long Island's little villages had forgotten how much they owed to the cyclers who poured into the countryside on warm summer afternoons. The ladies of River-head were not going to tolerate hussies riding through their community wearing outlandish clothing. To the Riverhead females, any woman who wore bloomers was shadier than the elms. One unhappy stranger who came pedaling through after dark had her bloomers immediately spotted by elderly harridans who hooted at her. A Chicago magistrate might fine poor Emmanuel Engstrom for hooting, but no justice of the peace was going to risk his position to discipline the viragoes of Riverhead. When the subject was discussed in the community's back yards it was generally the opinion of the women, old and young, that the bloomer costume had to go. The war cry of "Bloomers! Well, I guess not!" echoed through the streets. The female knickerettes of Riverhead were so intimidated by this frontal assault that they retreated, and the offending costumes went into moth balls.

At Freeport, on the Merrick Road, the women of the hamlet drew the line in no uncertain terms. When the rumor got abroad that a bunch of bloomer-clad pretties were going to invade their community, they put down their collective foot, stomped it in fact. In spite of the evidence that the entire thing was pure sensationalism—the bloomerettes were going to play a game of baseball—the women let their husbands know that attendance at the exhibition would constitute grounds for divorce. The town elders applauded this attack on big-city wickedness, and the antibloomer forces seem to have won again.

Most of this did not slow the "new woman" one bit. The police of Chicago could stop bloomer dances but could not prevent Hattie Strage from pedaling down Dearborn Avenue one Saturday evening in July, 1895, when the traffic was the heaviest and the bloomer fad at its peak. The smiling young lady was clad in a flesh-colored sweater and a pair of black tights that left few contours of her form to the imagination. She was promptly arrested on a charge of disorderly conduct and the police magistrate who inspected her costume fined her twenty-five dollars.

In some respects the bloomerette medal of honor should have been bestowed on Miss Ada Coleman of Mason, Ohio. It was on a Sunday morning, late in July, that Miss Coleman appeared in the sanctuary of the local Methodist Church to fulfill her obligation as the church organist. On the morning in question the young lady wore a pair of bright red bloomers! Mercifully John Wesley was beyond interrogation, but the members of the Ladies' Aid Society sizzled with indignation, not a little because Miss Ada's minister refused to excommunicate her. The editor of the *Chicago Tribune* grimly took notice of this invasion of God's house and intoned that the "bicycle had done its deadly work."[18] Furthermore, he hoped the Methodist Church in convention would stand firm against such degrading costumes. This last statement only points up the paper's hypocrisy, because it had just finished sponsoring a costume-designing contest for women's cycling outfits. With a judgment worthy of Solomon the paper had picked three winners, a long skirt, a medium skirt, and a bloomer costume.

The mayor of Chattanooga, Tennessee, called upon the city fathers to pass an ordinance to keep bloomers off the city streets because they were a "menace to the peace and good morals of the male residents of this city."[19] He proposed fines from $5 to $50, which leaves one wondering what sort of a threat was worth $50.

In a day when feminists were suggesting that God was properly addressed as "She," the leaders of the women's rights groups were not going to take that sort of thing without replying. Elizabeth Cady Stanton, a frontline soldier in the battle for equality between the sexes, rushed into print with a spirited defense of the bloomer costume. She contended that women had a perfect right to choose the dress they wanted to wear while cycling and pointed out that men had already reduced their cycling costumes to near nothing, a reference to abbreviated racing togs. She concluded, "We do not bother our heads about their cycling clothes, and why should they meddle with what we want to wear? We ask nothing more of them than did the devils in Scripture—'Let us alone!'"[20] It is doubtful that most women cyclers wanted to go *that* far, but they approved of Mrs. Stanton's sentiments.

There was no lack of females to defend the shorter costume. Frances E. Russell of Minneapolis answered Nellie Melba, the opera star, who had said that modest women would not ride bicycles, let alone wear bloomers. Miss Russell, noting that many society women—presumably modest by Melba's standards—played billiards, wrote:

> Which are really more modest, the wheelwomen with their honest outdoor exercise, or the billiardists playing to expose their feminine charms to the best effect? And which the more modest dress, the clothing that covers the body comfortably and conveniently, accepting the body as the Creator fashioned it for use . . . or the low-cut gowns of the society woman, stamped all over with the sex suggestiveness which will someday be considered low and vulgar?[21]

Miss Russell was seconded by President William F. Whitlock of the Epworth League of the Nostrand Methodist Church in Brooklyn, who defended the wearing of bloomers if they were voluminous and admitted they were more modest than gowns worn in the ballroom.

The opposition to the bloomer costume was dealt a blow when "touring trousers" were taken up by society people at Newport. That swank beach resort had long replaced Saratoga Springs in the hearts of the wealthy women who rushed to don bloomers in the summer of 1895. The newspapers suggested that young ladies had been wanting to adopt the costume for a long time, but had been waiting timorously for a leader to show up. In the second week of August, 1895, they found her and immediately shifted to rational dress. The paper did not say who the emancipated millionairess was, but once the rich took to bloomers it was difficult for the middle class to take offense, seeing that wealth was generally taken to be a sign of God's approval.

Lady cyclists not only were carrying the bloomer costume before them, they were absolutely belligerent about it. In the fall of 1895 a Chicago bloomerette was pedaling down Michigan Avenue when a man described as "dignified and elderly" made some unkind remarks that the young lady overheard. She promptly dismounted and rebutted the man's observations with a clenched fist brandished under his nose. His answer was a "derisive" laugh, an argument commonly resorted to by losers. The bloomer girl countered with a right to the jaw. The spectators cheered the lady pugilist, and the man beat a hasty retreat.

The bifurcated garments spread westward across the nation and took the Pacific Coast by storm. The Acme and Reliance bicycle clubs of Oakland, California, persuaded the manager of a local theater to have a "bicycle night," which was attended by three hundred belles clad in bloomers and escorted by males in knickerbockers. It was said that all the other members of the audience watched the bloomer girls instead of the play.

San Francisco had an enterprising restaurant owner who put his waitresses in bloomers and then watched the money pour in. But a New York City man did not fare so well. When he tried to force his girls to wear bloomers, he was faced with a strike. It was probably just as well for him, because the one waitress who did wear bloomers was responsible for sixteen gaping men who blocked traffic on the sidewalk outside. The proprietor was arrested for maintaining a public nuisance.

As the banner year of 1895 paled away toward the new year, a play entitled *Bicycle Girl*, described as a musical farce, played to big audiences in New York City. Down in Atlanta a man named L. M. Mayer caught the fever and composed a quickstep called "The March of the Bloomers." Tin Pan Alley, not to be outdone by a small-town hick, quickly produced "When Trilby Rides a Wheel," "The Girl With Bloomers On," and a smasheroo called "Her Bloomers Are Camphored Away." Before this nonsense was over one could also buy sheet music for "Get Your Lamps Lit," "Mamie, My Bicycle Girl," and the theme song of the complete lover, "I Love You, Bloomers, Bicycle, and All." One passes over the famous "Bicycle Built for Two" without comment.

As the madness spread, it took on crazy colorations. The papers ran the story of two Parisian *bicyclistes* who used their voluminous bloomers to conceal shoplifted goods, a practice that spread to the United States. One bloomerette from Rochester, New York, stole a Thanksgiving turkey from a home and outdistanced all pursuers on her bicycle. The LAW *Bulletin* exclaimed, "Woman, woman! Why, oh why?"[22]

The year closed with bloomers in the ascendant, but curiously, the dresses designed for noncycling became longer and more elaborate. As if to offset the effects of bloomer exposure and cater to males who thought cycling dress unfeminine—shortening the skirt would lead to cutting the hair—dress designers dropped skirts to the ground, produced leg-of-mutton sleeves such as had never existed before, and prescribed larger and larger hats, trimmed with bigger and bigger flowers. It seems that some were determined to preserve the mystery.

The fad continued with the opening of the season of 1896. However an ominous note sounded across the Atlantic Ocean. Under the headline "The Doom of Bloomers," it was revealed that French couturiers were moving away from the bifurcated garments. One had already refused to make any more bloomer costumes for his customers, noting that cyclers with small hips and legs looked ridiculous in the outfit while those more generously endowed were bad advertisements for their dressmakers.

Let the Paris dressmakers talk all they wanted, it looked as if the bloomer girl had come to stay with the bicycle. Indeed, it appears that she had just started to exercise her new freedom. In Tuxedo Park, that superselect real-estate development for the rich, the ladies were daring enough to get rid of leggings and gaiters. Golf stockings were substituted by the timorous, but most women where showing plain stockings and ankles, not to mention a tiny bit of calf. *Cycling Magazine* admitted that the effect was something startling to the beholder but made no further comment.

Equally startled was the anonymous poet who described the shock brought on by his first exposure to bloomers—with apologies to Edgar Allan Poe.

> When I saw you on your wheel, sweet Lenore
> Oh my brain did never reel so before.
> You were clad in knickerbocks
> And you wore such brilliant sox
> I could see 'em twenty blocks, maybe more.

I but gave a passing glance, sweet Lenore
At the natty sawed-off pants which you wore,
Then the cruel ground I hit
I had fallen in a fit,
And I've not recovered yet, sweet Lenore.[23]

Americans were ingenious, and discarding leggings was not the end of inventiveness. Clothing stores carried women's bicycle belts from which hung a small leather purse in which the bloomer girl could store small change, tickets, and feminine things. Rubber-soled cycling shoes for women came on the market, and hats proliferated like mushrooms. The newest creation in 1896 was a cloth toque called the "Langtry Toque redivivus," apparently a round hat with a brim caught here and there against the crown with black ribbons and a few quills. Fancy straw cycling hats of all shapes were available, all decorated with a profusion of imitation flowers including tulips, camellias, and cowslips.

Yet it seems that the bloomer craze, like the bicycle, had run its course by 1898. *Harper's Weekly* reported as early as 1896 that the "hideous and unsexing bloomers and knickerbockers worn by some women in the early days of the wheel craze"[24] had virtually disappeared. Although this was not quite true, nevertheless the bloomer fad did slow down, ultimately to pass away. In part this was because riding went into decline. Also, many women who set the beauty standards for the day did not adopt the bloomer costume and in some cases actually condemned it. Lillian Russell, for all her specially designed bicycle seat, opposed bloomers, and Lily Langtry told a reporter she had never seen a woman in "rational dress" who looked attractive. The "Divine Sarah" Bernhardt would not give her approval, and Nellie Melba's criticism has already been noted.

The bloomer costume might disappear, but "rational dress" in the form of the shortened skirt did not pass away. The *Minneapolis Tribune* noted that shorter skirts had become common in general outdoor wear by 1897, and no less an authority than the *New York Sun* said that the bicycle costume for women had brought about some desirable changes in women's clothing, a reform that had long been demanded by common sense. In addition, the heavy corseting that had gripped generations of American women with fingers of wire and bone was gone.

The bloomers were gone, but they certainly had been fun while they lasted.

CHAPTER 6

"It Has Put the Human Race on Wheels"

THE BICYCLE AS AN INSTRUMENT FOR SOCIAL CHANGE

BICYCLE INSTITUTE OF AMERICA

Riding Side Saddle

While some Americans were debating the pros and cons of the bloomer question, others were examining the impact of the bicycle on American society. Many praised the machine's utilitarian and sporting contributions, and a few applauded the coming of the birotate chariot on the grounds that it would affect broad sociological and political changes in American life. Here and there a fan contended that the bicycle would defend and preserve those qualities upon which the nation's well-being depended.

Back in 1884, when the ordinary held sway, the editor of *Outing* extolled the social virtues of the cycle. He maintained there was something peculiarly democratic about a conveyance that was comparatively cheap to purchase and maintain and was, therefore, within the reach of most Americans. Of course *Outing*'s primary purpose was to encourage cycling, and the editor, no doubt carried away by his job, apparently forgot that $150 represented almost half a year's wages for the majority of Americans.

Nevertheless, the feeling that the bicycle was an instrument of democracy continued to grow, and eleven years later another spokesman waxed eloquent on the same theme. He had just witnessed one of the bicycle parades that were held so frequently in the halcyon days. The parade, he said,

> forcefully suggested to every onlooker the thought that the bicycle is the most democratic of all vehicles. There were men high in the ranks of the professions and heads of immense business enterprises, side by side with the humblest patients or clients they are called upon to serve and the salesmen and saleswomen employed in their establishments.
>
> Not only is the bicycle democratic with regard to rules and regulations which govern its use on public thoroughfares, but it has been a minister to that community of feeling among men which marks true democracy. An example of this has been . . . the manner in which men of all grades have met in a common effort to secure from legislatures and the city council enactments favorable to the rights of the cyclist when awheel, or, it may be said, when paying his taxes or fighting his damage suits.[1]

Other friends of the bicycle extolled its "leveling influence." In 1896 a reporter for the *Scientific American* wrote:

> As a social revolutionizer it has never had an equal. It has put the human race on wheels, and has thus changed many of the most ordinary processes and methods of social life. It is the great leveler, for not 'til all Americans got on bicycles was the great American principle of every man is just as good as any other man, and generally a little better, fully realized. All are on equal terms, all are happier than ever before, and the sufferers in pocket from this universal fraternity and good will may as well make up their minds to the new order of things for there will be no return to the old.[2]

The worker who rode the plebeian cable cars and watched the rich trundle past in their four-in-hands undoubtedly was fully aware of the gulf that separated them. After all, to keep matched pairs of horses for a single year cost more than most Americans consumed in food during the same length of time. Therefore, the workingman pedaling down Riverside Drive or Michigan Avenue or Calhoun Boulevard in the same block with the rich might indeed have felt a fleeting sense of equality. That it could not last forever, and that the cycle-induced egalitarianism would be lost when the rich turned away to a more expensive toy, was beside the point.

In any event, creating a more democratic atmosphere was probably the least important social reform introduced by the bicycle. More significantly, the old concepts of social morality and proper conduct were undermined by the freedom conferred upon those who rode the wheel. As a result, a considerable part of American society had to re-evaluate its old ideas. For example, an article by J. B. Bishop in *Forum Magazine* said that parents who previously would not allow their daughters to go to the theater without chaperons were reluctantly permitting them to ride into the countryside without the customary supervision. Also, the bicycle had already begun to erode the barriers of etiquette that separated the sexes. Despite those who persisted in maintaining that a gentleman did not so much as lift his hat to a lady he did not know, cyclists contended that the comradeship of the wheel was such that "every rider feels at liberty to accost or converse with any other rider. . . ."

For those deeply distressed by the changes, Bishop argued that the bicycle was far better than the poolroom, because entire families could go awheel and this togetherness encouraged sobriety and decorum. Above all, cycling made companions of fathers and sons and bridged the generation gap of the nineties. According to Bishop, this "beneficial influence upon the character and habits of the latter, exerted, as it often is, at the formative period of the boys' lives, cannot be overestimated."[3]

Whatever the motivation, Americans rallied around the bicycle and banded together in clubs of various sorts, organizations that were outstanding expressions of the social aspect of cycling. And they were not organizations of people who just wanted to wear a special uniform. The clubs were approved because they contributed to the continuation and expansion of American virtues. They were not retreats but centers for the active, healthy growth of a more vigorous form of democracy. As *Outing* described it, life was no longer defined in terms of the "close closet work of the student, or the idling of the voluptuary, or the intense but intermittent strain of the professional, but the healthy, regular natural work of an American who understands that acting is living and healthy action [is] healthy life."[4] The Greeks never put it better.

For the most part the clubs between 1880 and 1893 were organized on lines laid down by Pratt in *American Bicycler*, which included a model constitution. The bylaws and rules provided for the election of officers, including the president, and all-important captains, guides, and buglers. The captain laid out the routes for the club runs and was responsible for touring discipline.

The bylaws were exceedingly precise about how the club should conduct its cycle tours. The morning air was broken at eight o'clock by "Assembly," blown by one of the three club buglers and taken quite openly from the tactics manual of the United States cavalry. The notes signified that the start was twenty minutes away and that all members should oil their cycles and make last-minute preparations for the tour. At twenty minutes after eight the bugle sounded again, and the members wheeled out their ordinaries and formed a line, with each man standing to the left of his machine. The cyclists then counted off by twos and stood ready until "Boots and Saddles" was blown, at which time each man turned his cycle to the left and put his left foot on the mounting step just above the small trailing wheel. Then at the command "Mount!" each cyclist vaulted into the high saddle of his rolling wheel, first making sure that the man in front of him had gained momentum—the book said "at least two revolutions." The call to "Form Twos!" then followed, and the club rode off.

They swept through the winding streets of the city with the captain in the lead, one of his buglers at his side, and his subcaptains distributed along the column. Once into the countryside, the command to "Ride at ease!" was sounded, and the riders were free to choose their own riding mates. The club streaked along elm-shaded lanes, the captain darting ahead and reconnoitering the hills to see if there were any curves at the bottom or, even worse, a horse and wagon that had to be passed. The rules were very precise for such encounters and reflect a sincere effort by the cyclists to earn the good will of the farmers. When meeting a horse, no bugle calls were sounded lest the beast become alarmed. Instead the captain held out his right arm, an indication that the cyclists following should extend their order to the interval of twenty yards recommended for passing on hills. Then the leader pedaled by the horse, going very slowly and speaking softly to calm the animal. At the same time he kept alert for signs the beast was about to bolt. If all was calm, the club rolled by the buggy, always being careful not to cut back in front of the horse until each man was ten yards ahead.

Animal, hill, and curve safely negotiated, the captain ordered his bugler to sound "No. 23, Cavalry Tactics, United States Army," which meant to reform in a single file. In this formation the club swept down on a sleepy village, whose entire population—men, women, children, and dogs—often came out to watch. Upon entering the hamlet the bugler usually gave a flourish on his instrument, and the merry music of the "Quickstep" sounded along the road, a call that conveyed no particular order to the club but was an expression of sheer exuberance.

Beyond the town the cyclists might stop for lunch and then ride back to the starting point. Even at day's end, tired as they were, the members maintained discipline. Brought to a halt by the bugle, they dismounted from the rear of the column forward, each man calling "Off!" as he touched the ground. The cycles were stored in the clubhouse while the bugler blew "Retreat," and the day was closed by the sounding of "Tattoo."

After 1890 bicycle clubs proliferated until every American town and village seemed to have one. As the number of cyclers increased and road conditions improved, the cycling club was generally transformed into primarily a social organization. Captains were no longer important in choosing the best routes for Sunday riding. Anybody could do that, especially if he paid attention to the weekly road reports printed in the newspapers or if he read the LAW road maps. "Boots and Saddles" fell into disuse. Cyclists became more disdainful of the horse and took fewer precautions when passing him.

The clubs built their own clubhouses when they could, and some, like the new fifty-thousand-dollar quarters of the Old Park Cycling Club, were pretentious. These meeting places became social centers for their members. During the cycling season the groups worked hard organizing tours, picnics, and teas, or planning monster parades. When winter came, except in the mild climates, the groups went inside. Since most of them lacked the facilities for indoor riding, they contented themselves with bowling contests, dances, and various other forms of entertainment. If things became too dull they could always go downtown and try to force the aldermen to repair the streets. Some clubs collected things: Chicago's Lincoln Cycling Club boasted locks of hair from the heads of two hundred prominent cyclists.

Parades were especially popular. The Mercury Wheel Club of Long Island held a lantern parade at night and gave prizes for the best-decorated and the best-illuminated bicycles, while fireworks flashed and boomed overhead. In the popular seaside resort of Long Branch, New Jersey, a parade of ten thousand cyclers rolled their decorated machines through the streets, while an estimated seventy-five thousand spectators watched. Before the parade, the Long Island Railroad had run excursion trains to the resort so the city folk could combine the cool air of the shore with the spectacle of so many bicycles.

On June 6, 1896, the *New York Herald* sponsored a parade it described as the "apotheosis of the wheel." Although the statistics deserve gentle suspicion, an estimated one hundred thousand people thronged the sidewalks along Riverside Drive and Western Boulevard as twelve thousand cyclists wheeled past. At Riverside Drive and 114 Street a judge's stand held U.S. Senator Chauncey Depew and Isaac Potter of the League of American Wheelmen, while on either side temporary bleachers seated fifteen hundred people who cheered lustily as the cycle units wheeled by. There were contingents of cycling policemen and cycle units from the Eighth, Ninth, Twelfth, and Thirteenth regiments of the New York National Guard, the officers rolling past with sabers drawn. Cycle makers were represented in the most obvious ways; the Greek god Zeus rode an Olympic Bicycle; Little Red Ridinghood was on a Wolf-American, while Dr. Livingstone's rescuer went past on a Stanley Bicycle. Not without reason did the *Herald* proclaim, "All New York Was Cycle Mad!" However, all that wheeling about in droves was for the hoi polloi. The "swells" had something better, or so they believed. For example, the New York club, presided over by Mrs. Robert Jaffray, Jr., held a "music ride" at "Professor Golden's Cycle Academy" in May, 1895, before turning to the outdoors. This high-toned kind of entertainment was the sort commonly practiced by clubs that aped the manners and make-up of the elite Michaux Club of New York City. The Michaux was organized in 1895. Michaux's founders, who wanted a place to ride during the winter, were Messrs. Wyndham-Quine, James Townsend, and Elisha Dyer, all socially prominent and the first a relative of Lord Dunraven, who later challenged for the America's Cup. The membership included Mrs. George Gould, Mrs. William K. Vanderbilt, and Mrs. Grenville Winthrop.

There were many activities at Michaux's rented quarters at Bowman's Hall. In the mornings members received riding instruction from the club's own teachers. In the afternoons the ladies could ride to the accompaniment of music—said to make cycling easier—and afterward enjoy tea served in the clubrooms. There was a balcony at one end of the riding hall for those who merely wanted to watch, although a gentleman member would never laugh at any mishap he might see on the riding floor below.

One activity the members enjoyed was known as the "Balaklava Melee," the palest of pale imitations of the gallant charge of the Light Brigade. In the Michaux Club riding hall four of the most daring riders donned fencing masks, grasped canes, and mounted their trusty cycles. Then they wheeled and circled around, all the while striking at the plumes on each other's heads. The last man to retain his feathers was declared the winner; the losers went off to see what could be done for a bad attack of ringing in the ears.

For the ladies there were "ten pin rides," wherein one snaked in and out through a line of bowling pins set on the floor. Even better than the "ten pin ride" was the *gymknana*, which was labeled as a new import from India, although it bore little resemblance to the land of the Khyber Rifles. Both males and females wore a prescribed uniform. The men were outfitted in white knickerbockers, red coats, red-and-white jockey caps, red stockings, and white shoes. The ladies wore white skirts, red-and-white striped shirtwaists, red leather belts, white straw sailors, red stockings, and white shoes. The bicycles were decorated with red and white ribbons.

The entire festival began with a grand march on bicycles, eight men and eight women participating. The march was followed by relay races, fancy-riding exhibitions, music, and a "bicycle dance" performed around a Maypole by little girls dressed in white with garlands of flowers in their hair. The evening was concluded by "dancing" the Lancers or the Virginia Reel on bicycles.

The superrich in America also took to cycles. John D. Rockefeller began presenting bicycles to those whose health he felt was in jeopardy. Mr. Rockefeller was partial to the Cleveland Bicycle, no doubt because he got started toward his first million in that city, and during one year he gave thirty-eight to associates who needed outdoor exercise. On one of his tours of that little Baptist college that Rockefeller endowments turned into the University of Chicago, John D. inspected the campus in the company of President William Rainey Harper and a covey of professors, all awheel. Amos Alonzo Stagg, that accomplished athlete and all-American football player, beat out the millionaire in a short sprint. The *Chicago Tribune* called on President Harper to challenge President Charles W. Eliot of Harvard to a bicycle race to establish the academic supremacy of the two institutions. President Harper demurred.

Other rich people rode bicycles. William Rockefeller was awheel and so was William O. Havemeyer, president of the sugar trust. In fact so many of the well-to-do cycled that the posh Metropolitan Club in New York City kept two hundred bicycles on hand for its members. Chauncey Depew, president of the New York Central Railroad, spokesman for the Vanderbilts, and a U.S. senator, learned to ride in Newport and commented that the machine was "harder to straddle than the civil service plank in the Republican platform."[5] However, he stuck with it, and by the end of the summer he had ridden every foot of three whole miles without assistance.

Depew was only keeping pace with his fellow legislators in Washington. The Capitol Bicycle Club had been formed in 1891. Five years later it was said, "Everybody who wants to be anybody has either learned to ride, is learning to ride, or wants to learn to ride the revolving wheel."[6] "Czar" Thomas Reed, powerful Maine political leader and future Speaker of the House, hoisted his 250 pounds on a bicycle. "Sockless Jerry" Simpson forgot his Populist constituency in Iowa long enough to try the same. Both stored their machines in the checkroom under the Capitol dome.

The "disease" even invaded President McKinley's cabinet. Teddy Roosevelt was too busy whipping the Navy into shape to ride a bicycle, but his wife was not. Neither was Secretary of State Richard Olney. Mr. Justice White of the Supreme Court doffed his robes long enough to pedal down Pennsylvania Avenue. It was also reported that the Army, the Navy, the clergy, and Washington society were all a bit stiff from unaccustomed exercise but smiling and buoyant withal. Not even the diplomatic corps was immune. The undersecretary of the British embassy, Cecil Spring-Rice, wheeled by on his way to a future knighthood. The Russian ambassador and his wife both cycled, as did the Belgian minister and Jerome Bonaparte.

The makers, however, were after the President's family, the one group in Washington that could put the final stamp of approval on cycling. William McKinley was too much the politician to become a cyclist—it simply did not fit with the dignified picture he had of the Presidency. But he did have a young niece; and an enterprising manufacturer came up with just the right model for a candidate who had run on a platform calling for maintaining the gold standard—a bicycle with gold-mounted trim! Grace was thrilled by the gift, but "Uncle Will" put his foot down and said the bicycle would have to go back. Then he lectured his family, private and public, on the impropriety of accepting bicycles from manufacturers.

The leaders of government were not the only ones to take to the cycle. Broadway was well represented by Nat Goodwin, who starred in *Nathan Hale*, John Drew, the first matinee idol, and W. H. Gillette, fresh from portraying Sherlock Holmes. Lillian Russell rode a jewel-encrusted bicycle, a gift from Diamond Jim Brady. Ellen Terry cycled on the streets of Boston while on tour with Henry Irving's company and reported that cycling helped her concentrate on the demanding roles she played.

In other places all kinds of people took to the cycle. Philadelphia laid claim to the first cycling club for Chinese, presided over by Woo Head and Sun Sing. They named it the First Chinese Bicycling Club of Philadelphia, an appropriate but not very original name. Although the City of Brotherly Love may have had the first Chinese club, it did not have the first Chinese school. That honor went to an establishment started down on Mott Street in New York's Chinatown to cater to rich merchants who wanted to learn to ride. Then there was the all-Japanese Rising Sun Cycle Club, which was described as being one of the best-uniformed and best-disciplined clubs to be seen.

Early in the spring of 1898 the Socialist Labor Party of America organized a Socialist Wheelmen's Club, and in May the members started riding from Boston through New England to New York City, distributing socialist literature along the way. *The New York Times* reported that the uniforms consisted of light brown jackets, blue sweaters, and ties and caps of socialist red. The effects of their propaganda are not recorded, but the ride demonstrated that Socialists could shift with the times.

Everybody got into the act. The *Minneapolis Tribune* noted that the Salvation Army had raised a mounted troop for work in the Colorado mining districts and predicted that before long, General Booth's organization would equip its soldiers with bicycles for city work. A Fat Man's Bicycle Club was organized in Brooklyn, with membership limited to men weighing 250 pounds or more.

Club members or not, the cyclers were out in great numbers, particularly in the cities of the East and Midwest. By 1895 tens of thousands were on wheels. And the numbers continued to grow. On one Sunday in August, 1898, an estimated 100,000 bicycles left New York City for the countryside.

Somewhere in those crowds were cyclists who had ridden one hundred miles in less than fifteen hours—the real hardcases of cycledom.

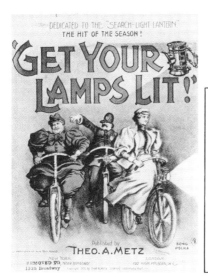

TOP, LEFT: SHEET MUSIC COLLECTION OF LESTER S. LEVY. TOP, RIGHT: *PICTURE HISTORY OF AMER ICAN TRANSPORTATION, POPULAR MECHANICS, 1952.* BOTTOM: COURTESY OF RAY BROSSEAU.

RIDING HIGH, BY ARTHUR PALMER, E. P. DUTTON, INC. 1956

INSTRUCTION BELT.

In instructing beginners in the use of the bicycle, the great difficulty has always been to get a substantial hold on the body of the beginner. This is effected in the best possible manner by our INSTRUCTION BELT—" Patented "—cut of which is presented here. The following advantages are claimed for it, viz: It lessens likelihood of falls while learning full fifty per cent.; thus saving damage both to rider and to his clothes and machine. In teaching beginners the instructor has, under the old method, to grasp them tightly around the arm or by various parts of their clothing; in the first way the grasp is sufficiently strong, when prolonged through a lesson of an hour or so, to seriously inconvenience the beginner by reason of the bruise which it causes to the arm; under the second method, clothing is most frequently warped and strained out of all shape and so damaged for further use. As will be readily seen, all this is avoided by use of the Instruction Belt. By use of our Belt one who has himself no knowledge of riding is able to instruct. This is a great advantage in small towns where dealers or riders are either not numerous or do not exist at all.

The Instruction Belt is made of best 3½-inch webbing, with straps of best black finished leather, strongly hand sewed and riveted; the handle is made of three-layer leather of same quality as straps, and is of large size and thickness, to afford a good hold. The whole device is packed neatly in card-board mailing case, with instructions for use, and sent, postpaid, on receipt of $1.25.

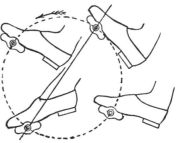

BICYCLE INSTITUTE OF AMERICA

Top, right: the science of proper pedaling. Middle, right: the disease dreadful—the bicycle hump. Bottom, left, and right: positions correct and incorrect.

Misadventures

Top, right: predictions of things to come if country roads are not improved. Right and bottom: mishaps and hazards of the road.

TOP, RIGHT: BICYCLE INSTITUTE OF AMERICA. BOTTOM: CULVER PICTURES, INC.

Options

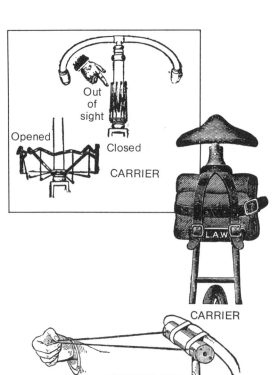

Out of sight

Opened

Closed

CARRIER

CARRIER

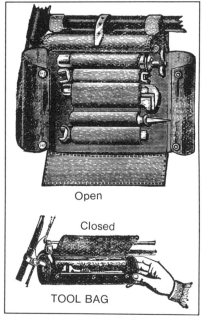

Open

Closed

TOOL BAG

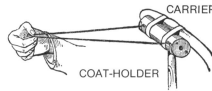

COAT-HOLDER

C

ROLLER BRAKE

STAND AND HOME TRAINER

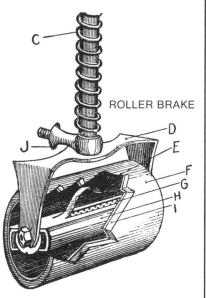

J

D

E

F

G

H

I

EXTRA GRIPS

BICYCLE INSTITUTE OF AMERICA

Cartoons from Puck

Top: a new status symbol.
Bottom: the idealism of early city planners.

RAMBLER BICYCLES.

PROSPECT AVE.

GEO. W. CHILDS · 5¢ CIGAR ·

GENEROSITY GOOD

C. L. SOLBECK

BICYCLES, REPAIRING SUNDRIES &C.

CULVER PICTURES, INC.

CHAPTER 7

"Let Him Ride to Death"

THE CRAZY FRINGE

BICYCLE INSTITUTE OF AMERICA

THE UNICYCLE

Like all sports, cycling developed its crazy fringe. Deeply absorbed with a machine that annihilated both distance and time, this fringe launched a determined campaign to prove what the bicycle could do. They also proved two other things: the strength of the human physique, and the durability of American products.

The madness took many shapes. One of the more common was determining how far one could cycle, concentrating on distance alone. It was not long before Americans were attempting to ride around the world, no doubt spurred on by Jules Verne's *Around the World in Eighty Days*. The first to make the trip was Thomas Beelen of San Francisco. He rode his fifty-inch ordinary to New York City, took a boat to England, rode across the island, ferried to the Continent, and then pedaled down through the Balkans to Constantinople. From there he rode into Persia, where he was forced to spend the winter because snow had closed the passes through the Hindu Kush, the "Roof of the World." The next spring Beelen started again. Chased out of Afghanistan by a government that looked with suspicion on a man who would try to pedal around the world, he rolled across the deserts of Baluchistan into India, crossed into northern Burma, and then entered southern China. The Chinese had had altogether too much experience with "foreign devils," and when they found one without his gunboat they made the most of the opportunity. Beelen was harassed unmercifully, but he made it to Shanghai, where he took a boat to Nagasaki. After a delightful trip across Japan to Tokyo, he sailed to San Francisco, passing through the Golden Gate three years after he began his historic trip.

The next Americans to complete the round-the-world trip were two young Midwesterners, W. L. Sachtleben of Alton, Illinois, and Thomas Allen of Ferguson, Missouri. These two bought their bicycles in Liverpool in June, 1890, crossed the Continent, and rode down into Turkey. In Armenia they climbed to the top of Mt. Ararat (whether on bicycles was not reported), then cycled across Persia and eventually on into China. Like Beelen they were non grata to some Chinese provincial governors, and occasionally they had to fight to retain possession of their machines. Once, backed with their bicycles against a wall, they were forced to use their guns (or what *Harper's Weekly* called "six hole Colorado logic") to keep a Chinese mob at bay.

Fortunately the trip was not always so bad, and the nearer they got to Peking, the better things became. Sometimes they were escorted by a small squad of Chinese soldiers. In all they rode over three thousand miles through China, traversing much land never seen before by Westerners. In Tientsin the viceroy received them cordially, even though the two Americans were outlandish figures in the eyes of the cultured Oriental: They were dressed in baggy knee breeches, Chinese sandals, and Russian stockings, with turbans wound around their heads. Spanning their waists were cartridge belts carrying their "Colorado logic."

From China Sachtleben and Allen ferried over to Japan and then, like Beelen, took ship for the United States. In San Francisco they replaced their worn-out cycles with new Victor Bicycles, rolled down to southern California, cut across the mountains at San Gorgonio Pass, and pedaled off into the desert. They arrived back in New York City in the summer of 1893.

Beelen and the Sachtleben-Allen team had their troubles, but their fate was far better than that of Frank Lenz. On May 15, 1892, the twenty-five-year-old Lenz mounted his Overman Bicycle and wheeled out of Pittsburgh on his way around the world, reversing the usual route and going from East to West. The young cyclist was under contract to *Outing*

Magazine to produce a series of articles about his trip. Lenz pedaled leisurely across the United States, stopping from time to time to visit bicycle clubs in the cities he passed through. After crossing the country he took ship for Asia, then cycled through China and down into India. At irregular intervals he wrote letters giving the next step on his itinerary, and his estimated date of arrival at each check point.

Cyclists following his trip got their first scare when in August, 1893, the *New York Herald* reported that Lenz was long overdue in Calcutta (he had been scheduled to arrive there on March 1). Six months later there was still no news; the Pittsburgh rider seemed to have dropped from sight completely. Finally, however, he reappeared, and cycling America breathed a sigh of relief. Keeping to his easy pace, Lenz pedaled across northern India and wintered there, waiting the coming of good weather to start the next leg across Persia and Turkey.

The following spring, in Turkey, Lenz vanished again. This disappearance was more ominous, because a strong anti-American feeling existed in Turkey at the time, manifesting itself in the form of assaults on missionaries. After six months of silence, young Lenz's family hired Sachtleben to go to Turkey to investigate. *Outing* immediately opened its own investigation, hiring an American detective to find out what he could. Hinting for the first time at foul play, the magazine insisted that the investigation was being made more difficult because Turkish officials were in league with the very people who had been responsible for Lenz's disappearance.

At Tchurouk the American detective made some tragic discoveries: half of a bicycle bell, some metal fittings from a touring bag, and two pieces of rubber tire that were being used to pad the saddle girths of a Kurdish horse. That was all he discovered, because the natives returned blank stares when asked if they had seen a man on an "iron horse." In November, 1894, an American tobacco merchant based in Constantinople speculated that the cyclist probably had fallen ill in one of the villages whose inhabitants were hospitable, and told Lenz's family and friends that he would conduct a personal effort to find the cyclist. But that winter and most of the spring of 1895 passed, and the fate of the American was still not known.

In July, however, fragments of information began to leak back to the United States that left no doubt about Lenz's fate. According to *Outing*, he had left Tabriz, Persia, in the spring of 1894, and somewhere between there and Erzurum, in eastern Turkey, he had been killed. Sachtleben brought back hearsay gathered from a man in Constantinople, who in turn heard it from a friend who was also a cyclist. The friend had allegedly stopped for coffee somewhere in the interior of Turkey and had been told by a soldier that he and five others had been on patrol when they had seen the machine coming along, raising a cloud of dust like a jinni out of Gehenna. The soldier and his comrades decided to shoot—if it were a jinni it would not be hurt, and if it were a man, it would fall.

The truth seems to have been closer to the story in the *Chicago Tribune*, which attributed Lenz's death to six Kurds, two sons of Khatto and two sons of Abduraman, all of whom had been arrested at the demand of the British vice consul. The men were tried for unpremeditated murder and convicted of the charge, but Levantine justice was never exacted, since all escaped and were never heard of again. Secretary of State Richard Olney tried to get the Turkish Government to pay an indemnity for Lenz, whose body was never found. But although Olney pushed for payment, the case got lost in more important world problems and what Sachtleben called "characteristic delays." Frank Lenz, bicycler, passed into oblivion.

Lenz's death put a quietus to round-the-world cycling trips, partly because of the dangers of Kurd hospitality and partly because Americans found they could ride as many miles as they wanted right at home. So they fell victim to a new mania, riding long distances cross-country.

The distance mania appeared early. By 1889 a few bicycle clubs were awarding special medals to the member who had logged the most miles during the previous cycling season. Some clubs also tried for collective records. In 1889 the Buffalo Ramblers reported that club members had ridden a total of 189,329 miles in one year. The organization had one man who covered 5,675 miles during the season.

Probably the record for such cycling was established by a young man named Tom Winder, who "rode the border" of the United States. Winder, who was sponsored by the Eclipse Bicycle Company, set out from New Orleans along a route that took him through Houston, San Antonio, Los Angeles, San Francisco, Portland, and on to Seattle. Then he turned east through Spokane, Grand Forks, St. Paul, Chicago, Buffalo, and Bangor, and finally south to Boston and New York. After resting for a while, Winder mounted his bycycle and pedaled into the Deep South to Savannah, Mobile, and home to New Orleans. He covered 21,000 miles in 274 days, averaging a hardy seventy-five miles each day.

Then there was Frank Beedleson, who rode his bicycle from San Francisco to New York in 1893. The throng outside the offices of the *New York Herald* broke into cheers when the elapsed time of the trip was announced—sixty-six days! And while the applause reverberated against the buildings of Newspaper Row, the modest young man of twenty-four *stood on his only leg* and waved back at the crowd.

A different version of the long-distance mania, collective in nature, was the relay. The mastermind behind the first cross-country relay was William Randolph Hearst, the publisher of the *New York Journal.* Hearst was locked in a circulation war with Joseph Pulitzer, and both were alert to any and all opportunities to advance sales at the expense of the other. A cross-country spectacular was sure to draw readers. Hearst fell back on his popular "Yellow Kid" cartoon character for a symbol, and called the relay the *"Journal-Examiner* Yellow Fellow Transcontinental Bicycle Relay," a mouthful if there ever was one. The cross-country route was divided into 220 relays of about fifteen miles each, with a team of two riders assigned to each relay.

On August 25, 1896, a yellow-clad cyclist pedaled away from the *Examiner* office in San Francisco at high noon, the first of the long string of relays crossing the country. Pumping hard and using the railway snowsheds across the Sierras, the riders passed Reno in one day and got to Terrace, Utah, in two. On Sunday, August 30, the cyclers went through Creston, Wyoming, looped around the Medicine Bow Mountains, and rode south toward Laramie. Six days out from San Francisco, the relay passed through Kimball, Nebraska, and headed east toward the valley of the South Platte. A day later a team flashed through Kearney, and on September 2 another went through Grand Junction. All this time the crowds in New York followed the progress of the cyclists on a giant map hanging over the front of the *Journal* office, waiting anxiously for the reports that were sent by telegraph to the city.

Fate and bad weather caught up with the cyclists in Iowa, and it took almost two days, September 2 and 3, to ride over the muddy roads of the Hawkeye State and Illinois.

In Indiana the riders picked up speed, and on the evening of September 4 they wheeled through the twilight into Bryan, Ohio, and then on toward Erie, Pennsylvania. Twelve hours later the relay was east of Utica. The next day, Monday, September 7, the last cyclist, professional racer Fred Titus, rode triumphantly up to the steps of City Hall, where Hearst awaited him on a reviewing platform. The total elapsed time was thirteen days and twenty-nine minutes! The old Pony Express had covered the 2,000 miles from Sacramento to St. Joseph, Missouri, in ten and a half days. The cyclists had raced 3,400 miles in thirteen days, or about 30 per cent faster than the horsemen.

Naturally not every bicycle fan engaged in these extended versions of cycling mania, but there was something special for the ordinary bicycler in the Century Riding Club of America. This organization was created to encourage those who wanted to ride one hundred miles all in the same day. The club awarded a gold bar each time it was done.

The whole idea was the object of a contemptuous indictment by the *New York Herald* in 1893.

> The fellow who is ambitious to ride a century every Sunday belongs in the category with the prize pie eater and the one who enters gorging and guzzling contests. He is moving toward the fool's grave more rapidly than the other fools and we should not throw a tack in his way. Let him ride to death. He never will be missed. He has mistaken the doctrine of the "survival of the fittest" for the "survival of the toughest." Let us hope he will die young and without offspring to help afflict a fool-ridden world.[1]

Yet two years later the number of those who went out to ride their "century" had increased like flies in May, and century riding clubs had changed their requirement to riding one hundred miles in fourteen hours.

On January 1, 1898, a New Yorker named Teddy Edwards announced that he was going to ride a hundred miles a day every day in the coming year. Each morning Edwards arose around 8:30 and had a rubdown, followed by a breakfast of clam broth, oatmeal, a rum omelet, and an assortment of breakfast edibles. Then, contrary to all advice, he smoked one or two cigars. By 10:00 A.M. he was on his bicycle and away.

In late summer, having ridden one hundred miles every day since January 1, Edwards left the city roadways and struck out across the nation. In September, Edwards was the main attraction at the convention of the League of American Wheelmen being held in Indianapolis. The delegates cheered him to the rafters and wished him good luck as he wheeled eastward again toward New York City. Edwards expected to reach home on September 10, but three days after leaving Indianapolis he came to grief. Somewhere along the way he contracted typhoid fever, and a physician ordered the intrepid cyclist out of the saddle. Edwards had to be content with 25,000 miles for the time elapsed.

Colossal . . . except when one remembers that Edwards was *trying to break* two records already standing. He failed to outride John George of Philadelphia, who had set a year's record of 32,479 miles in 1897, and John Noble, who rode 253 centuries in one year.

As time passed, the idea of riding a mere hundred miles in a day gave way before the onslaught of determined Americans who wanted to cover even more distance in less time. Twenty-five-year-old Gus Egloff of the Century Club of New York set out in June, 1899, to ride eight centuries in eighty hours—eight hundred miles in a little over three days! Gus rolled out on June 11, fortified by the determination to break the American record of six hundred miles in one ride. Egloff completed the first five hundred miles in a little less than fifty-one hours, excellent time that could be attributed to the teams of cyclists who paced him so he would not fall behind the required speed. At the end of five hundred miles, Egloff dismounted, had a rubdown to get the kinks out of his tightening muscles, took some light refreshment, and was off again.

Gus finished his eight centuries in an elapsed time of 82 hours—and kept right on going. On June 15, he finally stopped. Living on ice cream for 108 hours and twenty minutes, sleeping only six hours all told, Egloff had ridden one thousand miles.

Six weeks later Charles Lehritter of the same club mounted his bicycle to make the longest continuous ride in American history. He pedaled away at 4:16 P.M. on Saturday, August 19, and rode for seven days and nearly eight nights. During this time he was off his cycle less than seventeen hours, fifteen of which were spent in sleeping. Contrary to most people who did this sort of thing, Lehritter ate rather heavily of boiled chicken, eggs, and beef tea, most of which he consumed while riding along behind his pacers. On August 27, he decided to stop, having ridden his bicycle 178 hours and covered 1,500 miles! Egloff had averaged a spanking 9.3 miles per hour on his run; Lehritter averaged 8.4 on a ride 50 per cent longer.

As might have been expected, the "new woman" was not to be left out. It is impossible to say exactly who rode the first women's century, but in July, 1894, Mrs. E. E. Witchie became the first woman in the Midwest to cover a hundred miles in one day, the distance from Anoka, Minnesota, to St. Cloud and back. Mrs. A. E. Rhinehart of Denver was on record as having ridden 17,152 miles in 1896, including 116 centuries! As if such a record were not imposing enough, on ten successive days she completed a century each day, and in the famous *Journal-Examiner* cross-country relay she carried a message nine miles up the mountains in thirty minutes.

And women had a go at the same thing Egloff and Lehritter did. Mrs. Irene Brush of Brooklyn was the first woman cyclist to ride four hundred miles according to the rules of the Century Club, and she did it in less than two days. Mrs. Brush was described as being of "athletic build," surely a euphemism for a twenty-five-year-old who weighed a spanking 165 pounds and stood five and a half feet tall.

Miss Jane Yatman of New York went Mrs. Brush one century better. In July, 1899, about two weeks after Mrs. Brush's "quadruple," Miss Yatman rode off down the roads of Long Island. In the next fifty-eight hours she was off her bicycle less than six, and at the end she had ridden five hundred miles, a new woman's record.

If women could ride a hundred miles, then why couldn't children? In August, 1897, the Century Road Club of New York sent 473 starters out on a run. Of those starting, forty-two were women and one was a seven-year-old boy! Of the group, 460 finished, including all the women and the boy, Master Walter McGrath of Philadelphia. It so happened that the century was young Walter's fourth of the season. A year later he added four more to his credit.

By all odds, the most virulent form of cycling lunacy came with the endurance contest called a six-day bicycle race. In the earliest contests, which started in 1883, contestants pedaled twelve hours out of twenty-four, the prize going to the racer who covered the greatest distance during the period. From time to time during the race the management required sprint runs just to liven up the proceedings.

Endurance races began to grow in popularity after 1890, even though in 1892 *Outing* condemned these contests, saying that they were not calculated to elevate the sport in the eyes of noncyclers. "Prowler" criticized the six-day race as a contest in which the managers were at loggerheads with their riders and both were so foul-mouthed that decent women were prevented from attending. Adding to the generally low level of the affair were the bicycle clubs with their "silly and inane club calls," a blend of "Yips" and "Rahs" that produced one "pandemoniacal uproar."[2]

Despite the carping by "Prowler," six-day bicycle races remained popular throughout the craze and for several decades thereafter. Usually the contests were held during the winter, to assure that cycling fans would be in the stands and not out on the cycle paths. Those held in Madison Square Garden were the most famous and were typical of the sport.

The Garden had an oval board track, ostensibly measuring ten laps to the mile. The ends were banked sharply on the curves, and a wooden fence was supposed to prevent cyclers from going over the top and out into the crowd. A black stripe was painted eighteen inches from the bottom of the pine track so the speeding racers would have something to guide themselves by. This line was duplicated at the top of the track as a warning that the cyclist was perilously close to the edge. At the Fourth Avenue side of the Garden, just below what was called the "bad Fourth Avenue turn," were tents for the racers, cots, and oil stoves for keeping warm by and preparing the frugal meals the men ate. At the other end of the track was a bandstand from which music continuously assaulted the ears of fans. The officials and the public address system, a giant megaphone suspended from a tripod, were in the center of the bowl.

The rules for six-day races were relatively simple. The winner was the man who covered the most miles in the time alloted (contestants generally rode at least twenty hours a day), with the proviso that everybody had to ride a minimum of 1,350 miles to qualify for any prize money. After all, the managers of the race wanted no collusion on the part of the racers against the public, especially since betting was frequently heavy. The prize money varied, but for the race of 1897 it amounted to $4,200, with $1,300 for first place down to $75 for the last man. On the face of it, the total prize money seems inadequate, but it was enough to attract riders from Paris, Brussels, Stockholm, and other European cities.

On the opening day of the 1897 race, ten thousand spectators packed the Garden as the racers mounted bicycles held upright by their starters. Then a shout almost lifted the roof as the starter's gun sounded. The racers set an easy pace, saving their strength for three or four days later, when it would be needed. Fans drifted in and out during the daytime, built up to the biggest crowds at night, then dwindled after midnight, only to begin swelling again the next morning. During the long night hours two hundred or so die-hard fans watched the cyclers spin around the boards. Lurking beneath and behind the stands were overcoat thieves who waited for the spectators to leap to their feet to cheer. As soon as the posterior was off the overcoat, the thief snatched it and was gone.

A third of the way through, some racers began to show the effects of the grind. One man rode round and round, mumbling all the while that the scorekeepers were cheating him on the count and threatening to run over them if they did not credit him with more laps. By the third day the only thing that jolted the mesmerized racers was the shout of the crowd, which spurred the tired men into sprints against each other and momentarily made them forget their muscles howling at the strain. *The New York Times* called them "whirling demons who ride between walls of shrieking faces."

On the fifth day the chief of police brought police surgeons into the Garden, who checked the pulse and temperature of each contestant. They reported all were in fairly good condition, considering the grind. However, the pace was beginning to tell in other respects. One racer was described as "surly" because after a break he refused to go back on the track. The previous year the same man had tried to throw his cycle into the crowd. A fellow contestant in the 1897 race lost a tire on the sharply banked turn, jammed his front fork, and smashed his head into the fence at the top edge of the track. The injured cycler was rushed to the hospital, but three hours later he was wheeled back onto the track and shoved into the race.

Finally the race came to an end. The winner was a Chicagoan named Charlie Miller, followed in second place by a cyclist named Schineer, both of whom had repeatedly asked their managers if they could sleep but had been cajoled into finishing. In the allotted time Miller had pedaled 2,093 miles; Schineer had covered 2,026. While the crowd whistled and rocked the Garden with their stamping feet, Miller stepped up to receive a spray of flowers and a kiss from Anna Held, the darling of the musical theater. He also got a total cash prize of $3,550. Of this, $1,000 was for personal appearances to be made later, $550 was from the maker who furnished the machine he rode, $200 was from the manufacturer of the saddle, $500 was from the tire maker, and $100 was from the firm that had constructed his special handlebars.

Miller told newsmen that his ankles had swollen rather badly after the third day of the race, and that the cigar smoke and the dust rising from under the boards had been so bad that all he could see was the black line ahead of him and the wall around the track. He became so hypersensitive that the very nailheads in the track had jarred him "fearfully," and he thought his bones were coming apart. During the race he ate three pounds of boiled rice and a pound of oatmeal, and he drank three gallons of strong coffee and twenty quarts of milk. In six days he had been off the track a total of ten hours, of which *only four* had been spent in sleeping.

Unhappily Miller's victory lost a little luster when it was announced subsequently that the Garden track was short, and as a result, the mileage covered by the racers was not as great as had been originally represented. The race managers said the short track was an inadvertent mistake, but the *Times* said that the scandal would give cycle racing a tremendous setback. The League of American Wheelmen shrugged that it was not responsible; its sanction for the race only meant that the racing was carried out according to the league's rules.

None of the criticism prevented the next annual contest from starting on December 7, 1898. Schineer was in fine fettle, having conditioned his legs during the summer by walking up and down 33,000 steps every day at Chicago's Masonic Temple. Unfortunately, the program didn't help. By the second day of the race, collisions on the board track were multiplying, and riders were beginning to drop out, but crowds of as much as 15,000 cheered those who kept at it. On the fourth day Charlie Miller forged ahead and stayed there. After his victory, in the presence of thousands of cheering fans, he married his fiancée. For his wedding Miller wore the ultimate in racing costumes. The groom's racing tights had one white leg and one pink. Atop this Miller wore a shirt, also in pink and white but with the colors reversed from the tights. On the back of his shirt was embroidered an American eagle surmounting a shield, and around his waist he wore a silk American flag as a sash. Whatever life had left in store for Charlie Miller, he enjoyed his hour of glory.

The six-day race for single cyclists was doomed, however. New York and Illinois in effect outlawed such contests by forbidding any rider to pedal more than twelve hours out of any twenty-four. As a result the managers shifted to teams of two men each. The fans continued to come out, but the glory days and nights of the supercyclist were past. The six-day contests lasted well into the era of the Great Depression, but after 1900 no man would come close to Charlie Miller's two triumphs as a human cycling machine.

Elsewhere and at other times, Americans tried to do pretty foolhardy things. For example, William Seels of Woonsocket coasted down the steps of the Capitol in Washington, D.C., in fifteen seconds flat. Seels got a good start at the top and hit his maximum speed sixteen steps from the bottom, at which point he became airborne. He landed at the base of the steps in a heap of tangled spokes and bent rims but suffered no broken bones as a result of the sudden stop.

One cyclist challenged a speeding express train. Cycle and iron horse raced side by side, the engine on the tracks and the cycle on the path alongside. With his head down and pumping for all he was worth, the cycler could not see that the path ended as the tracks crossed a bridge. Bicycle and rider shot off the bank, sailing thirty feet into the mud flats below. If there was a cycling saint in heaven he was on the job that day, because the bicyclist regained consciousness after half an hour and struggled out of the muck with nothing worse than a broken collar-bone and two sprained ankles. He had apparently landed as he had taken off—pedaling like a fiend.

During the early summer of 1899, C. W. Murphy laid plans to use a locomotive in a race against the clock. A wooden roadway was laid between the rails on a five-mile stretch of track, while a large windscreen was built out from the rear of a railroad car. When all was set Murphy mounted his Tribune Racer, got inside the protecting screen, fixed his eye firmly on the black stripe down the center of the track, and off man and locomotive raced. When the run was over Murphy had officially ridden a mile in 57⅘ seconds. It was some years before Barney Oldfield drove an automobile that fast. Man had made sixty miles an hour on his own power!

Not all who peopled the shimmering outer fringes of the cycling world were fast or fortunate. One who lost his luck was Frank Donahue from Fort Wayne, Indiana, who billed himself as "Professor Arion." Arion was a slack-wire artist who used a bicycle in his act. He had brought gasps from crowds at Niagara Falls and other cities with his innovation. On the night of August 1, 1897, the Ridgewood Amusement Park on Long Island was crowded with summer vacationers who had come to watch Arion do his bit. Rumor had it that the slack wire, which was slung between two telephone poles a hundred feet apart and rising seventy-five feet into the air, would be charged with five hundred volts of electricity when Arion rode his bicycle across it that night.

At 9:30 Arion and his machine were hoisted to the top of one of the poles. While the crowd gaped, he steadied himself on his platform and settled his bicycle on the wire. Then he mounted the saddle and threw another wire across the one connecting the poles. To the crowd's amazement and applause, both he and his bicycle lighted up—his costume was wired with tiny lights, and so was his machine. Smiling at the upturned faces, he grasped the balancing pole and started across the wire.

But partway over his smile disappeared. Twenty feet out Arion lost one of his pedals, and in trying to catch it with his foot, he lost his balance and fell. One report said he made a grab for the slack wire but was jolted loose by the shock. Others said he dropped straight down.

In any case, Arion died in the arms of a doctor, while women fainted dead away in the August night and the crowd fled in horror. There is little evidence that Frank Donahue had many imitators.

Well, maybe one, but he was an Englishman, and everybody knew about mad dogs and Englishmen. Eight days after Arion fell to his death, a parachutist named Luton rose in a balloon over London. Then, mounted on a bicycle attached to a parachute, he cut himself loose at three thousand feet. Falling all the time, Luton pedaled his bicycle to open his parachute and thus settled safely to the ground. One is left with a vision of a cyclist suspended midway between clouds and terra firma and pedaling like hell.

If a man could pedal on an electrified wire, why could he not pedal on snow? Jules Lee, who had accompanied Peary on one of his excursions above the Arctic Circle, in 1897 maintained that the bicycle could be used efficiently on future polar expeditions because the gravel-like character of the snow would permit traction. He told a reporter that he had seen mile after mile of snow on his trip across Greenland, snow suitable for cycling, and that if he ever went North again he would certainly take his bicycle with him. He allowed that pneumatic tires would be worthless in polar regions but suggested that tires made of woven cotton would stand up in the frigid weather. Ruefully, the cyclist admitted that he did not expect Peary to try the idea on his next trip. Peary agreed.

Two months later, when newspapers were filled with stories about the Klondike gold rush, the *New York Herald* described a syndicate that planned to solve the cost of transportation to the gold field by using a cycle. Extra-heavy machines would be constructed with solid rubber tires and rawhide-wrapped frames that would permit them to be touched in the subzero weather. Mounted on either side of the frame and just ahead of the sprocket would be a wheel that could be folded out to convert the bicycle to a four-wheeled vehicle that could be pushed. The predicted payload of five hundred pounds would be fastened over the front and rear wheels of the bicycle. So far, so good.

The syndicate was familiar with the great effort required to carry supplies up and over the steep Chilkoot Pass, the most direct route to the gold, and it was there that they planned to try the specially made bicycle. It was suggested that all a man had to do was to push or drag the cycle ten miles up the trail to where the first pack would be deposited, and then fold up the auxiliary wheels and pedal back to pick up another load.

Unfortunately, the Chilkoot Pass was so steep that men climbed with their noses against the snow in front of them, and in places it was negotiable only with the aid of ropes. Therefore, to *pedal* down that incline would mean ending up in the mud on the beach at Skagway. Allegedly the syndicate was only waiting for some unidentified matters to be cleared up in the West before launching its scheme, but the only answer from Seattle was a burst of raucous laughter from sourdoughs who had been over the pass.

Apparently the giving of costly, ornamented cycles had some currency during the peak of the fad. A New York dealer told a reporter he had sold a male customer a silver-plated bicycle, costing five hundred dollars, for his wife's anniversary present. Another silvered gift bicycle with pearl-handled grips cost a thousand dollars. However, the dealer went on to say that very rich people—Miss Emily Vanderbilt, W. C. Whitney, Frank and Ellen Gould, the children of Jay Gould the financier—all ordered stock bicycles, although very good ones. Only the nouveaux riches went for such ostentation.

Such was the notorious Diamond Jim Brady, who was never one to hold back a dollar when it came to show. At the height of the fad, Brady hired the Pope Company to build him a dozen gold-plated Columbia Bicycles. Plating such as this was beyond the considerable competence of Colonel Pope's plant, so it was recommended that Brady take the machines to Tiffany, the jeweler. When Tiffany's refused to plate the frames, Brady built his own plant, plated his own bicycles, and then tore the place down. Nobody knows how much these golden bicycles had cost him.

But best of all was the bicycle he had made for Lillian Russell. Not only did it have a custom-fitted seat; the machine also had mother-of-pearl handlebars, and wheel spokes encrusted with chip diamonds, rubies, and sapphires. Miss Russell carried the bicycle back and forth to Saratoga in a plush-lined morocco leather case. Rumormongers at Rector's Restaurant said the cycle had cost Diamond Jim not less than ten thousand dollars.

Even if one was not rich, one could still dream about riding a be-jeweled bicycle. Two such fancy rigs, one a man's, the other a woman's, were offered as prizes in the *New York Journal's* popularity contest for cyclers. (William Randolph Hearst was not going to let up until he had milked the bicycle craze for all it was worth.) The big prizes were ex-pense-paid bicycle tours through Europe. But what caught everyone's eye were the bicycles that went along with the tours. These two machines had been decorated by Tiffany's, which seemingly did not draw the line on William Randolph Hearst as it had on Diamond Jim Brady, and they were something to see. "His" was filigreed in silver in the style of Louis XVI. "Hers" was done in the fashion of that royal womanizer, Louis XIV. Both cycles had sterling silver lamps, sterling bells, solid silver cyclometers, silver-mounted tool bags and saddles, and carved ivory handlebars. For the riders themselves, there were sterling silver "bicycle watches." Small wonder that New York cyclists followed the voting through the entire summer of 1897 until late August, when it was announced that the winners were R. Weber and Miss Florence Wright.

In Pittsburgh F. F. Howe snorted at such silliness and got out his own custom-made bicycle for a parade. Howe was an electrician, and if Tiffany cut to last, so did the man from Pennsylvania. His bicycle was equipped with an eight-inch electric gong and "searchlights" of 200 candlepower, while over his head floated an umbrella fringed with multicolored miniature lights. Howe was smarter than Professor Arion, and his lights worked off batteries. F. F. Howe might have been eccentric, but he was *no* lunatic like all those others.

Or so he thought.

CHAPTER 8

"*Diamonds Flash from His Tie*"

CYCLE RACING: THE AMATEURS

The popularity of automobile racing in the United States is testimony to the American predilection for speed. The attachment goes back a long way, to the advent of the bicycle. As one journalist put it at the height of the bicycle boom:

> man finally had hit upon a device which makes his own body the source of power. He had placed wheels upon his feet, and as a result finds his powers of locomotion multiplied by five and even ten. . . . We have become a race of Mercurys, in fact, and the joy which is felt over the new power amounts to a passion.[1]

Before the bicycle, the horse had been the fastest thing available to human beings, but the swiftest of these was not within the financial reach of the common man. Of course one could go fast on a train, but in such circumstances the man was a mere passenger, and only the engineer got the thrill from his grip on the throttle. However, the steel steed, which was cheaper than a horse and was propelled and guided by the rider, made it possible for Americans to go faster than they had ever gone before. When E. F. Leonert raced a mile in one minute and thirty-five seconds, beating the time of the great pacing horse Salvator, the issue of speed was resolved in favor of the bicycle. Of course, not every cyclist was truly a speedster; the fast men called "cracks" came few and far between and were the product of strict training. Nevertheless, that did not keep most cyclists from turning the cap visor around, crouching over the handlebars, and cutting loose down the street. Imagination did the rest.

The bicycle had hardly been introduced to the United States before racing became an accepted sport, growing more and more popular as the machine itself attracted Americans. Ultimately newspapers carried extensive coverage of races on their sports pages, and racing cyclists became the men of the hour. Ultimately, too, the sport underwent a major shakeup amid charges of cheating, chicanery, and roughhousing.

The beginnings were modest. *Harper's Weekly* recorded that the first one-mile bicycle race ever run in this country was won by Will Pitman in 1878, shortly after Albert Pope began grafting the cycle to the American way of life and his hand to the nation's pocketbook. Pitman looked out from the pages of the weekly with a flower in his buttonhole, his head thrown back in the regal pose of a champion, and his handlebar mustache sweeping down and around the corners of his mouth. However, his time for the mile was only three minutes and fifty-seven seconds, or about the same pace as a fast runner in the 1960's. Although this was good for the period and splendid for the old ordinary on which he raced, in less than twenty years his time was reduced by more than one half. Eventually the quest for speed, not to say money, saw the development of special racing tracks and complicated racing techniques.

Cycle racing fell into two basic categories: road racing and track racing. The earliest form of cycling contest seems to have been the road race, which undoubtedly sprang out of the cycling tours conducted by clubs. These races were also encouraged by the willingness of individual cyclists to challenge each other on the streets. In words of a later time, some cyclists were willing to "drag" with anyone who presented himself; or as they put it in the nineties, anybody who thought he had a "turn of speed" would accept "brushes" with all comers.

Road racing generally started on May 30 and served as a signal that the cycling season was officially open, at least in the Northern sections of the United States where most of the craze was concentrated. From time to time bitter complaints were lodged against the practice of commencing on Memorial Day, these protests coming for the most part from local encampments of the Grand Army of the Republic. The veterans of the Union Army felt the day was theirs, and since they had already used their influence successfully in the matter of pensions, there was every reason to believe they could put down a handful of whippersnappers. Waving the flag—the "bloody shirt" that had won so many elections for the Republicans after 1865—the GAR said it was no more appropriate to have cycle racing on a day set aside for honoring the dead than it was for Confederate veterans to dedicate a war memorial on the same day. The organization was not above giving a tug or two to the heartstrings, as a cartoon in the *Chicago Tribune* illustrated. A veteran of the Union Army was shown leaning on his only leg, pointing to a perfect river of cyclists that streamed past, and saying, "We thought Decoration Day belonged to us, but the bicyclists seem to have gotten away with it this year." None of these complaints were heeded, however, and on Memorial Day fans eagerly jockeyed to get the best spots along the roadway.

Almost any town or city with pretensions of being important had a road race, although it may not have been an annual affair. At Chicago, Cleveland, Buffalo, Toledo, Minneapolis, Denver, Los Angeles, Waltham —everywhere around the nation road races blossomed. They all seem to have been conducted along the same lines. To begin with, they were amateur contests. Professionals could not make a living on the prizes offered, and they were hardly willing to risk losing because of a break-down, or a pothole, or some such happening against which they could not guard. They much preferred to race on better surfaces and for different prizes.

Generally the weekend cyclists who entered road races were men of varying abilities, and for the sake of fairness they were handicapped by officials of the League of American Wheelmen or some sponsoring agency such as the Associated Cycling Clubs. Usually the time periods between starting groups were small, and as a result collisions at the start were frequent. A few days before one of the Irvington-Millburn races in New Jersey, entrants were warned they should really ride their older machines lest they wreck their new ones in the crush. Once the starters sent the groups away, the prize simply went to the man who crossed the finish line first, providing that he had traversed the entire course.

From the standpoint of the number of cyclists involved, the greatest of the road competitions was the Pullman Road Race, held in Chicago. The Pullman Race had its origins in a rollicking contest held on Thanksgiving Day in 1883. That first contest was a form of chase called hare and hounds, the general object of which was for the hare to get to the Chicago suburb of Pullman before he was caught. In the first chase one of the rabbits won the contest, and the route he took became the course for the Pullman Road Race of later years. Apparently the first bicycle contest was held in 1886. From then until 1893 the annual race was run over the same course of a little less than fifteen miles. In 1894 the course was shifted to the North Side, along a nineteen-mile run laid out from Chicago to Evanston, but after 1895 the contest was transferred back to the South Side. On the whole the races were very popular; the contest of 1893 drew 325 entries, that of 1894 had over 400, and the 1895 race had 515. By comparison, the Millburn-Irvington Race in New Jersey, the nearest competitor in number of cyclers, never seems to have had more than two hundred entrants.

The Pullman Race of 1895 was a classic of its kind. To begin with, the mob of entrants all had to be handicapped. Of the 515 entries, only five started from scratch, that is, without any handicap at all. One lone cyclist, who should have been congratulated for his audacity in entering at all, was awarded a head start of twelve minutes, and from there the handicappers worked back at intervals of fifteen seconds to the scratch riders. It was just as well. The vision of the crush that would have developed in trying to get all those racers off the mark at the same time is frightening. As it was, fifty starters were required to get the job done.

When the race was finally launched, the cyclists streamed into Lincoln Park in such numbers that pedestrians were prevented from crossing the street. In the frantic race, to go down was to stay down. When one of the racers, H. J. Jacobs, fell from his bicycle, a victim of the heat, the following cycles simply ran over him. He joined the ranks of the injured, which numbered fifty before the day was over.

It is doubtful that the thousands of spectators who lined the course really saw much after the first rider passed, since a cloud of dust obscured their view. If it was confusion at the start and obscurity during the race, it was bedlam as the cyclists raced across the line, giving their all in one last burst of speed that they hoped would change their position by one place. To the cheering at the finish was added the uproar that came from the corps of judges, who shouted the number of each man into a phonograph that recorded the order of finish—probably the first time such a device had ever been used for keeping records of a sporting event. After the judges replayed the record, they announced that Homer Fairmon was officially the winner of the race.

Unhappily that was not the end of the contest. Critics charged that the race was filled with skullduggery too heinous to contemplate, including the supreme crime of not riding the full and exact course, an accusation aimed at the declared winner. A subsequent investigation revealed that the charges of short-coursing were true. Before it was all over at least twenty racers had been disqualified, and the race had to be run again. But an odor of fraud clogged the air, and Chicago road racing went into a short eclipse.

Although such unfair practices did not reach the proportions elsewhere that they did in Chicago, racing frauds were found in other places around the country. The 1895 Linscott Race, between Waltham and Malden, Massachusetts, was run over a muddy course; yet the first man across the line wore a spotless sweater. Seeing that he had not started first and that all the other racers were covered with muck, it was thought best to disqualify the man.

The taint of the 1895 Pullman Race soon disappeared, and in 1897 the Chicago race was revived. The contest was scheduled for July 4. But fate in the form of one of those stifling humid days that Chicago frequently endures intervened to postpone it; with horses and humans dropping dead, it was decided not to add to the mortality rate by holding the race.

The delay lasted only a day, however, and on Monday, July 5, the racers struck out. First off the mark with the biggest handicap was Eddie Marcus, all three hundred pounds of him. Marcus, the famous Chicago fat cyclist, was racing without his equally obese friend, Baby Bliss, who did not bother to start. Eddie had gone only about a foot when a gargantuan thrust broke a pedal crank. But the fat man merely got another cycle and wheeled off. He had to, because he had bet seventy-five dollars and "numerous" cigars that he would ride the entire course.

Eddie Marcus disappeared in the pack, and forty minutes after he had started, C. A. Anderson raced first across the finish line. Those who had laid their bets against Marcus watched the judges close down their stand and rubbed their palms in anticipation of Eddie's money. But they did not know their man. Twenty-five minutes after the judges had gone home, Marcus rolled across the finish line, huffing and wheezing but finishing nonetheless. For this perseverance he was awarded the one thing every three-hundred-pound man needs—a square meal.

Not all races had a happy ending. In fact, one assumed the proportions of a Greek tragedy, man struggling against fate and going down to defeat. On May 30, 1895, Denver conducted its own road race, with 156 intrepid and determined men entered. Group by group the men rode away, determined to complete the twenty-one-mile course. However, a freak blizzard swept down the slopes of the Rockies, striking the thinly clad cyclists. The winner barely had the strength to gasp, "Am I the first?" before he collapsed into the arms of the judges. Eventually, twenty-six others wobbled across the line. According to the *Chicago Tribune,* one of them was a "raving lunatic." The report was undoubtedly exaggerated, but the course certainly was littered with broken men and machines.

In spite of its general popularity, one thing detracted from road racing as a spectator sport. As in sailing races, it was difficult to tell who was winning. Since all starts were from handicap, it was hard to decide whether the racer who had just passed was a scratch man who had dashed out in front, or a high-handicap man working like mad to stay ahead of the pack racing up from the rear. In the main, it was a lot easier to go to the cycle track and watch the cracks chase each other around the boards than it was to choke to death in the dust from a road race.

As a result, the most important bicycle races were held on a specially prepared track, usually a third of a mile in circumference, with professionals on the cycles and the stands filled with roaring spectators. The first such race was conducted by the Worcester Bicycle Club in 1883, just a step ahead of the Springfield Club, which rapidly established itself as the early center for bicycle racing. Eventually myriad tracks came to exist in the United States, ranging from the dusty, dirt-surfaced ones of the Midwest to the more sophisticated board, asphalt, or concrete tracks in the East.

At first track races, like road races, were amateur contests between gentlemen who would give every ounce of effort to win a cup, but none whatsoever to win money. But as soon as cycle manufacturers realized it was good publicity to promote winning racers, the simon-pure amateurism of cycle racing began to wither away. The makers went out to attract the fastest racers, whom they then subsidized in return for the racers' willingness to ride the bicycle the company made. This practice gave rise to the term "maker's amateur," which was used to distinguish these riders from those who still clung to the strict amateur status. As soon as some "amateurs" began accepting expense money and other gifts from manufacturers, the line separating those who rode for the fun of it and those who rode for money became blurred, and the change in the direction of professionalism was accelerated.

In the meantime significant changes occurred that altered the nature of cycle racing. The racing bicycle was dramatically redesigned to a lightweight machine whose sprocket was made larger to increase the gearing and the speed. In addition, friction was progressively reduced as American makers learned to make better bearings and as pneumatic tires replaced the old rubber tires. Improved track surfaces also helped to cut seconds from races. The men themselves underwent a regular training regimen designed to strengthen leg muscles, lung power, and endurance. Very important also was the introduction of pacing teams, which not only encouraged the racer to put out his maximum effort but also acted as windbreaks to decrease wind resistance and thus increase speed.

Americans were accustomed to mechanical improvements, but the training techniques were relatively new, although prize fighters had long trained for bouts. As a matter of fact, the more important bicycle racing became, the more it was necessary for a racer to have a good handler and a well-designed program of individualized training. Preparation for the racing season began in February with light gymnasium work, followed in a few weeks by long, slow rides on the bicycle. During this period the bicycle sprockets would be changed to increase the gearing, and the racers were encouraged to make longer and more frequent bursts of speed to get used to the difference. Three months of this regimen was considered enough to put a man in racing fettle. But it did not come cheaply, since a personal trainer cost between eighteen dollars and thirty dollars a week, plus expenses and a share of the prizes. If the racer was a real "flash" he would have a valet as well. Amateurs, not up to this sort of expenditure, frequently shared one trainer among several would-be racers, at a cost of about five dollars for each man per week.

As racers became more professional, some of the early color and flamboyance disappeared from the sport. It is unlikely that "Midget" Michael, for instance, the rage of the cycling world in 1897, ever gripped the hearts of Americans as A. A. Zimmerman had a few years earlier. "Zimmie" was a member of a tribe now extinct, the free-ranging, loose-training natural athlete who was really an amateur at heart. As with many of the sportsmen of this dawn-age of professionalism in American sports—Rube Waddell, "Chief" Bender, Grover Alexander, John L. Sullivan and others—Zimmerman loved to compete but hated to train. And as with the men above, it does not seem to have made much difference. Albert Mott described in *Harper's Weekly Magazine* Zimmerman's preparations for an attack on the record for a paced mile in 1895:

Mr. Zimmerman roomed next to the writer at a hotel in Asbury Park, and with his jovial disposition added to his position as one of the entertainers [racers], it may at least be said without offending the proprieties that all the rules of training were by him held in abeyance for a week. Mr. Zimmerman was chatty—he was convivial. He daily and nightly joined with zest in every boyish prank and sport until tired nature bade his companions seek their rest. In the small hours of the morning when they did so Mr. Zimmerman kept the pace by taking to the veranda and smoking cigars with whoever was enticed by his agreeable companionship to sit it out with him. On the night, or morning rather, of the day he performed his racing feat, he so far made a concession to it as to retire about four o'clock. With three hours sleep, a hasty breakfast, "a spin with the boys", a heartier dinner he appeared on the track in the afternoon, and rode that mile in 1.57' ⅘" without apparent distress. [2]

It should be added that "Zimmie" was only twenty-five at the time, a hale and hearty young man having a good time.

However, as racers progressively reduced their times for the different distances, it became apparent that such carefree practices could no longer be maintained, and cyclists who trained on cigars and late hours gave way to the dedicated racer who prepared like Midget Michael. Michael, the premier middle-distance racer of the midnineties, kept regular hours as a start, going to bed at eight and getting up at seven in the morning. He breakfasted on toast, eggs, and tea, then rode forty to fifty miles to "get up a good sweat"(!) or substituted for this by running eight to ten miles a day. He told one reporter that he pedaled an average of sixty miles a day to get into training. Others of the "new breed" of 1896 were described as living soberly, saving their money, cutting down on their entourages, staying away from the bookmakers, and going to bed at night.

The award system was also undergoing a change. In the early races, which were between men who were amateur by definition, the prizes were usually cups, bicycles and their accessories, tires, cyclometers, cigars, cycling shoes, napkin rings, and the like. By 1895, however, *The New York Times* was sponsoring a race and advertising a gold medal "worth $50" as the first prize, not to mention other awards of gold-nugget watch charms, uncut diamonds, and other things that might readily be converted into cash.

In other instances the prizes were obviously subterfuges by which race managers hoped to circumvent the rules of the LAW on racing and the awarding of prizes to amateurs. In some races the prize was livestock, which caused one paper to comment that the coming of the racing circuit to a town rivaled the appearance of Barnum's circus. In other events the awards for so-called amateur contests were house lots, a horse and buggy, small gold bricks or pieces stamped with their value in cash, and checks that were ostensibly to be used in purchasing gold watches or diamonds. It seems quite clear that the primary purpose of this was to provide something the racing cracks would be willing to go all out for, something more valuable than trophies. Chairman Gideon of LAW's racing committee tried to hold the amateur line; he said that diamonds, nuggets, and gold medals were intrinsically cash and hinted that racers who accepted them would be suspended.

The amateur-versus-professional war developed fairly early in the history of cycling. In 1891 *Outing* said it could not bring itself to believe that amateurism was dead in the sport, or that cyclists would refuse to race in contests where "glory and laurel wreaths were to be the only reward."[3] The magazine insisted that the attractiveness of a contest to racers was *not* in direct proportion to the value of the prizes awarded. Clearly *Outing* did not realize what was happening to the sport.

The quarreling and bickering over professionalism continued until late in 1893, when the racing board of the LAW decided to divide racing cyclists into various classes. Prior to this time the LAW had required racers to produce affidavits testifying to their status as amateurs. However, no less a person than Chairman Gideon admitted that any crack rider could "produce unlimited strange and mighty oaths" from his parents, club officials, or a manufacturer that he "never, no never, did, could, would, had or might receive one penny from . . . persons directly or indirectly as a result of his riding."[4] It was in the attempt to solve this problem that the LAW divided the racers into three categories, Class A, Class B, and Professional.

The Class A amateur got nothing but prizes from his riding and was not even allowed to accept expenses from a cycling club or any other group that might sponsor his appearance in a contest. The Class B amateur was something else, an amateur who could accept pay for his work. *Harper's Weekly* could hardly restrain itself in condemning the hypocrisy of such a classification, which it labeled as an attempt to maintain control over cycle racing and at the same time stay on the good side of the manufacturers. The magazine admitted that the makers indirectly gave life to racing by sponsoring the riders and in many cases putting up the prizes themselves, but for *Harper's* the Class B status took competition-for-competition's-sake out of the sport and made it a "game for gain."[5]

The *Boston Globe*, on the other hand, stated that nobody in his right mind would expect a man to travel around the country paying his own expenses for a few "tin medals." "Of what use are a couple of hundred bicycles, a dozen horses and buggies, clocks, pianos, etc. to a man who has to hustle to live?"[6]

As it turned out, Class B racers developed an unenviable reputation, springing partly from the situation they were in. Now that the classification had been made, the makers came forward openly as sponsors. They were always alert for promising riders coming up. They hired managers and trainers for their racers and generally supervised the entire business of fielding a professional group of amateurs. They took good care of their riders financially, too. The result was the appearance of a flashy new athlete on the American scene. *Harper's Weekly* said, "Diamonds flash from his tie, his linen, his badge, and from as many fingers as his taste will permit them to. His rest at night is unbroken and long—if the poker hand is not too distracting. A porter carries his luggage and a careful trainer sees to his diet and that his exercise is just right to keep his speed at top notch."[7]

Many of the Class B amateurs became masters at sharp practices and plotting. Scarcely had the group been designated than rumors began to circulate that some races were rigged. A reporter for the *Minneapolis Tribune* suggested to his readers that since the men were working for cycle makers and their jobs depended on winning a race every now and then, the riders sometimes got together and agreed on who should win each race. He also hinted that some referees appointed by the LAW's racing board were getting kickbacks for fixed races.

In other instances Class B riders went on strike if conditions were not all to their liking at the race meet. The strike sometimes took the form of deliberately riding slow races, to the disgust of a crowd that had paid to see cracks make assaults on records. One paper labeled these cyclists as "over-inflated, grasping, young men" who had become "arrogant, unreasonable, and filled with too much self-importance and self conceit."[8] A race in Minneapolis illustrated what they could do. The Class B stars had come to town "all very nice, very fraternal, very sportsmanlike and all that"[9] for a two-day meet. But when the time came to go on the track they refused, since some of their bicycles had not been delivered and ostensibly no racer would ride a wheel not his own. Then, while the crowd fumed and the manager wrung his hands, the riders folded their arms and refused to ride until the sponsors came up with a special race for a prize of seventy-five dollars. The cycles finally arrived, but only in time for one race, much to the anger of the customers who had been promised several contests.

The next day the racers got into a quarrel with the referee for setting an impossible time limit on a race (to counteract loafing and to force the cyclists to ride the fastest race possible, the referee was allowed to fix a maximum time limit for some contests). As a result, the riders refused to race and terminated the meet.

Referee Magazine rushed to the defense of the Class B men, who it said were frequently at the mercy of race managers. They were also preyed upon by the local referees—"local boobies" they were called—who knew no more about their duties and responsibilities than they did of "the location of their souls."[10] As detailed by the magazine, the sins of management were many. The racers were frequently the recipients of prizes that fell far short of their announced worth; the men were forced to ride on tracks that were unsafe; they were the victims of unfair handicapping, which gave big starts to the local favorites in the hope that they would be able to beat the "flyers"; and they were compelled to race against unjust time limits. Nevertheless, *Referee* admitted that the Class B men had been pretty much a law unto themselves.

By 1895 the stench arising from the Class B situation was so overpowering that the demand was made for the LAW to eliminate the class altogether, or, even more drastic, for the league to get completely out of racing. Some critics argued that racing took too much of the league's time and money and distracted from the promotion of cycling in general and the movement to improve roads in particular. There was additional pressure from those who were not particularly concerned with maintaining the amateur status of the sport. The manufacturers were getting tired of bearing the financial burden of a scheme that was no longer returning enough publicity to warrant the expense. The *Minneapolis Tribune* called passing attention to the Toledo manufacturer who had fielded a racing team costing around ten thousand dollars a year, and in return had gotten nothing but "thirds" and "unplaced" finishes. It occurred to the makers that if they stopped subsidizing Class B contests by refusing to pay the racers or furnish most of the prizes, they could shift the entire burden to the managers of the races. After the tremendous upsurge in cycling popularity in 1895, the makers saw no necessity to advertise machines when they were already falling behind in supplying the demand. Very well, let Class B fall by the wayside, and let the riders stand forth for what they were—professionals.

So it was done. Early in 1896 the LAW abolished Class B racing and tightened the restrictions on the amateur Class A. According to the new regulations, the LAW racing board reaffirmed its right to scrutinize all prizes offered in contests and to limit them to a value of thirty-five dollars. It listed infringements that would result in suspension, such as entering a class race that one's record did not entitle him to run, giving false figures to referees and handicappers, using obscene language on the track or swearing at other racers or track officials, and failing to pay entry fees. The league struck hard at the old cycling-club practice of recruiting the best talent to race under club colors by forbidding an amateur to race in any contest more than a hundred miles from his home. In addition, amateurs had to sign affidavits attesting that their status agreed with the league's definition.

Nevertheless the League of American Wheelmen and its racing board remained under constant attack. The LAW held stubbornly to the proposition that all cycle racing in the country should be under its jurisdiction, but it could not win. The end of the struggle for control of the sport came with the creation of a second group, the National Cycling Association, a purely professional group under whose auspices races were held around the country. The National Cycling Association, the "cash league," fattened on the LAW's troubles. For example, the LAW had always opposed racing on Sundays, partly because it could not control the betting that accompanied every race. When the cycling clubs of California wanted to race on the Sabbath, the league threatened to suspend participating clubs from membership. The result was a wholesale exodus of the California clubs from the organization. And the sorrows continued to pile up. The Amateur Athletic Union, which had remained faithful to a marriage of convenience with the LAW, divorced itself when the league sanctioned a race meet that the AAU had blacklisted as professional. In the meantime the president of the league was publicly accused of giving his friends jobs as handicappers in order to build a personal "machine" inside the organization.

The quarrel went right down to the turn of the century, with the LAW hanging tight but finally losing the fight. The National Cycling Association continued to sweep up dissident groups. It made little difference that the International Racing Association supported the LAW. The professional promoters continued to build their tracks and sign up the best racers, and when the NCA got control of most of the big-city tracks, it meant they had gained effective control over cycle racing. No matter that *Outing* wistfully predicted a resurgence of amateur racing as a reaction to the "riot of professionalism," the fact remained that by 1898 cycle racing was for the most part a professional sport controlled by professional promoters. In 1900, *Outing* called upon the league to give up its involvement with racing and return to the drive for better roads. The league capitulated.

CHAPTER 9

"Clear Out If You Value Your Life"

CYCLE RACING: THE PROFESSIONALS

BICYCLE INSTITUTE OF AMERICA

COASTING ON EAGLE

So professionalism took over bicycle racing in the United States, with LAW-sponsored meets competing for a time with those of the National Cycling Association, and with the racers sometimes trying to beat each other and sometimes not. It was the failure to go all out in the races that caused the customers to squirm.

For example, late in the summer of 1895 the racing brethren, led by Fred Titus, "Dute" Cabanne, and Charles Murphy, rolled into St. Louis. Murphy approached the other two with the suggestion that since there were only three big races on the card, each of them should be allowed to win one contest. Cabanne fell heir to the One-Mile Open, since St. Louis was his hometown. Murphy was to get the One-Mile Handicap Race, and Titus would be allowed to win the Two-Mile Handicap. According to Titus, both he and Cabanne stayed out of Murphy's race, covering themselves by complaining publicly that the latter's handicap of thirty-five yards was unfair and more than they could overcome from scratch. As a result, Murphy won the race easily. However, in his race Titus could not surmount the handicap given to an outsider, and he lost. But that mattered little, since the One-Mile Open was coming up, and Cabanne would be allowed to strut his stuff before the home folks—or so he thought.

A Kansas City reporter who interviewed Titus and Cabanne after the race told what really happened.

> "That Murphy is the most underhanded racing man on the circuit," said Titus boldly. "We should have known better than to have trusted him."
>
> "I set the pace as agreed, Dute following closely after, with Murphy back in the bunch. Within a short distance of the tape I pulled out to let Dute have the pole which he was unable to take, however, because his wheel was lapping mine on the outside. That is why he also turned out. What does that sneak Murphy do then but jump to the place left open by me.
>
> "Of course, it was too late for Dute to do anything then, and Murphy won the race with ease. . . . It was one of the most contemptible and sneaking steals ever made on a race track but only what might have been expected of a man like Murphy."[1]

Murphy excused his failure to allow Cabanne to win by explaining that his sponsor, having heard of the agreement, had ordered him to ride out all the races. Titus' rejoinder was to call Murphy a "Judas, sneak and renegade . . . and a disgrace to his profession." Not one of the three men seems to have felt the slightest remorse over such blatant rigging, so it is no wonder spectators complained and the LAW banned all three for life. "Life" did not last very long, though; Murphy was pardoned the next year, although Titus and Cabanne had to wait another year before the league would let them race again. Cabanne moaned that he had lost four thousand dollars in prize money because of the suspension.

Cycle racing was more than simply getting on the machine and pedaling off as fast as one could. The ways of winning a race, or preventing a faster man from winning, were many. A third-class rider with no chance even to place third would sometimes be hired to "dump" one's competition for a fixed sum or a cut of the purse. At other times a fast man would be hemmed in during a preliminary heat, which would be run at a deliberately slow pace to prevent him from getting into the finals.

Such stratagems could also be worked by pairs or "teams" of racers. In 1898 a pair named McFarland and Stevens worked together, one man concentrating on winning while the other devoted himself to hindering the racer who was considered to be the closest competitor. As the *Chicago Tribune* observed, the man outside the team in a three-man race did not stand much of a chance to win. McFarland's motto was,

"Be honest, but get the money, no matter what the sacrifice." That the system worked pretty well is attested by the fact that in Philadelphia McFarland won the One-Mile Open while Stevens was getting third; and Stevens captured the next race and McFarland got third. The man who got second surely had a hard time of it.

Sometimes a race was more like a fencing match, especially in two-man races over short distances. When Eddie "Cannon" Bald and Tom Cooper met in Chicago, the two men circled the track for several laps, neither willing to let the other fasten on the pace cycle and thus get the initial advantage. While the crowd hissed and stamped its feet, the referee made the two come back and start over. In the second attempt Cooper caught the pace cycle as it went by, and Bald perforce had to strike out after him.

At other times the tactics were more direct and less ethical yet. Elbowing one's opponent was common, although this was difficult to do if the racer stayed well down over his handlebars. In a race in Louisville, Cannon Bald and Tom Cooper, who seem to have disliked each other, pushed and shoved each other for 150 yards. During the jousting Bald seized Cooper by his sash and nearly jerked him off his machine. One can imagine what Cooper gave him in return, since it was Cooper who was disqualified. A counter to these rowdy measures was to lay back out of harm's way and then "jump" for the tape, shooting by before elbows could be brought into play.

In some instances the tactics seem to have been derived from horse racing, since they involved "pocketing" the most dangerous opponent while a confederate shot by to take the prize, which he then split with other members of his team. An example of this ploy would find "X" trapped behind one racer while a second came up on the outside and pinned him in the box. For good measure, a third would ride up in the rear just to make the pocket tight. Then a fourth would come by on the outside and ride on to win. Such pocketing stratagems were regarded by the racers as just a part of the game, unethical maybe, but not illegal. When the racing board threatened to suspend all riders who split prizes, the professionals merely grinned and went about their business.

Getting out of the pocket called for a cool head, a firm touch on the handlebars, a special burst of speed, and the willingness to gamble with one's good health. One always had to be careful not to become the victim of a treacherous invitation. For instance, the side man on the pocket would sometimes ease off to the outside, presenting an opening around the front man, an enticing opportunity for the cornered racer to escape. But trying to shoot through could be dangerous, because the side man would only be waiting for the attempt, at which time he would close the pocket again and dump the trapped man on the boards. Such falls were common in racing and help explain why professional cyclists did not use toe clips on their pedals, but liked to be able to swing their feet free at all times.

One of the better escape techniques was for the pocketed rider to pull up until his front wheel overlapped the rear wheel of the man closing the box in front. Then, while still riding at high speed, the pocketed man gave a quick twist to his handlebars and "slapped" the wheel of the closer, knocking it toward the inside of the track and doubtless scaring the hell out of the rider. The involuntary response to this maneuver was to overcompensate to the outside, and when the front man swerved out, the pocketed cyclist shot through on the inside and escaped. It was a trick for the strong at heart and certainly not for the amateur. One sure solution to the pocketing bit was to get ahead at the start and stay there for the entire race, but this was possible only in the sprint races of less than a mile.

For a brief time there were some professional women's teams that traveled around the country. The ladies rode like the men; after one race in Minneapolis, a French import, Lisette, loudly complained that the Americans had pocketed her all night. That the ladies of the troup might have departed from the accepted rules of decorum was hinted at by a Chicago gazette, which titillated its readers with a description of how the lady racers stripped nearly to the buff before being rubbed down by their men trainers. The paper also said that obscene language was bandied about and predicted darkly that the day would come soon when the ladies would don tights as racing costumes.

One practice that altered sprint racing to a degree, and middle-distance racing to a great extent, was the introduction of pacing teams, something Americans picked up from the English. The pacer's work, especially after the tandem bicycle was introduced, was simple—he got out in front and set the speed for the racers who came behind him, at once fixing a fast rate that made for record breaking and providing a windscreen for the racers themselves. To many fans, the pacers were simply hired wind cutters, but most racing cyclists accepted them as being absolutely essential to winning races and setting new records. For sprint races the pacers were not often used, but occasionally a pacing team would be employed if a rider or the manager of the meet thought there was a chance of setting a new record in one of the sprints. To some degree, the use of pacers helped prevent pocketing, because they set such a fast pace that the slower men who would have created the pocket were burned out and left behind.

As time passed, the pacers were improved. In order to provide a bigger windscreen, the pacing cycles grew from tandems to quintuplets, then to sextuplets, as the racers called for more dead air and pacers who could go fast enough to call up every bit of speed the cyclist had in him. Even so, pacers found it impossible to maintain high speeds throughout a long race, so they were relieved frequently, one pacing crew sliding in to pick up the racer while the other rolled up to the top of the track and out of the way. To do this smoothly, without slowing the racer or throwing him off stride, called for a good deal of skill and constant practice. Riding pace also demanded a certain amount of courage, because a blown tire or a broken chain created an even more serious probelm than a high-speed blowout on an automobile. The crew of the sextuplet just "abandoned ship" when they heard a tire blow, taking to the boards as the lesser of several evils. Eventually the number of pacers that could be used in a match race was fixed ahead of time. When Midget Michael raced Frank Starbuck at the Manhattan Beach Track in 1897, each man was restricted to twenty-four men, whether four "sixes" or six "fours" was not specified.

Without question the greatest of the middle-distance men was Michael, the scarcely five-foot Welshman who dominated that class from 1895 to 1900. Michael was a demon trainer who was riding him- self to death, according to what he told a *Chicago Tribune* reporter in 1897. He admitted to being nervous at the start of a race, but once the pace was set he lost all such feelings. Then, to use his description, he just settled down over the handlebars, focused his eyes on the rear wheel of the pacing bicycle, and tried to get as close to it as he could. Shutting out as much of the world as he could, he pedaled where the pacer led him, high on the straightaways and down on the curves, rising and falling like a bird as he circled the track. For a few miles he still heard his trainer calling out the time and giving advice, but later the only sound that came to him was the purr of the tires. After twenty-five miles he said he lost all power of hearing or feeling and frequently got the impression that he was really motionless. Most of his actions became purely instinctive. As pacer after pacer came and went, he simply followed them, changing from one to the other without thinking about it.

In a way it was difficult to call such a race a contest, because if Michael is to be believed, each man was oblivious to everything going on around him, concentrating all his efforts only on keeping up with the pacers and paying little attention to his opponent. If such a contest sounds monotonous, it can only be said that Michael's races packed the stands with spectators.

Cycling produced some unique things in the United States. Out of the melee called a race, out of the flurry of flying elbows and straining muscles came Marshall Taylor, the first black American athlete to achieve national recognition and acclaim, many decades before the color line was broken in most of the major professional sports.

It is not known when black Americans began to ride bicycles, but it had to be at a time later than whites, if for no other reason than that the early bicycles were so expensive. Nevertheless, Negroes took to the machine like everyone else, and there is reason to believe that the old ordinaries found their final homes in the South.

The color line was first drawn when it came to membership in the League of American Wheelmen and participation in league-sponsored racing meets. In its early years, when the cycle was expensive, the question of Negro membership in the league did not really come up, but by 1890 it had become an issue that the organization tried to solve by ignoring it. However, the problem did not go away, and two years later some LAW members were arguing that the league was a voluntary social organization and that each local unit had the right to exclude whomever it wanted. The larger question raised by this debate was what would happen if a local unit of the league voted to accept Negroes as members. Did membership in the local club also carry membership in the national organization, and if so, did this mean that black members could attend league conventions?

Some local clubs already had black members. One was the Post Office Cyclers of Newark, New Jersey. The postal riders had been invited to participate in a bicycle run sponsored by another club, but when the latter organization discovered the postal crew had a black member, Mr. L. A. Sears, it withdrew its invitation. The Post Office Cyclers in turn unanimously elected Mr. Sears club president. But incidents like this did not stop discrimination, and the usual result was that Negroes organized their own cycling clubs. To point a moral, a Brunswick, Georgia, cycle club for black women ceremoniously excluded their white sisters from membership.

By 1893 the problem could no longer be avoided by the League of American Wheelmen, especially since white members from the South were challenging the inclusion of Negroes. The matter came before the LAW convention of 1893, whose delegates probably had seen "Prowler's" statement on the question in *Outing* magazine. "Prowler" maintained that the antiblack faction ought to be content with local option on the question of membership and observed that "hoodlums" were worse for the organization than black people.

This attitude mattered little to some delegates. A Kentucky cycler put forward a motion to change the constitution of the league to allow only white people to be members. This motion, which had to be carried by a majority of two thirds, split the convention almost exactly, 108 votes for and 101 against. The foes of discrimination had good reason to be discouraged, because in the year following, when the matter came before the convention again, the lily-whites won the day. The constitution was amended, and Negroes were excluded from membership in the League of American Wheelmen.

Outing kept its editorial mouth shut at this point, but the *New York Tribune* said that "wheelmen generally must look with disfavor upon the outcome of the convention of the League of American Wheelman at Louisville. . . . Fair-minded men will condemn the exclusion of colored men."[2] In Chicago the *Record* said that "the League of American Wheelmen has taken a step backward, and if it endures a decade it will regret its action. Does the desirability of securing a few thousand more white wheelmen justify the gratuitous exclusion of a worthy race?"[3]

Apparently the amendment was ignored by some. Miss Kitty Knox from the all-black Riverside Cycle Club of Boston showed up at the LAW's meet in Asbury Park in 1895. She was the focus of all attention when she did a "few fancy cuts" in front of the clubhouse, and that night Miss Knox seems to have been the belle of the ball. The next day the newspapers said that local grumblers were going to get the LAW to look into the fact that Miss Knox had held a membership card for the last six years.

Not all cycling groups followed the LAW's lead, however. The Illinois branch of the American Cycling Road Association, an independent group, did not draw the color line, and when some members insisted that the organization do so, the officers said that such a position would be a violation of the Constitution. In 1896, when several riders threatened to pull out of the Pullman Road Race if the all-black Douglass Club sent a racer, officials responded that they would not only allow the man to enter, but that they would see that he got fair treatment. In 1897 a black man finished the race, so obviously the color line was not drawn.

Nevertheless, it was a system of racial intolerance that Marshall Taylor had to face when he began racing in the 1890's. Taylor told of his setbacks and successes in his autobiography, *The Fastest Bicycle Rider in the World*, written in 1928, a book that is remarkable for the absence of bitterness against the men who treated him so unfairly.

Taylor was born in Indianapolis in 1878. Eight years later he rode his first bicycle, a machine that belonged to one of his young white playmates. When he was twelve years old the Negro youngster became the clean-up boy at Hay and Willit's bicycle store, and soon he was giving trick-riding exhibitions on the side. It was one of Taylor's employers who entered him in a road race when he was only thirteen, a race he did not win. In 1893 the lad was giving lessons for a bicycle salesman, H. T. Hearsey, who entered him in the Indianapolis-Mathews Road Race. The move was surrounded with secrecy, since Taylor had already antagonized the local white racers. A few months before, one of the cracks of the day, Walter Sanger, had set a new record of two minutes and eighteen seconds for the mile. Encouraged and paced by his white friends, Taylor had followed this by lowering the time to two minutes and eleven seconds, a feat that apparently caused him to be barred from racing in Indianapolis. As a result, the manager of the Indianapolis-Mathews Race was afraid the white riders would not race if they knew Taylor was entered.

On the day of the contest Taylor waited until the others got started, then pedaled away from the line with a tremendous handicap of several miles to make up. As Taylor moved up, he endured "vile names" thrown at him when the other racers discovered him in the contest. In spite of threats, he flashed through the pack, then rode hard along the deserted stretches because he feared ambushes. He had a bad moment outside Marion, where he was met by a crowd of twenty-five white men. But Taylor's fear turned out to be ill-founded; the whites were a group of admirers who had come out to pace him the last leg of the trip. The black cyclist finished a full hour ahead of the pack. He gave the first prize of a house lot to his mother, along with the promise never to ride that distance again.

At this time Taylor changed jobs and went to work for Birdie Munger, a white racer-turned-manufacturer, who made the young man a new racing cycle weighing only fourteen pounds. Munger's sponsorship of the promising young black cyclist brought upon himself the same kind of ostracism that Taylor had to accept, and so Munger moved to Worcester, Massachusetts, taking Taylor along. The youngster found the Eastern city more receptive to his color than Indianapolis. He immediately joined the YMCA. From that base, and with Munger's encouragement, he made his racing debut in a LAW race at New Haven. He took first prize, a gold watch, which he promptly handed to Munger as a token of his gratitude. It must be pointed out that the LAW's attitude toward blacks at this time was ambivalent: it would not allow them to join, but it would allow them to race, an act of hypocrisy that was frequently pointed out to the organization.

From New Haven on, Taylor's career was on the upswing, but so was the prejudice against him. In the Irvington-Milburn Road Race in New Jersey, he was riding neck-and-neck with the eventual winner when a man stepped out of the crowd and threw a bucketful of cold water in his face. Taylor later called it an accident and said that the offender had been the white racer's trainer who was only trying to give his man a lift, but Taylor was being charitable about the incident. In self-defense, therefore, he had to develop various tricks. For example, he found that a good tactic was to lay back in a long race, pretending to be exhausted, and then, when the other racers relaxed, shoot out ahead and stay there. In developing this technique he built up a tremendous last-lap kick that stood him in good stead when he went on the board tracks.

In 1896 Taylor turned professional for the races at Madison Square Garden. He promptly caught the fans' attention by winning the Half-Mile Handicap against such famous racers as Bald, Cooper, and Arthur Gardiner. He also broke his promise to his mother and entered the six-day race, finishing in eighth place with a respectable 1,786 miles, a great accomplishment for an eighteen-year-old man. However, this marked Taylor's final experience with marathon racing; he never went back to it. Instead he contented himself with racing the sprint distances, and thereafter when he entered races of more than five miles he frequently had troubles.

It is safe to say that most of Taylor's vicissitudes came not from distance but from the attitudes of fellow racers. Taylor later wrote that many of the topflight racers were "too big" for prejudice. Among these he listed Zimmerman, who became a lifelong friend and who gave Taylor tips on when to start his jump for the tape. A. A. Windle was another who seems to have taken Taylor under his wing. And of course there was Birdie Munger. But the number of men who were too big to hold Taylor's color against him was deplorably small.

Professional bicycle racing was not exactly a quilting bee, but Taylor was subjected to more than his share of roughneck riding. His competitors pocketed him at every opportunity, ran him wide on the curves, and fouled him repeatedly. He placed second in a race at Trenton, New Jersey, in 1897, only to have the third-place rider come up afterward and start strangling him. The police interfered, but Taylor remained unconscious for a quarter of an hour and was unable to finish the day's racing. *The New York Times* roundly condemned the culprit, who claimed that Taylor had ridden him into the fence. The *Times* also contended that while the majority of the white riders deplored the assault on Taylor, they "had approached the limits of fair riding in attempting to get an advantage over the colored lad."[4] A Boston paper was more direct, saying that the other riders had deliberately tried to "throw" Taylor, that "the same dirty tactics have followed the plucky little colored rider all around the circuit," and that it was "to the everlasting discredit of the men who are in on the schemes."[5]

One paper said that Taylor rode all his races in deadly fear and that frequently he was threatened with bodily harm if he competed. It was suggested, and Taylor did not deny it in his own memoirs, that when he was threatened he would generally ask to be excused from participating, and if the judges refused permission he would then keep well back of the bunch and out of the competition.

In the season of 1897 Taylor was locked in a head-to-head struggle with Cannon Bald for first place in the national standings when he apparently fell victim to a conspiracy to shut him out of winning. There was some kind of trouble at the Woodside Track in Philadelphia—just what it was Taylor did not say—that resulted in his being barred by the managers of the races in St. Louis. Taylor then hoped to catch up with Bald in the Baltimore races, but the promoters also refused to allow him to race there. According to Taylor and his manager, this prevented him from winning the national championship that year.

The next year Taylor jumped to the NCA and went south early in the year to train at Savannah, Georgia. There he had some unspecified trouble with another racing team, and shortly thereafter he received a letter. "Mr. Taylor," it said. "If you do not leave here before forty-eight hours you will be sorry. We mean business. Clear out if you value your life." It was signed, "White Riders." Taylor left. One thing about the incident rings false, and that is that a Georgian would have addressed Taylor as "Mister." One is permitted to believe that the threat was manufactured by other professionals who saw an opportunity to cut Taylor's training short.

"Major" Taylor (he had adopted this *nom-de-wheel*) was better off in the season of 1898, since he was racing under the sponsorship of the Iver Johnson Cycle Company. But at the start of the season he was well back in tenth place in the national standings. He was getting knocked about more than all the other riders put together, but he was still riding. At Asbury Park, he won the One-Mile Sprint, and after his victory his friend Zimmerman was there to shake the black man's hand and proclaim that Munger had been right when he had predicted Taylor would be a champion. When the other racers flocked into the black man's tent after the contest he hardly knew what to anticipate, but they also congratulated him, the first time any of the big competitors had ever done so.

In Green Bay, Wisconsin, Taylor won all the professional races on the August program. One of the local papers said that all the cycle racers acknowledged Taylor's ability but still did not want him to win because he was black. "If it were possible to make him all white," the paper commented, "all the boys would gladly assist in the job." However, it was predicted that it would be almost impossible to keep "this little negro boy who came into the cycling world entirely unheralded from winning the cycle championship of America in the season of 1898."[6]

The season of 1898 did have a peak for Taylor. His manager, William A. Brady, a noted sports promoter, challenged Midget Michael to a race, two best-out-of-three heats of one mile each, five thousand dollars for the race and winner take all. The offer was accepted, although the tiny Michael was stepping out of his middle-distance class to race a sprinter. On August 28, thousands of spectators packed the stands at the Manhattan Beach Race Track. The betting, which had always accompanied cycle meets, became feverish as first one contender and then the other won a heat. The drama boiled down to the final heat. Taylor won the toss for the pole position. While the racers got ready, the big pacers circled the track waiting for the starting gun.

Both men got away fast, but it became evident that the sprints had told on Michael. He called on his pacers to go steady, and when Taylor heard this he knew he was going to be the winner. Calling up all his reserve strength, he kicked up to his own pacers and commanded them to go all out. The young black racer won the final heat, after which *The New York Times* called him the premier sprint racer in the world. It is difficult to know exactly where all the prize money went; Taylor says his manager gave him a thousand dollars for winning the race, a sum that he then split with his all-white pacers.

If Michael went out of his class to race Taylor in the mile, Taylor surely got out of his when he agreed to race Michael a month later over twenty-five miles. It was a dull contest in which the young Welshman played around for a few miles, just to warm up, and then simply ran off and left the Major behind. Michael won by three laps.

Taylor was accorded the national championship for that year by the LAW, but because of the split between the league and the National Cycling Association there were several claimants, and the title was clouded.

In 1899 Taylor set new records in almost every sprint distance—the quarter-mile, third-mile, half-mile, two-thirds mile, three-quarters mile, one mile, and two mile races. On the opening of the season at the Charles River Track in Boston the black streak took home $875 for a single day's racing. From there he swept through the Midwest, getting ovations simply for taking warm-up spins around the track.

Then in August, 1899, Taylor went to the international races held in Montreal. Cheered by the massed thousands, he won the One-Mile Open championship, barely nosing out Tom Butler by a half a wheel. He also won the Two-Mile Open and might have won the Five-Mile except that somebody punctured one of his tires just before the start and he had to ride on a flat, a punishing task that he gave up after two miles. Nevertheless, he had firmly established himself as an international champion, the first black American to do so.

Four days later he was in Boston to race in the LAW championship races. The field ganged up on the black rider and kept him in a pocket most of the time, and Taylor was beaten by Tom Butler in the One-Third-Mile Sprint and again by Butler in the One Mile for Professionals. That year the national champion was Tom Cooper, who raced under the colors of the NCA.

In 1900, however, Taylor was proclaimed the national cycling champion with no conflicting claims from anybody. In 1901 he raced in Europe with considerable success, then came home to continue his activities for another three or four years. After that the same decline that struck at cycling in general diminished interest in racing, and Taylor slowly faded from the scene. In the *Encyclopedia of Sports*, Walter Badgett, who raced from 1898 to 1918, ranked Frank Kramer, champion from 1901 to 1916, as the best cycle racer the country ever produced. Kramer was followed by Eddie Bald, and in third rank, along with several others, was Major Taylor. Taylor had made his mark as the first black champion.

The physical punishment Taylor took raises the question of just how dangerous it was to whirl around the small wooden bowls called racing tracks. The answer seems to have been not very, in spite of the jostling and mayhem that existed, although every now and then racers collided and knocked each other unconscious.

Yet sometimes the accidents were deadly. In 1897, in Danbury, Connecticut, two amateur wheelmen were practicing for the approaching Memorial Day road race by taking warm-up runs on the local track. Pedaling in opposite directions at a speed of about sixty miles an hour, heads down in the scorcher's crouch, they collided in front of horrified witnesses. One cyclist was killed and the other was seriously injured. A little over a month later two men in New Jersey had an identical accident, and one was carried off with a broken back. That same year at a crowded Cleveland racetrack fourteen racers and six spectators were injured in a single accident, although there were no fatalities.

These accidents involved amateurs, however. Indeed the only fatality among professionals was a Minnesota racer, Joseph Brieber, who ran up the embankment of a curve on a track in Lima, Ohio, shot over the heads of the spectators, and split his skull against a post. Walter Sanger, riding in the same race, told authorities that Brieber had passed him with his face set and riding like a wild man. Physicians tentatively diagnosed the cause of such irrational riding as a burst blood vessel.

Of course there was potential danger any place the bicycle buffs gathered, especially during the racing season. The Jackson Park Track in Chicago was very crowded during the month of May, 1897, as the amateurs prepared for the annual Pullman Road Race. As a result accidents were exceedingly common, and as cyclists smashed into each other, arguments followed. On a Sunday afternoon tempers really flared, and a cyclist named Schroeder stabbed another named Durken. From his hospital bed Durken explained that a punctured tire had caused him to swerve into the path of his assailant, whereupon Schroeder had threatened that if Durken ever did it again he would get killed. Words led to more words and then to a stabbing, after which Schroeder leaped on his bicycle to escape, only to be run down by other cyclists in the park. Other witnesses said that the two men had been quarreling for some time, and Schroeder contended that Durken had been cutting in front of him all afternoon. Fortunately Durken recovered from what turned out to be a minor wound.

Yet for the most part it can be said that cycle racing was far from the most dangerous sport. But was it lucrative? Before the LAW divided racers into Classes A and B, only a crack could legally make a living at racing, although some made a good one at it. In 1891, A. A. Zimmerman was rumored to have taken prizes worth $6,000 for the season. Two years later the papers reported that Zimmerman took $20,000 in prizes, while the three racers who trailed him, Johnson, Windle, and Tyler, all averaged about $12,000. This was probably true, since 1893 was Zimmerman's best year, and the total for prizes in LAW races that year was $125,000.

After Class B racing was established, riders could take cash from their sponsors. During the peak of the racing mania the top maker's amateurs were rumored to be drawing salaries somewhere between $10,000 and $20,000 a year, but these figures were probably exaggerated. As for professionals, in 1897 Eddie Bald told a friend that he had cleared $15,000 the year before and expected to do better that season.

For a while, match racing appears to have been a good business for those who won. In 1897 Midget Michael was rumored to have taken about $18,000 for the season, $6,500 of it in just two weeks of racing. He won a $1,000 match against Lucien Lesna, the Frenchman; picked up $400 in an exhibition; followed that with $3,000 won in a three-cornered match race; and then beat Lesna again for $2,000. In addition he got a salary from the bicycle maker who sponsored him, not to mention a share of the side bets his manager got down. Just about the only expense Michaels had was maintaining his pacing teams at a rate of $15 for each man each week. This seems ridiculously small, but it was customary to pay the pacers a bonus if a new record was set.

In other words, cycle racing could be profitable if one were not back in the pack. However, the big incomes were just for the best professionals, the men who were consistent winners during the racing season. Strung out behind them was a host of lesser lights who were lucky to meet expenses. These were the racers who could be hired as "wreckers" to take care of one's competition. In some meets they competed for a percentage of the profits, and in the rural areas, this might mean a percentage of nothing at all. There is some evidence that the lesser professionals would enter amateur races under assumed names just to pick up a few prizes to sell for cash. However, this was what one might expect when the number of professionals on the LAW roster jumped from 90 in 1895 to 1,973 a year later. There were just too many racers for the amount of prize money.

Whatever the pay, a cycle racer had to make his fortune quickly because a rider stayed at peak performance only for about four years. Besides, there was always the danger that something else might come along to seize the public's attention and cause cycling to fade from the picture.

The Bicycle as Entertainment

MUSEUM OF THE CITY OF NEW YORK

CULVER PICTURES. INC.

SMITHSONIAN INSTITUTION

The Bicycle Clubs

TOP: KANSAS STATE HISTORICAL SOCIETY, TOPEKA. MIDDLE: CULVER PICTURES, INC. BOTTOM: MUSEUM OF THE CITY OF NEW YORK.

Bringing the Outdoors In

Top: velocipede riding school, 1869, from *Harper's Weekly*
Bottom: the fashionable Michaux Bicycle Club, 1895

CULVER PICTURES, INC.

Going Places

Top: Frank G. Lenz, murdered in 1894 in Turkey, while on a world tour on two wheels.
Bottom, left: on the road. Bottom, right: the whole world over — map of bicycle tracks.

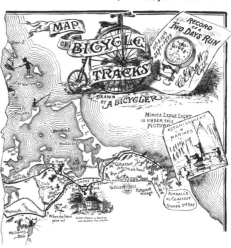

BOTTOM, LEFT: CULVER PICTURES, INC.
BOTTOM, RIGHT: NEW YORK PUBLIC LIBRARY PICTURE COLLECTION.

At the Races

The trainer's quarters

Alf Robb receiving "consolation" and a rubdown after a header

Alf Robb, the English champion

The first turn after the start

The leaders after the first night's racing

Madison Square Garden in New York is host to the
International Six-Day Bicycle Race, October, 1891.

CULVER PICTURES, INC.

At the Races

Left: Mile-a-Minute Murphy, a champion racer. Top, right: Llewellyn H. Johnson, the American amateur champion. Bottom: Major Taylor, the champion who rode over racism—for a while

LEFT: BICYCLE INSTITUTE OF AMERICA. TOP, RIGHT: CULVER PICTURES, INC.
BOTTOM, RIGHT: CULVER PICTURES, INC. BUTTON: BICYCLE INSTITUTE OF AMERICA.

At the Races

TOP AND BOTTOM: CULVER PICTURES, INC.
BUTTON: BICYCLE INSTITUTE OF AMERICA

Ads on Wheels

MISS ANNIS BURR PORTER ON HER QUAKER WHEEL

ALL: BICYCLE INSTITUTE OF AMERICA

Sin and Salvation

TOP: CALIFORNIA HISTORICAL SOCIETY, SAN FRANCISCO. BOTTOM: CULVER PICTURES, INC.

CHAPTER 10

"I Am the Scorcher Full of Zeal"

THE CLASH BETWEEN CYCLERS AND NON-CYCLERS

BICYCLE INSTITUTE OF AMERICA

RIDING BACKWARD

Generations of Americans who have been reared in the mystique of the automobile assume that the gasoline buggy was the first vehicle to terrify the nation's horses and arouse the nation's farmers, but the case is otherwise. The first machine to panic horses, provoke pedestrians, and incur both urban and rural hatred was the relatively quiet and outwardly inoffensive bicycle. In the early days it made little difference that cyclists claimed to have the same rights on the roads and streets as other vehicles. In actual practice the bicycle and its rider were at the mercy of just about everybody and were harassed without letup.

As early as 1883, long before bicycles swarmed like locusts, politicians moved to protect horses from the birotate chariot. An Ohio legislator who claimed to have observed two instances wherein horses had been frightened by bicycles proposed punitive legislation, but he was allegedly restrained by the opposition of the League of American Wheelmen. For a short time in 1884, Jersey City had an ordinance prescribing the proper conduct of cyclists vis-à-vis the horse. The city ordered that if the driver of a buggy or wagon raised his hand on the approach of a cyclist, this signal constituted a warning that the horse was getting skittish. The gesture repeated was a command for the cyclist to dismount immediately and wheel his machine around the beast. The law was soon repealed.

Similar ordinances were proposed elsewhere throughout the eighties and early nineties, although the vigilance of cyclists prevented the enactment of most of these proposals. In 1891 the Illinois legislature pondered a bill that would compel cyclists to dismount when meeting teams of horses. The measure—which "Prowler" said was patently unconstitutional—did not pass. At the same time, propositions were put forward in other parts of the country that bicycle riders should be held liable for damages that resulted when horses became frightened at the approach of the machines.

As late as 1899, long after the bicycle had carried the nation by storm, it was necessary for a Minnesota supreme court justice to hand down a decision that it was "not the duty of a party lawfully traveling upon a public highway upon a bicycle, when he sees a horse and carriage approaching, to stop and enquire whether a horse will become frightened, especially in the absence of apparent reason for doing so."[1] The judge's syntax may have stunned cyclists a little, but his decision was applauded by all who rode bicycles.

In other areas cyclists were objects of discrimination. In 1883 the commissioners of New York City forbade cyclists to use the paths of Central Park. They relented two years later to the extent of allowing cycling only along certain paths. However, even that limited entry was restricted to those who belonged to a regular cycling organization and wore the club's uniform and badge while awheel.

Such restrictions seem to have been common elsewhere in the United States. In 1895, with the cycling avalanche about to descend, the civic authorities of Minneapolis were excluding bicycles from the many parks that surrounded the city. Surely, commented a local paper, the authorities realized that the "platoons of baby carriages" ranging the parks also crowded pedestrians off the paths and onto the grass. The paper also testily called the attention of the police to the fact that children rode their velocipedes on the sidewalks and created more "chaos" than half a dozen bicycles. How about arresting those "youthful terrors?"[2]

The bicycle also had its legal tribulations, arising in part because there was no legal definition of what the bicycle was, and therefore no way to determine what regulations it was subject to. In New York a decision favorable to the plaintiff was handed down in the case of *Israel Baldwin vs. The Fraternal Accident Association of America.* (The case was first argued in 1894, but no decision was given until three years later, an indication of how swift justice was at the time.) Baldwin held an accident policy that paid what today would be called "job insurance." While cycling one day, he fell from his machine and was so badly hurt he could not work. He promptly applied for payment, and the Fraternal Accident Association gave the lie to its name with equal dispatch. The company reduced its payment below the amount specified in the policy, on the ground that cycling was a "game" and that the policy did not cover injuries received in sports contests, which were classified as hazardous occupations. The court finally held for the plaintiff, a verdict that was lauded by "Prowler," who claimed that cycling was no more dangerous than driving a carriage or riding on a railroad train.

But cyclists did not win them all. In Michigan, the supreme court— cyclers had a penchant for carrying their suits right to the top—considered a damage case in which a cycler riding on the sidewalk had struck and seriously injured a young woman. The defense denied negligence on the part of the rider, basing its argument on the fact that the accused had struck a rock with his front wheel, causing him to lose control and hit the pedestrian. The court did not agree, pointing out in its decision that the street was available for cycling and that it was the responsibility of the cyclist to give due warning of his approach.

Often communities were caught in the bind between the enthusiasm of the cycling fraternity and pressures from noncycling pedestrians. If pressure from bicyclers forced local authorities to permit riding on the sidewalks, the local government ran the danger of damage suits. Newark for a time allowed cycles on its walks, but after a pedestrian was injured the court held that it was illegal to allow vehicles to use the walk and that the city was liable for damages. Ultimately, most sizable towns passed ordinances governing the use of roads and sidewalks by both carriages and bicycles and so paved the way for the elaborate codes controlling the use of automobiles in the present century.

Regardless of legal decisions, cyclists had two natural enemies who did not surrender slavishly to the wheel. Teamsters and cab drivers continued to wage an unrelenting war against the machine. To an era that seldom sees a wagon on the streets and has forgotten the original meaning of "teamster," this sounds most strange, but a hundred years ago the men who drove teams of horses considered themselves kings of the road. Stephen Crane, who also penned newspaper articles about cycling, described their attitude in a novel entitled *Maggie*, about a girl whose brother Jimmie became a teamster in New York City. Jimmie sat on his lofty seat high above the crowd and looked with contempt at pedestrians—and, one might add, bicyclers.

> Foot passengers were mere pestering flies with an insane disregard for their legs and his convenience. He could not comprehend their desire to cross the streets. . . . He was continually storming at them from his throne . . . [and] he swore at the men as fools, for he himself could perceive that Providence had caused it to be clearly written that he and his team had the inalienable right to stand in the proper place of the sun chariot.[3]

The only things this young teamster feared were the flying hooves and the plunging momentum of fire engines, which, like time and tide, waited for no man. The very moment Jimmie heard the clanging of the steamer's bell he drove up on the sidewalk, "threatening untold people with annihilation."

Enough teamsters had the same attitude as Jimmie to make a difference, and in the cities they seem to have been a law unto themselves. They made turns anywhere and anytime it pleased them—U-turns were the order of the day—they gave no signals, and frequently they actually drove *against* the flow of traffic. Cab drivers, who saw the bicycle bite into their income, joined the teamsters in becoming the enemies of cyclists. Sometimes horse drivers quite literally turned out of their way to strike a wheelman down.

For example, in 1883 *Wheelman* magazine noted that drivers had developed the "playful custom" of breaking up bicycle parades by driving their animals through the columns, even though a judge had held that cycles had the same rights on the streets as other vehicles. Truth to tell, draymen paid little attention to what the law said about cyclers' rights, looking upon the latter as good-time Charlies who prevented an honest workman from making a living. One driver, a heavy-jawed, scowling man named Rothpetz, rode the tailgate of another wagon and led several other teamsters in spitting tobacco juice on cyclists who came close to the rear. The judge who later fined Rothpetz said, with some understatement, that there seemed to be a disposition on the part of drivers to annoy cyclists.

Certainly the law was no comfort to the victims of Andrew Weiss, a coachman in New York City, who took advantage of a warm April day to shoot five cyclists before he was arrested while taking aim at a sixth. He knocked a man and a woman off a tandem, upset a second man, then got a third man and a boy on separate shots. In general he was the terror of the street.

Weiss had his rural counterpart in a man named Jacob Heitz, who drove his wagon down a Long Island road and refused to pull over to permit a cycling group to pass. When the cyclists persisted in ringing their bells, the teamster retaliated by pulling his team and wagon at right angles across the road, blocking passage altogether. Then Jake just sat there, displaying all the patience of his namesake, while a hundred men and women dismounted and walked their cycles around the obstruction. But Jacob Heitz was not quite finished with the city dudes. When the column pedaled off again, he whipped up his team and charged down on the rear of the cavalcade, scattering them like quail. To say that pandemonium reigned is to put it mildly; women were unseated in bunches of five, and there was enough screaming and shrieking to satisfy the most sadistic. When one of the men cyclers seized the bridle of the off-horse, Heitz laid the butt of his whip across the man's head. The berserk teamster was finally seized and lodged in the local jail, having done little to cement friendly relations between those who drove horses and those who rode cycles.

It was also difficult for pedestrians to accommodate themselves to the bicycle. Throughout the history of the nation, pedestrians in towns and cities had been free to go where they wanted, when they wanted in relative safety. In traffic it wasn't too difficult to dart in and out among the horse-drawn vehicles, although there was some danger in trying to outsmart the men who handled the cable cars or the electrical cars that later provided mass transportation. At crossings, even though drivers of wagons and cable cars could not be bluffed, at least they gave some warning of their approach—the *clip-clop* of hooves, the rattle of iron tires, or the jangling of a streetcar bell. With the bicycle it was different. The big problem for pedestrians was that the cycle was almost noiseless in its approach and bore down on the unwary without warning.

People on foot eventually realized they could not monopolize the streets, but sidewalks were a different matter. The man afoot felt he was entitled to primacy there, and he fought hard to keep it. For the most part cyclists did not insist on pedaling on the walks; but from time to time they did, especially after the sprinkling carts had been out or rain had converted the dirt streets into quagmires. Frequently cyclists took to the walks to avoid potholes, the omnipresent street hazard of the period. But it was on the sidewalks that the law waited to pounce.

By 1893 cities and towns from southern California to the Atlantic coast were instructing policemen to keep cyclists off walks, although the difficulty of enforcing such ordinances, especially in small towns, made most such laws a dead letter. Two generations later Americans would become familiar with the speed trap, a device for enlarging the incomes of rural magistrates around the country; but long before such traps were set for heavy-footed motorists, there were "sidewalk traps" to snare cyclists. In 1895 the *New York Herald* warned that the entire city of Hackensack, New Jersey, was a trap for those who pedaled on sidewalks to avoid mud puddles, and that Long Island constables were dragging cyclists before justices of the peace for riding on the walks of sleepy little villages.

There was often a significant difference between this system and the speed traps of the automobile age. No law officer can force a driver to *exceed* the speed limit; but the police of Babylon, Long Island, and other villages were accused of digging trenches across roads and creating their own water-filled puddles, all to divert the cycle traffic onto the sidewalks, where the minions of the law waited in ambush. The cyclists protested, but there was not much they could do except to encourage the building of better roads so they would not have to ride on the walks.

Occasionally they enlisted powerful support. In June, 1897, no less a person than John Jacob Astor the Younger, himself a cyclist, wrote to the village fathers of Rondout, New York, protesting against an ordinance forbidding cycling on the sidewalks. Astor pointed out that the village did not keep the main road repaired, and therefore in bad weather the cyclist was forced to the walk. He further contended that a fine of ten dollars for violating the ordinance was excessive, indeed "it was all a hard working clerk or mechanic may have when starting on a three days' trip."⁴ The paper did not record the town council's reply to this letter, but one believes that John Jacob Astor probably got his way.

Sometimes the harassed cyclist struck back. Take the case of Mrs. Ann Ball, widow, of New York City. On June 15, 1897, Mrs. Ball was riding her bicycle along a street that was so badly torn up by workmen that she went onto the sidewalk. Surely anyone who has been frustrated by the perennial breaking up and re-laying of streets can sympathize with her. However, Mrs. Ball had pedaled only three blocks when nemesis appeared in the person of a mounted policeman who warned her to get back into the street. The lady complied, but just as soon as the officer turned his horse away Mrs. Ball rolled back onto the walk and continued for another five blocks.

The same policeman trotted up to the lady again and placed her under arrest, in spite of her contention that she had permission to ride on the walk. The assertion caused the officer to dismount and grasp the lady's bicycle, probably with the idea of preventing her from riding away. At that juncture all hell broke loose, and the policeman came under an assault that made his service in the Sioux Campaign look like a cakewalk. Mrs. Ball leaped from her machine, blacked both of the poor man's eyes, tore off some of his uniform buttons, and left him hanging on for dear life, madly blowing his whistle for help.

Six more of New York's finest rushed up to reinforce the hero of the Indian wars. It took all seven to carry the kicking, screaming bicyclette to the station house a mile away—where she was released on a technicality. The revised city ordinances forbade the driving of "carts" and "wheeled carriages" on the walks, and it was argued that the bicycle was neither of these but a "vehicle," a nice distinction that the judge probably grasped with all the alacrity of a drowning man seizing a straw. No charges were brought for resisting an officer in the performance of his duty. What his fellow officers said to the man is best left to the imagination.

While the cyclist may have sinned against pedestrians by pedaling on the sidewalk or running them down in the crossings, he was repaid in full measure. Charles Pratt wrote in *The American Bicycler* that early cyclers were objects of much harassment from the noncycling public, especially from "roughs" and children. In addition to shouting epithets, Pratt said that the youngsters "cut certain pranks," which was his way of saying that they made every effort to knock the rider off his machine with rocks, tin cans, and sticks that bombarded fragile spokes and almost equally fragile cyclists. Pratt noted that one pioneer cyclist had made a practice of concealing a cowhide whip beneath his coat and using it indiscriminately on both boys and dogs when they tried to unseat him. Pratt himself felt that a "little vigorous language" was usually sufficient to discipline the street urchins and cautioned the cyclist to "supplement his rights with the gentler obligations of courtesy," since cycling was in its infancy and on trial in the eyes of the public.[5] The man with the whip was probably more effective.

The street urchin who preyed on cyclers got his best chance after the pneumatic tire came into common use; the delicate fabric of the air-filled tube was made to measure for the urchin with a good-sized needle in his hand. Grace Denison, in one of her chatty columns for the female cycler, admitted that a small boy with a stout bodkin could break the spirit of anyone who left a bicycle untended. From the introduction of the pneumatic to the collapse of the cycling fad, the tire fiends never let up in their assault, even though laws prohibiting the deliberate puncturing of tires were passed by virtually every town and city of any consequence in the United States.

Sometimes the puncturers went in for large-scale attack: *The New York Times* reported in 1896 that the resort roads of Long Island were littered with tack-studded strips of leather, the work either of cranks or, it was hinted darkly, of tire repairmen who knew how to encourage business. As a matter of fact, the *Times* noted, something new had been discovered, short pieces of wire bent in such a way as to always point up and into the tire, a variation of the medieval caltrop for disabling cavalry horses. Even broken glass was strewn along the roads to supplement the attack, and it was a common sight to see groups of unhappy people walking back from what had started as a pleasant Sunday's ride.

One cycle club, in a desperate attempt to frustrate such crimes, put up twenty-five dollars as a fund to be used to prosecute any person caught puncturing tires. So small an amount of money did not stop the vandalism, nor did the hundred dollars put up by the Brooklyn Good Roads Association. Indeed the youngsters of New York's Lower East Side decorated newly paved streets with tacks and then stood on the walks to laugh at the unfortunate cyclers. Since nothing could be proved against them, they went scot free. No wonder a cycling "superstition" had it that "to see a small boy beside the road is a prophecy of a puncture."

However, boys were not the only enemies of the cycle. Horses eventually accepted the inevitable and settled down to live with the cycle, but not dogs. When not contending with small boys with sharp instruments, the cyclist had to endure the canine. The moment a man mounted a bicycle, his best friend forgot its role and raced into the streets, yapping and snapping at the heels of a rider who was generally having enough trouble just staying upright.

Around 1890 cyclists came up with a handy device known as a "dog paralyzer," a rubber bulb filled with ammonia, one squirt of which was said to teach dogs their manners. Unfortunately, the device leaked and turned out to be more of a liability than an asset. Then a more reliable weapon was perfected, called the ki-yi gun, which was leakproof, had a range of twenty feet, and would shoot twelve times without reloading. It also used ammonia and was an immediate success, so much so that the *Minneapolis Tribune* intoned that "every person in the land will rise up and call the inventor of the ammonia gun for dogs blessed."⁶ It was also a versatile weapon: George Nicholson of Lynn, Massachusetts, gunned down a holdup man with his.

Other approaches to solving the dog problem were louder and potentially more lethal. Some riders exploded a Fourth of July "torpedo" under the animal's nose to turn him away. Others used pistols on dogs.

In one instance, at least, it was thought that the cyclers had overstepped themselves in the dog war. In the spring of 1896, canine fanciers in Peekskill, New York, were enraged over the sudden deaths of forty animals in four days. This was not the first time such a thing had happened; every year for the last four, the dog population of the town had suffered a sudden drop, a sort of canine Black Death that coincided with the opening of the cycling season. There was no direct evidence that the animals had been poisoned, but one paper did report, "Wheelmen now ride the streets of Peekskill in peace."⁷ Probably not, since a nickel's worth of carpet tacks could pay them back.

On the whole, cyclers seem to have been more sinned against than sinning, at least in the early days. For example, Samuel F. Scott of New York City hired a horse-drawn cab and, as he rode past a cyclist in the street, leaned out and kicked the poor wretch off his machine. Better yet, consider the plight of Florence Merrow, who posed for "living pictures" before a screen in Koster and Bial's burlesque house. Florence was pedaling along the avenue, followed by the appreciative smiles of the male population, when she came upon Mr. and Mrs. George Wilkin crossing the street. It is quite possible that Florence's cycling did not encourage a feeling of confidence, but surely it should not have inspired hate. Mr. Wilkin got out of the way, but his lady stopped dead in the street and gave the burlesque beauty a ringing clout with her purse, a shot worthy of John L. Sullivan, which laid rider and cycle in a heap. Then, while Flo and her steed were *hors de combat*, the irate Mrs. Wilkin proceeded to jump up and down on the spokes of the front wheel. When Florence finally struggled to her feet she turned to Mr. Wilkin—an interesting choice of opponent—and treated the poor man to language he had never heard from a lady. Wilkin took refuge in flight, but Flo whistled up a policeman, and the embarrassed man and wife ended up before the desk sergeant. Mrs. Wilkin pleaded confusion and said somewhat indignantly that so many cycles were coming at her at the same time that she lost control of herself. She denied that she had struck Florence Merrow, but insisted that she herself had been hit so hard by the machine that it had lost its front tire as a result. As for the mangled spokes of the wheel, Mrs. Wilkin contended that Florence had stuck her own foot through them when she got off the pavement. Who knows? Wilkin gave Florence a check and left muttering something about having been "the victim of extortion to the extent of $6.50."[8]

In defense of Mr. Wilkin, it must be admitted that by 1897 the life of a noncycler was freighted with anxiety. The heroes of the day were racing cyclists; and while not every man who straddled a bicycle seat was a Midget Michael or a Major Taylor or a Cannon Bald, that did not keep the run-of-the-mill American male from emulating the fast cracks.

So the bicycle speeder was born, the scorcher, who darted in and out through the traffic, head down, rump up in the air, and feet flashing in the pedal stirrups. Even most cyclers regarded him as a menace, and to pedestrians he was as lovable as a dynamite bomb. This high regard the scorcher reciprocated.

> I am the scorcher!
> Please observe
> The curve
> That appertains unto my spine!
> With head ducked low
> I go
> Over man and beast, and woe
> Unto the thing
> That fails to scamper when I *ting-a-ling!*
> Let people jaw
> And go to law
> To try to check my gait,
> If that's their game!
> I hate
> To kill folks
> But I will do it, just the same.
> I guess
> Unless
> They clear the tracks for me;
> Because, you see,
> I am the scorcher, full of zeal,
> And just the thing I look like on the wheel.[9]

It was such sentiments that caused *Outing's* "Prowler" to say in June, 1893, that while an occasional spurt on a smooth road was enjoyed by all cyclists, riding all out was just as intemperate as drinking too much alcohol. A month later he condemned scorching as reprehensible and called on all decent wheelmen to help the police in stamping out the offense. If "Prowler" thought it was bad in 1893, all he had to do was to wait.

Before another year had passed, scorchers were scattering pedestrians at street crossings in larger cities, and irate citizens were clamoring for the police to do something about the situation. Such a demand was easier to make than to fulfill, because the scorcher had the edge on mounted policemen, and the ordinary foot patrolman was just not in the contest. As a result, an officer's order to halt was usually answered by a mocking laugh and the derisive command to "Chalk it down, old man!" as the cyclist sped off down the street.

The officer on foot was not entirely without means of getting back at those who mocked him as they raced away. Billy clubs were found to be useful against cyclists. The ideal tactic was to race alongside the scorcher and jam the stick between the spokes of the rear wheel. However, the policeman of the era was usually a man of girth, little given to sprinting, so often he simply threw his stick at the rear wheel. In either case the attack brought down both rider and machine, leaving the former sadder and wiser and poorer for the repair bill. Sometimes patrolmen were stationed a block apart, and when a speeder flashed past the first officer he signaled ahead with a lantern. Hopefully the man up the block would then rush out to arrest the offender.

In the main the police tried to control speeding in two ways; they fixed speed limits for cycling, and they put policemen on cycles so the offender could be apprehended. However, taxpayers being what they are, there were never enough cycle policemen to supervise the thousands of people who took to their wheels on weekends. In spite of the speed laws, then, it was generally possible to get out and "eat up half a mile of asphalt" without meeting an officer, and in the larger cities scorchers proliferated. Nor were they discouraged by the fines that were handed out by police magistrates, exactions that ranged all the way from five dollars in New York City to the choice between a twenty-five dollar fine or thirty days in jail in New Orleans.

The plain fact was that cyclers could be something of a problem, and the roles of tormentor and tormented were frequently reversed. For example, a scorcher pedaling along in the Lower East Side one day struck a woman crossing the street, and her angry husband and a friend promptly fell upon the offender. At that same moment a pack of ten bicyclers rolled by. Seeing what was happening to their compatriot, they dismounted and rushed to his aid. Using fists and bicycle wrenches, they succeeded in freeing their comrade, and all eleven rode triumphantly away. Shades of Hell's Angels!

Small wonder then that sometimes even the most peaceful citizen had a tendency to run amuck when hit by a scorcher. In New York a cycler and a pedestrian went down in a heap; and while both men lay on the pavement, a bystander walked over and stamped out the spokes of the bicycle wheels. A fight ensued. The jumper later was fined ten dollars, but he had the satisfaction of knowing that it took more than that to repair the two bicycle wheels. Or consider the plight of Henry Lamont from the same city, who took time off from tending bar to go for a spin. He had the misfortune to collide with two pedestrians, who remonstrated with Henry in a most effective way. They knocked him down, blacked both his eyes, and bit him on the ear and wrist. It was incidents like these that prompted *Scientific American* to publish a list of "Do's and Don'ts." The list included a bit of sage advice: "Don't go back and apologize when you knock a man or woman off their pins. *You may mean well but you will find the person knocked down unreasonable and sometimes impertinent.*"[10] How about that?

The forces of law kept trying to slow down scorchers. In Washington, D.C., an ordinance was put forward that said the handlebars of a bicycle could not be more than four inches below the level of the saddle, an obvious attempt to curb fast riding by eliminating the scorching position. Furthermore, all cyclists in the nation's capital had to adopt a position that would enable them to see a full one hundred yards ahead at all times, a thing difficult to do if one assumed the nose-down position of the fast rider. And in New York City and in other towns the police began sweeping up speeders in wholesale lots of twenty or more.

Nevertheless, some bicycle riders continued to be guilty of reckless riding, and the number of accidents involving bicycles continued to mount. In 1897 the *Chicago Tribune* said that three hundred mishaps involving cycles had been reported to the police during the months of June and July. In a tone of rising alarm the paper said, "As a source of accidents the wheel knows no rivals. . . . even the deadly trolley has been forced to yield the palm."[11] According to the *Tribune* the three leading causes of accidents were scorching, unwarranted boldness on the part of beginners, and just plain inept riding.

The New York papers had long maintained that Chicago was the accident capital of the cycling world, but that same summer they reluctantly admitted that the epidemic had struck Manhattan. One Sunday's list of accidents involving bicycles included cycles running into wagons, wagons running over cyclists, and cyclists running over pedestrians. This forerunner of automotive carnage took its toll in scalp wounds, broken thighbones, skull fractures, and lesser abrasions and bruises too numerous to mention.

Many of the collisions were the direct result of intensified competition for city streets and country highways in the last part of the nineteenth century. As the population grew, so did the number of vehicles necessary to carry on the normal activities of life—the wagons, streetcars, carts, and hansom cabs. Then, to streets already crowded came thousands of bicycles. The result was trouble.

The U.S. census does not include the number of cycles in the country as of 1890, but it does list over a million and a quarter such machines in 1900. The great majority of these were to be found on the packed city streets. For example, on a Sunday in June, 1896, while an estimated 100,000 New Yorkers cycled out of the city and dispersed for a day in the Long Island countryside, another 50,000 stayed and contributed to New York congestion. On a spring evening a year later a reporter for the *New York Journal* estimated that 25,000 cyclists were on wheels on just one of the city's streets. The same congestion seems to have been common in the rest of the country's major cities. The result was an undeclared war for the right of way on the nation's streets.

Nonriders insisted that cyclists as a group believed they had the right of way on all roads, from country pikes to private gravel paths. Like some automobile drivers half a century later, cyclists seemed to think that ringing a bell or tooting a horn automatically cleared the way for them. The results were collisions, and the number of pedestrians hit by careless cyclists grew. The worst part was that sometimes this carelessness killed innocent people. Young children were more frequently involved in fatal accidents than adults, although cyclists were not always at fault in these cases. Darting out in front of a bicycle was common long before the even more perilous act of running out in front of a passing motorcar.

Sometimes cyclists were the victims in traffic accidents. In June, 1897, a young cyclist in New York was run over and killed by a two-horse dray whose driver had sent his team up the wrong side of the street against the traffic. A month later a milk-wagon driver ran over a one-armed cyclist. When brought before the police the driver pleaded guilty of assault, the first time the plea had been entered in such an accident. The *New York Journal*, which later took the credit for starting the Spanish-American War, boasted that the confession was the result of its determined editorial attack on such criminals.

Other cycling accidents, frequently fatal, involved streetcars. As the U.S. population increased, the transportation problem became critical. For several decades prior to 1890 carriages and horse-drawn streetcars had monopolized the streets, but neither had proved adequate to the demands of the cities. As a result, the cable-drawn car and the electric trolley added their bulk and speed to thoroughfares already swarming with vehicles.

Although Americans generally believe the cable car was unique to San Francisco, the fact is that all major cities of the nation had cable-car lines in the late nineteenth century. Thousands of pedestrians learned to avoid the smooth metal plates guarding either side of the cable slot. But not cyclists. They quickly discovered that the plates made an ideal roadway for the pneumatic tires of their machines. Riding the cable-car plates became common in cities, even though the practice was admittedly dangerous: One young fellow in New York who was changing from one slotway to another shot out from behind a wagon and met an oncoming car head-to-head. He did not survive.

Few cyclists had the temerity of one young Chicagoan. Pedestrians along the State Street cable-car line looked up one day in the summer of 1896 to see a cyclist rolling along with one end of a rope tied to the front fork of his bicycle and the other end fastened in some unknown way to the moving cable. In other words, the cyclist had hitched a ride. As the spectators watched with mounting horror, the young man was pulled down toward a stopped car that had released its grip on the cable. But at the last minute the cyclist leaned forward, cut the rope that bound him to the wire rope, and calmly pedaled away. The comments of the cable-car gripman are not on record.

The time came when the cable was replaced by the overhead electric wire and traction companies tore up the cable slot, but the area around the trolley tracks continued to exert a powerful appeal for cyclers. Bicyclers, imitating racing cyclists, pedaled behind the streetcars, using them as windbreakers and capitalizing on what modern stock-car racers call the "draft," the tendency of the front vehicle to draw the rear one along in its wake. However, when a streetcar stopped for fares the man on the cycle had to shoot around it, and in doing so he sometimes collided with an oncoming car. The results were usually fatal, although one Brooklyn man had the presence of mind to dive off his machine into the woven-rope fender of the approaching trolley and thus save his life. In such cases one's sympathy tends to lie primarily with the motorman of the car, but it is difficult to understand the attitude of the man who ran his streetcar up behind cyclist Frank Eggers on a New York street and knocked him into the path of an oncoming trolley. Maybe the motorman wanted to give the cyclist a gentle bump to get him out of the way, but if so, he overdid it.

Another dangerous cycling pastime was to ride on the strip of pavement between the two sets of track, a smooth surface that had not yet been worn down and broken up by the iron tires of delivery wagons. Such a practice called for iron nerves. In 1894, the *Minneapolis Tribune* commented that the way bicycle riders zipped single-file along the level path between the trolley lines would make one's hair stand erect like the "quills of the fretful porcupine." The paper added, "Often the passengers on some car have their blood chilled by seeing a wheelman glide by the fast-moving car in which they are riding with his handlebar almost grazing the side."[12] A Cincinnati man was scorching down the asphalt between the tracks when the "hot" trolley wire broke and the loose end snaked around his neck. The charge knocked him sideways, and it was alleged that only his rubber tires saved his life.

Wheelmen did not give that sort of thing a second thought, nor did they heed the warning of the Chicago paper that pointed out:

> It is impolitic, to say the least, for a cyclist to dispute the right of way with a cable train or an electric car, yet on the evidence of the police and those citizens who have witnessed the many accidents and hairbreadth escapes of the last two months this is almost a daily occurrence on every thoroughfare used by wheelmen and crossed by carlines.[13]

The paper added that almost one fifth of the three hundred serious accidents to cyclists in two summer months involved streetcars, and that the two-wheelers were at fault in every instance.

Some attributed the increase in the number of accidents during the heyday of the bicycle to the fact that more women were cycling. Until the bicycle came along, the American female seldom was involved in street collisions simply because few women drove vehicles except on farms. The bicycle changed all that, and the American woman, albeit usually a young one, took to the streets on her machine, the controller of her own destiny and, as it turned out, of the fate of others.

In 1895 women drivers were accused of being poor judges of speed and distance and of having trouble making up their minds which way to turn. It was this indecision that caused a chain collision at the junction of Broadway and Rockaway Road in Brooklyn. The result was a heap of ten bicycles, which the *New York Journal* said resembled a gigantic mound of broken watches. Fortunately no one was hurt seriously, but accidents like that caused teamsters to complain that they could not stop their wagons and wait for an hour while some bloomer-clad, feather-headed female made up her mind which way she was going to turn. Teamsters said they would rather drive past a circus parade than try to pass a woman on a bicycle.

One sure indicator that the accident rate was rising was that some enterprising Americans saw a chance to make a dollar out of it. A mutual insurance company in Boston informed its policyholders that henceforth bicycling would be regarded as being twice as dangerous as driving horses, riding on a railroad, or traveling on seagoing vessels. Policyholders who objected to having cycling defined as a "hazardous occupation" had three options: they could stop riding, pay a double premium, or drop the policy. Other companies rushed into the field. The Aetna Insurance Company of Hartford, dead in the center of Albert Pope's bicycle empire, naturally did not attack cycling, but it did offer a double indemnity policy for both injuries and death arising from cycle accidents. Another company offered death coverage of a thousand dollars and agreed to pay the same amount for the loss of both legs. Less serious injuries were paid off in smaller amounts.

Insurance was not the answer to the problem of how to cut down the number of accidents, however. In fact there could be no real control over the bicycle until the rights of cyclists as well as their responsibilities were defined by law. Finally in 1897 the bicycle was accorded the same legal rights as other vehicles and cyclers the same privileges as other drivers. Municipal corporations were declared liable for injuries arising from negligence in maintaining safe roads, although in states where "Sunday laws" were still in force a cyclist could not recover damages. Otherwise, riders were given the right of legal action against those who willfully or negligently caused accidents or injuries. On the other hand, cyclists were enjoined generally from riding their bicycles on the walks. "Immoderate rates of speed" were held to be dangerous, and deaths arising from such practices laid the individual cyclist open to the charge of manslaughter. The courts did not then, as they do not at present, define speeding very precisely.

Cyclers were pleased with all the legal concessions made to them, but they were less happy about accompanying regulations controlling the use of bicycles. When it came to the latter, organized wheelmen were no different from most human beings; they wanted laws enforced against other people, but took a dim view of enforcement against themselves. Scattered here and there among the aficionados were some who realized that if the sport did not police itself, an outside agency would do it. Some cyclists tried what today would be called public relations. The local consulate of the League of American Wheelmen in Riverside, California, passed a resolution commending the city government, its police force, and the townspeople for "bearing with our faults and mistakes" and *not* passing laws to harass cyclers. The group also unanimously condemned scorchers and advocated fixing speed limits. However, such acts were rare, and besides, most cyclists were not affiliated with clubs and were therefore beyond their jurisdiction and control. The result was that local government, cities, towns, and states all tried to control the cycling craze.

Most of the measures to control cycling aimed at solving several problems: the necessity of giving warning to pedestrians, maintaining visibility at night, controlling the cycle, and trying to insure safety for all involved in the steadily increasing flow of traffic. The problem of alerting pedestrians seems to have been the first to require the attention of authorities. The horse-drawn vehicle had never been a serious menace to life and limb, but the bicycle slid up on the unwary with all the stealth of an Apache scout, rolling swiftly and silently along on its air-filled tires. As a result the pedestrian frequently did not know danger was near until it was too late, and he could quite honestly ask the hackneyed question, "What hit me?"

The result of this was an early attempt to force the bicycler to use a warning device, occasionally a horn but more often a bell. New York City passed an ordinance in 1893 calling for such apparatus to be used, and so did remote Elkhart, Indiana. The Midwest town went a step further than the metropolis and required a cyclist to carry an affidavit testifying that he had ridden a bicycle at least two months, a requirement that may be fairly taken as the ancestor of the automobile driver's license. Warning devices were also required in other cities; some added that all rubber-tired vehicles, even the horse-drawn cabs, had to carry such devices.

Then New York City took another step toward the present. It was pointed out to the aldermen that a policeman racing madly after a scorcher was as much a menace to life and limb as the cyclist himself. Therefore, it was recommended that each police machine be equipped with a continuously sounding bell that would warn all others out of its path.

Cyclists were not necessarily eager to obey these reasonable and in-expensive regulations—"reasonable" in the sense that wheelmen should have been willing to take all steps to guarantee the safety of pedestrians, and "inexpensive" since Sears, Roebuck and Company would sell their absolutely top model, nickel-plated, double-stroke bell for fifty-five cents. If that was too costly they would send their "siren whistle," which would reproduce any sound "from a groan to an unearthly shriek," for only five cents. One can only speculate on the effect of an "unearthly shriek" suddenly coming from behind an unsuspecting pedestrian.

In Emporia, Kansas, the reaction to a bell ordinance seemed to support E. L. Godkin's famous warning against letting any more states into the union until Kansas was civilized. The town council required cyclists to sound their cycle bells at street crossings and alleyways, and when cyclists did not see fit to obey the law, the local police went to work. Almost a hundred riders, including doctors, lawyers, merchants, and the sons and daughters of all, were haled before the police magistrates and warned. The response of these nineteenth-century scofflaws was to stage a gigantic burlesque of the law, during which they made the night air hideous by beating on pans, ringing cowbells, blowing horns, and generally confirming noncyclers in the opinion that those who rode the two-wheeled machines were a menace to law and order. Having made their point, the cyclists of Emporia calmly went back to disobeying the law.

The *Boston Globe* lampooned bell ordinances in a series of satirical cartoons. One ring of the bell meant that the pedestrian should jump to the right, two rings mean "Jump to the left," and three rings warned the unhappy man afoot to turn a back handspring. On the other hand, if the poor earthbound mortal heard "Hey, you!" accompanied by one or more rings of the bell, he was to run straight ahead because the cyclist was a woman. If he heard a continuous ringing of a bicycle bell, the pedestrian should immediately climb the nearest lamppost, for the ringer was a beginner who might strike from any direction. Finally, if the man on the sidewalk heard bells from both sides of him, his only hope for survival was to prostrate himself and put his salvation in the hands of the Almighty.

Cyclists in general tended to disregard bell ordinances. In spite of a Minneapolis ordinance requiring all bicycles to have bells attached, it was admitted that not more than one out of twenty fulfilled the requirement, nor were the offenders being arrested. By 1897, the bell requirement was almost national in scope, but there was no way of telling whether or not such devices were actually being used.

As with the bells, so it was with lights. When cycling became popular, many people who worked all day discovered that the only time they could ride was after night had fallen. Darkness increased the probability of accidents; it did no good to ring a bell if the pedestrian could not see the oncoming machine. Therefore, the demand that cycles be equipped with some kind of light began to increase. But cyclists found the demand inconvenient, because kerosene lamps were always running out of fuel, and the constant jarring of the ride had a tendency to extinguish them. As a result, it seems that cyclists either did not own lamps or ignored them when they did. Consequently, the police and some private citizens were forced to do their duty. Thomas DeWitt, all iron-gray hair and bushy beard, stalked into the 68th Street police station in New York City in the summer of 1896 and announced that he did not like cyclists "in principle." Then he threw all his 230 pounds and the West Side Protective League, an antisaloon organization, into the battle to enforce the ordinance requiring lights on bicycles after dark. DeWitt prowled the cycling streets, making citizen's arrests or goading the police into acting. Offending cyclists were arrested in batches and hauled into the courts, much to their indignation. They got some relief, though, when Teddy Roosevelt, the Chairman of the Police Commissioners, ordered that violators of the cycling ordinances should not be thrown into the "tank" with common criminals or be "subjected to the indignities of imprisonment in a regular cell."[14]

There was a similar light law in Chicago that the city government announced would be stringently enforced, but throughout the summer of 1896 this meant only that the police stopped offenders, gave them a warning, and took their names for future reference. About all this practice accomplished was to contribute to an increase in the use of aliases. Even then Chicagoans had a strong feeling for self-protection.

Sometimes government got an assist from private citizens. A young lady from Passaic, New Jersey, was fined five dollars for riding without a light. Her enraged father, after straightening things out with the police, took the family ax and chopped her bicycle into shards of metal.

Finally the State of New York took cognizance of the cyclist's problem and passed the Collins Act of 1899. This law provided that if a cyclist ran out of oil or his lamp became defective, he could continue to pedal as long as he went no faster than six miles-per-hour and sounded his bell every thirty feet. However, the Collins Act did have an interesting provision that the police probably looked upon with a certain amount of relish. The law stipulated that a policeman who arrested a cyclist for breaking the law could accept five dollars as security for appearance in court the next day. According to the lawmakers, this provision was put in to save men and women the "humiliation" of being escorted publicly to the station house for committing a minor misdemeanor. But what a windfall it promised to be for an enterprising and ambitious member of New York's Finest!

It was not to be, however; the Chief of Police interpreted the law differently and said the offender had to go to the station and deposit the money with the desk sergeant. The chief said that he had every confidence in the rank and file of the department, but that he did not propose to have them "holding trial on the sidewalks" or extracting bail without first taking the prisoners to the station. There is little doubt that he did the right thing, but it is ironic that all the while, other officers were busy skimming the cream off the Tenderloin District and the city's saloons and prostitutes.

The only real solution to the problem of how to cut down on accidents in heavy traffic was a revision of the rules of the road. This was finally done in New York City in 1897, when its aldermen produced a new traffic code. More complicated than that used to control horse traffic, the system became the foundation for the automobile ordinances of the present. Most important, pedestrians were to be given the right-of-way. Maximum speed was fixed at five miles-per-hour for horses, eight for bicycles. All vehicles had to show a white light from thirty minutes before sunset until a half an hour after sunrise. Cyclists were not permitted to coast on city streets, and they had to have their feet on the pedals and both hands on the handlebars at all times. Cyclists had to mount and dismount on the right-hand side of the street and had to sound their bells before passing. The law stipulated that bells could not be more than three inches in diameter. This last can be seen as a faltering step toward noise abatement that succeeding generations did not see fit to follow. Trick riding, like reckless driving at a later date, was expressly forbidden on the city streets.

A generation of automobilists would probably find nothing seriously wrong with these provisions, but they came under instant attack from horsemen. An assault was launched by the Four-in-Hand Club, an association of those rich enough to own and drive those expensive equipages, in cooperation with the Liveryman's and Boarding Stableman's Association. They objected to the pedestrian right-of-way clause, since starting and stopping heavily loaded drays was difficult and time-consuming. The drivers also complained because bicycles were allowed to go faster than horse-drawn vehicles. As a counterirritant, the horsemen proposed that the code be amended to require that all bicycles appearing on the city streets be equipped with brakes.

Cyclists fell on the liverymen's suggestion with scorn and arguments than can only be labeled as specious. They answered that if brakes were required, the bicyclist would never really learn to control his steed but would rely abjectly on the mechanism, never learning the "flying dismount" that the cyclemaniacs thought was necessary. They ridiculed the language of the proposal, which called for brakes of a certain "power," hooting at the idea that the device had any power at all—it was man-power that set the brake! They contended that if a cycler felt he had to have brakes he would buy them and put them on his own bicycle, but that it was wrong to force a "useless adjunct" on people who did not need it and were better off without it. They argued that requiring brakes would mean "confiscation of the poorer classes whose wheels are mostly of the make of two or three years ago";[15] the brakes to be offered for sale would not fit the older machines and, therefore, the poor would be legally deprived of the right to ride their bicycles. And what was wrong with that argument? Hadn't the lawyers of the rich argued before the Supreme Court against the income tax on the ground that it would confiscate the meager fortunes of the widow and the orphan? The soon-to-be-perfected coaster brake put an end to all this foolishness, for the new brake became standard equipment on most machines.

Generally speaking, as the cycle began to disappear from downtown areas and no longer contributed so heavily to congestion, traffic and light ordinances were less frequently enforced. However, the course of the future had been laid out. When the automobile began to crowd streets, the ideas and concepts of the older cycle ordinances were applied to the new but similar situation.

CHAPTER 11

"Scarcely Jackassable"

THE DRIVE FOR BETTER ROADS

BICYCLE INSTITUTE OF AMERICA

RIDING DOWN STAIRS

No sooner had Albert Pope set out to make himself a tycoon and the United States cycling conscious than bicyclers discovered something was amiss. It was pointless to have a machine that enabled a man to outspeed a horse if the surface he traveled on was bad enough to bring him to a halt. When it came to springs, the ordinary was not much different from the old boneshaker. On an average American street the rider of either took a merciless pounding—not enough to endanger his health and bring on a hernia, as was darkly predicted by some, but sufficient to make cycling uncomfortable and to utterly destroy the illusion of speed. The plain fact was that before the bicycle there was no great pressure for good roads. Horses were relied on to cope with the difficulties of bad roads, whether in the cities or the country. Those who lived in cities and who could not afford a horse used streetcars, whose tracks made smooth streets unnecessary.

But horses and streetcars were not bicycles. In order to achieve the freedom and the economy of transportation that adherents claimed for the machine, it was mandatory that city streets and country roads be as level as possible. From the very outset, then, cycling fans were outspoken advocates of street and highway improvements that interested neither horsemen, traction owners, nor railroad magnates.

As far back as December, 1884, Charles Bates, president of the League of American Wheelmen, had spoken of the need for highway improvement. In *Outing* Bates took American farmers to task for misunderstanding the relationship between good roads and agricultural profits. He accused farmers of being the outstanding opponents of road-improvement programs, adding that even where they were not actively opposed to improving the roads, they were at least guilty of electing legislators who would not push hard for changes. Since the agriculturalists constituted the largest body of taxpayers in the nation, this meant formidable opposition. Bates claimed that much farmer opposition arose from false ideas about road-improvement costs. He inadvertently put his finger on the heart of the problem when he noted that there were fifty thousand bicycle riders in the country in 1884, and that twenty-five hundred rode "habitually." So few habitual riders were not enough to persuade a legislator to court political disaster by advocating a public works program that would benefit such a small group, while laying a tax burden on a majority that was hardly concerned.

Progress in improving roads and streets during the 1880's was negligible, but the LAW did not lose heart. Throughout the decade it hammered away at the need, although most of the discussion and debate was confined to the meeting rooms of cycling clubs. However, in 1889 the league formed a Committee on the Improvement of Highways, and from then on the publicity barrage intensified.

Not a little of the movement's ultimate success was due to the appearance of the safety bicycle. A few years later, the number of American cyclists increased by 2,200 per cent! There was an important difference between fifty thousand cycle owners plugging for better roads in 1889 and over a million organized and led by the LAW in 1897. In fact it was in marshaling cyclemen in their struggle to improve roads that the LAW made its most important contribution to cycling. In the middle of the nineties the LAW was an important organized group that got things done.

The opening shot of the LAW's revitalized campaign for good roads was a little handbook on road making that was distributed free to members. Twenty thousand copies were quickly circulated. This booklet was followed by "The Gospel of Good Roads," a pamphlet that used photographs to contrast the improved highways of Europe with the hopelessly bad roads of the United States, probably in an effort to excite patriotism in the "Gospel's" readers. Sixty thousand copies of the pamphlet were passed out, and in addition some newspapers reprinted the work on their own initiative. On the whole, the league was so satisfied with the resulting publicity that in November, 1891, the organization established the *Good Roads Magazine*, which sold about a million copies in the next three years. This publicity campaign was financed partly by Albert Pope and A. H. Overman but mostly by the league. Five years later it was estimated that the cycling organization had spent $210,000 on education for improved roads.

The campaign gained an important ally when the Massachusetts Institute of Technology, abetted by the league and Albert Pope, created an instructorship in highway construction. The instructor's primary task was to teach budding civil engineers the techniques of building better roads, probably the first such course in the nation.

The work of the national LAW was but a part of the overall drive. The Connecticut and New York divisions conducted their own campaign to dramatize the need for road improvement in 1891. They sponsored an amateur photography contest, offering prizes for what were called "stuck-in-the-mud" pictures, or, as it was put, "photographs . . . show-ing the common spectacle of the farmer's team and wagon on rough and muddy roads in their worse condition."[1] It was hoped that "before and after" snapshots would be sent, showing first the farmer in difficulty and then the comparative ease with which he could move produce to the market after the road was surfaced. For the best collection of three such photographs—which meant of the worst roads—the divisions would give a prize of fifty dollars.

There was no question that country roads needed repair and a better system of maintenance. American folklore is replete with stories that sum up the general condition of rural highways. Such a story involves the traveler who came to a mudhole in the road and found another wayfarer stuck in the mire up to his chin. When the first man asked if he could be of help, the second refused, saying that he was completely safe since he, in turn, was standing on the back of a mule. When Charles Dickens visited Ohio before the Civil War, he started a leg of his journey early one morning in high spirits and prepared to enjoy even the roughest roads.

It was well for us, that we were in this humour, for the road we went over that day, was certainly enough to have shaken tempers that were not resolutely at Set Fair, down to some inches below Stormy. At one time we were all flung together in a heap at the bottom of the coach, and at another we were crushing our heads against the roof. Now, one side was down deep in the mire, and we were holding on to the other. Now the coach was lying on the tails of the two wheelers, and now it was rearing up in the air, in a frantic state.[2]

Dickens' description was written a generation before the cycling craze, but the roads had changed very little in the intervening years. Perhaps it was put most succinctly by the wag who described such mucky arteries as

Wholly unclassable
Almost impassable
Scarcely jackassable![3]

Seven years after launching its good-roads drive, the league was still trying to make the highways at least "jackassable" and was still offering prizes for the best pictures of bad roads.

There was a perfect outpouring of good-roads propaganda, much of it aimed at the farmers who were potentially the greatest users of the improved roads and, at the time, the people responsible for keeping the roads repaired. Generally speaking, each farmer was charged with the upkeep of the road along his property. After the spring rains were over most farmers went out, filled in the deepest potholes, graded the shoulders a little, and let it go at that. However, "that" was hardly good enough for cyclers who wanted to ride on country lanes on Sunday afternoons.

The necessity of converting farmers to the gospel of good roads produced a bombardment of statistics aimed in their direction. The *Chicago Tribune* in August, 1895, raised its editorial hands in amazement over the fact that Illinois had built less than a thousand miles of improved roads in the decade preceding 1895. The paper quietly called attention to the fact that the value of farmland along improved roads was almost double that of land along unimproved roads.

Just off-stage was Albert Pope, not entirely disinterested of course, telling the cycling public and every one else that it cost an astronomical one and a half *billion* dollars to feed the nation's horses and mules. If better roads were constructed at a cost of only $4,000 a mile—or a total of twenty billion dollars to construct good roads everywhere in the nation—the American farmer would save $700,000,000 annually on fodder, since better roads would eliminate the need for so much horse-power. Pope called the massive feed expenditure a "big annual tribute to mud."

The good-roads advocates found a valuable ally in the United States Department of Agriculture. The department shouldered some of the organizing burden by sponsoring Good Roads Parliaments, national organizations with the same objectives as the LAW's Committee on the Improvement of Highways. Much of the work was spearheaded by General Roy Stone of the U.S. Bureau of Roads, a tireless speaker in behalf of better highways and the man who can be called the father of the interstate highway system. In 1898 Stone called for a "Grand High-way" across the nation from the Atlantic Ocean to the Pacific, an artery that would connect with two other systems running north and south. One of the latter would be on the Atlantic coast, following the path of the old Boston Post Road; the other on the Pacific would approximate the Spanish Camino Real. Stone proposed to finance the construction by assessing property owners along the road a maximum of two dollars an acre, while outlying landholders would be taxed in proportion to their distance from the highway. The levy would be paid over a period of about fifteen years to minimize the burden.

It was the problem of financing that forced the cyclists to realize that highway improvement was a political matter, because the burden had to be laid on the taxpayers. Therefore, the cyclers moved as an organized group to put pressure on legislators. In southern California they talked about electing men who could be counted on to vote for improved roads. As early as 1891 *Outing* called upon the entire body of wheelmen to refuse their votes to candidates who were unwilling to support the good-roads programs, and it called upon both political parties to put planks in their platforms advocating such improvements. Although at the time the parties ignored the wheelmen, three years later the Demo-crats of New York did call for "improved highways of travel throughout the state in the interests of our citizens, and particularly of the farmers and bicycle riders."[4] In 1896, when the forces of Free Silver went out to do battle with the Gold Bugs, cyclists belonging to both parties again tried to get them to include good-roads planks in their national platforms, but to no avail. Faced with this reluctance, some cycling groups let it be known that their votes were available to any candidate who would support road improvements, party affiliation be hanged.

This sort of organized power to deliver votes was not lost on some politicians, especially state legislators. When the league held its convention at Asbury Park, New Jersey, in July of 1895, *The New York Times* observed that the meeting had become a rendezvous for politicians spanning the spectrum from mayors and ex-mayors to United States Congressmen. At the same time, *Scientific American* noticed that politicians were making bids for cycling votes by promising to deliver better highways, commitments they would have to fulfill because the cyclists were a determined lot who meant to get what they wanted.

Spurred by publicity, the movement swept on, gathering converts and momentum as the decade passed. By 1898 Missouri had Good Roads Associations in half of its 115 counties, and the Federal Department of Agriculture supported them by publishing material on how to build better roads. Indiana's Governor Mount, who was himself a farmer, plumped for better highways; as a result of his efforts, the state came to have a good system of "free graded" roads. Some might consider this an extremely modest advance, but when the LAW met in Indianapolis, Mount was invited to address them as a special mark of their approval of his efforts. Wisconsin had several county organizations that were advised by the Federal government. One Wisconsin Congressman built a section of model road at his own expense and brought farmers from around Menominee in to inspect it, and at the State Fair in Milwaukee a similar strip was exhibited in hope that farmers would be converted to the good-roads movement.

In New Jersey a pioneer law for state aid in road building had been passed in 1891, under which two-thirds of the property owners along a stretch of public road could petition for improvements. The state then paid one-third of the cost of the work, while the property holders along the right of way paid ten per cent and the county paid the remainder. The first sum of money paid in the United States for state aid to road improvement was $20,661.85 put up under this law. The result of the law was a far-ranging job of road reconstruction that made New Jersey the nation's leader by 1896. When the farmers of the state were asked to evaluate the program, they admitted that it was of more benefit to the rural areas than any other thing that had happened, and that it had increased the value of their farms and decreased the number of animals they needed to do hauling jobs. Significantly, others pointed out that the existence of a good system of improved roads would hasten the coming of free rural mail delivery.

New Jersey had set the pattern, and in the other states that passed road laws, a similar system of combined payment was the usual way of financing improvements. Even then, however, the problem of money wasn't solved. In New York the idea of good roads became so popular that farmers made applications for help far in excess of the amount of money appropriated for the work. The sum set aside for such improvements was a niggardly fifty thousand dollars, an amount that bore all the earmarks of a sop thrown to farmers and cyclists to keep them quiet.

It may also reflect the fact that everyone seems to have wanted good roads, but nobody wanted to pay for them. Even the league's *Bulletin* took its members to task for always talking about good roads while at the same time being unwilling to contribute to their construction by doing such minor things as paying for a bicycle license. And the New York State legislature in 1897 turned down a bill calling for a levy of one-tenth of a mill on all property in the state, the money to be used to improve roads. The sum that such a tax would have raised was estimated to be about $500,000.

For cyclists living in cities and towns, improving streets was as important as repairing country roads. Unfortunately, city streets had to be shared with horses, wagons, and other vehicles. For this reason problems abounded when it came to trying to keep a smooth surface. The calks on horseshoes constantly tore the asphalt paving; and when wagons and horses took time out from making life miserable for bicycle fans, the ubiquitous ditchdigger stepped forward. During the last decade of the nineteenth century the great cities of the United States were growing even greater, bulging with newly arrived immigrants and big with their own natural increase. This growing population necessitated the laying of more and more sewer pipes and gas mains, and the work kept the streets in a constant state of impassibility. To say that the cyclists found this discouraging was to understate considerably.

They had reason to be discouraged. It was contended that any bicycle that held together on Atlanta's Peachtree Street would remain intact on any other street in the world. When Rudyard Kipling visited New York in 1892 he described the streets of the metropolis as "first cousins to a Zanzibar foreshore." There were "gullies, holes, ruts, cobblestones awry, kerbstones rising from two to six inches above the level of the pavement; tram lines from two to three inches above the street level; building materials scattered half across the street; lime, boards, cut stone, and ash barrels generally and generously everywhere."[5]

New York's Public Recorder Goff, understandably partisan since he was an avowed advocate of cycling, said that the metropolis "enjoyed the proud distinction of being the only city in the world from which it is impossible to get into the country over a good road."[6] Meanwhile New York papers were complaining that across the river in Brooklyn, a cyclist could go anyplace on an asphalted or macadamized road.

With the Brooklyn example before them, in 1897 the New York City branches of the LAW raised the hue and cry against bad streets to a crescendo. Cyclists filled the good streets with bicycles and complained bitterly about those in disrepair. They even spilled over onto the bridle paths of Central Park, and wheelmen complained that they had been "badly used" when the police drove them off. They flocked to meetings at Madison Square Garden and aired their grievances, attacking the mud in the streets and the bad roads.

The political pressure that cyclists exerted in New York and other cities was enough to bring about results. In Chicago the powerful interests of the street-traction magnates who had long before purchased the favor of Chicago's aldermen, were overturned. In 1897 the cycle riders were instrumental in killing two propositions giving franchises for laying streetcar tracks down the center of Jackson Street. They followed this victory with a campaign to "boulevard" the street. The dictionary lists no verb "to boulevard," but such a thoroughfare was restricted to pleasure vehicles only, wagons and trucks being excluded. The friends of the bicycle covered the city with yellow ribbons bearing the legend, "Jackson Street Must Be Boulevarded!" Simultaneously they buried the aldermen under petitions. The resulting ordinance called for the improvement of the street along the lines advocated by the cyclists; ultimately it came to be called the "Yellow Ribbon Ordinance," open acknowledgment of the power of an organized group.

In other cities the authorities capitulated to the persuasive efforts of wheelmen and improved some relatively short stretches of street. In 1895 Nicollet Avenue in Minneapolis was paved with asphalt, with the result that every evening between 8 P.M. and midnight it was a solid mass of cyclists, all taking advantage of a superior surface. Smaller communities like Camden, New Jersey, saw cyclists hold mass meetings, form Good Roads Leagues, and adopt the motto, "We want GOOD streets: do you?" All summer long in 1897 they plumped for improvements and got them.

Meanwhile engineers were busy learning about road construction. Where possible, roads were macadamized. In rural areas this simply meant that they were surfaced with gravel, but in city areas the gravel base was generally asphalted to give a smoother surface. The result was streets that were a joy to the cyclist. General Stone advocated two separate surfaces, side by side, in the rural regions, one a smooth dirt road and the other a hard-surfaced stone one. The wagons would use the dirt road in dry weather and then shift to the hard-surfaced one during the rainy season. Presumably the cyclist would use the graveled road all the time.

Of course, engineers had to learn as they went along, since MIT's program had not yet produced its crop of "road masters." They experimented with different surfacing materials, the most unusual of which was tried in Chino, California, in 1895. An unidentified experimenter mixed molasses with sand and proposed it as a smooth, hard surface for roads and cycle paths! In the middle of July it would have resembled a gigantic strip of flypaper. Even cyclists got into the engineering act when they pointed out that steamrollers used to pack the gravel exerted less pressure per square inch than the tires of ordinary wagons. As a result, the surface of the road was constantly being rutted by vehicles that were in effect heavier than the machinery used to prepare the roadway. It was embarrassing but correct.

The road builders faced other problems, such as the lack of machines to do the work. The day of the great, self-propelled monsters that mixed their own material and laid an entire lane at one time was long in the future, and most road building was done with horse-drawn scrapers, wagons to haul the fill, and lots of manpower. For that reason, builders were ever on the alert for cheap labor. As a result they encouraged the growth of one of the country's most infamous institutions, the convict road gang.

Unhappily, cyclists stand as one of the earliest groups to advocate the widespread use of convicts as road builders. In 1891 *Outing*, while agreeing that there was some basis for opposing the use of convict labor when it competed with "honest labor," asked why a prisoner couldn't be used on public works, since the prisoner was a charge on the public. A year later "Prowler" observed that there still were some people who felt road work would be degrading to the "poor, dear convict," then added that "if honest labor in God's pure air is degrading then I support that the gentlemen are correct."[7] A Minnesota paper came up with the novel idea of putting scorchers to work on the roads instead of levying fines against them.

The controversy bred strange bedfellows. The *New York Journal* reported in 1897 that the Michigan Federation of Labor had come out in support of convict labor for building roads, a seemingly strange thing for a union to do until it is understood that it was composed of skilled men who were not afraid of the competition from unskilled pick-and-shovel men. The support given by cyclists and some unionists to the system of convict labor on roads seems to have born fruit by the 1890's. Iowa passed a law allowing the inmates of the state prison to be put to work breaking up rocks—the familiar symbol of the penitentiary—which would then be distributed to the counties for use in surfacing roads. A "road law" in Kentucky provided that prisoners in the county jails and workhouses who were sentenced to hard labor could be put to work on roads. In fact, the term "hard labor" in such sentences came to mean simply road work. Even municipalities used convicts. Two hundred inmates of a county work farm were brought in to repair the bicycle path from Washington Avenue to Prospect Park in Brooklyn. It is debatable how much work they accomplished, because they were surrounded by bloomerettes who had pedaled down to watch them. With a perfectly straight face the *New York Journal* contended that the men had been put to work to keep them from going crazy in their cells for lack of anything to do.

But if the LAW was to be criticized for advocating the road gang, it must surely be applauded for its sensitivity to another problem. In 1898 the league stated that it was not enough just to have good roads, properly graded, but that highways must also be pleasing to the eye. The organization said that the nation had to pay attention to adorning the roadside with trees and shrubbery. The League of American Wheelmen reached out across the decades to touch hands with Ladybird Johnson's Highway Beautification program. Unhappily, neither enjoyed much success.

At the same time that cycling organizations were pushing hard for street and road improvements, they were also working on another project, the construction of cycling paths for their exclusive use. Not all cyclists favored the project. Some argued that the hard-won recognition of wheelmen's rights on the highways would be jeopardized, for cycle-paths laws would be "class legislation" and therefore bound to create an unfavorable reaction against cyclemen. As a result, they might lose the right to use public roads and instead be confined exclusively to the paths. Despite this opposition, the supporters of cycling paths were successful—perhaps in part because taxpayers concluded that cycle paths, three to four feet wide, were cheaper than improved streets. The drive resulted in a far-flung system of bicycle side paths that became downright grandiose in conception.

Brooklyn was the first city to construct a path exclusively for bicycles. In June, 1895, before the city became a borough of New York, the park commissioners completed the Coney Island Cycle Path, five and a half miles long and probably the most famous in the country. By mid-June the ground had been plowed, rolled, surfaced with crushed limestone, and made ready for the cyclers. Newspaper photographs, long since faded, show a pleasant, shaded roadway running between rows of stately trees. On June 15 the path was opened with a gala parade. Thousands of people lined the sidewalks to watch. Sprinkling carts spent all morning laying the dust so the spectators would have a good view as the cycles rolled past. By noon the crowd had grown to thirty thousand.

Then, while Mayor Charles A. Schieren of Brooklyn smiled his approval, the band struck up and three hundred uniformed militiamen wheeled onto the path, followed by the grandest cycle parade the country had yet seen. Allowing for exaggeration on the part of the reporters, probably ten thousand cyclers rolled down the path that day, only the first installment of the thousands who would use it before 1900. One after the other, the divisions glided past. Although males outnumbered females twenty to one, it was the women who caught the reporters' eyes. The parade was acclaimed later as a "triumph for the cycling girl," whether "bloomerite" or "knickerite." Even little girls came in for their share of admiration, especially the three who pedaled by in white costumes with sashes that bore the proud name of the Brooklyn Good Roads Association.

To say that the Coney Island Cycle Path was an instant success is to give it faint praise. One month after it was opened, the road had carried such heavy traffic that it required repairs and resurfacing where the bicycle tires had scattered the gravel around the path. All that summer and fall the traffic streamed toward the resorts in the morning and then, about four in the afternoon, began to flow back toward the city. As the *New York Times* put it, the stream did not subside until most of Brooklyn had gone to bed and even the dogs had stopped barking. Those who ran the amusement parks and the beer gardens on Coney Island were said to be overjoyed.

The path was so popular that six months after its opening, it had to be widened. Three extra feet were added to the original fourteen. In addition, milestones were set up so cyclers could check their cyclometers for accuracy. The following year saw no diminution in the flow of cyclers on the path. Once again the road was widened, this time doubling its width along its entire length. In 1897 the entire road was rebuilt again, allegedly because it had been poorly constructed at first and did not have a firm foundation. The odds are that the builders, like the contractors who laid the highways of the 1920's, simply had no concept of how much traffic the path was going to carry.

Elsewhere bicycle riders took up the cry for their own highways with less success. A public meeting in Manhattan protesting the absence of cycle paths brought nothing tangible. Chicago showed a similar resistance, and it and other large cities contented themselves with trying to improve the streets. Sometimes they paved strips adjacent to the curbs on either side of the street to provide some smooth surfaces, but riders complained that teamsters cut into these areas and forced cyclists out into the middle of the street. The New York legislature finally passed a law making driving a wagon on a cycle path a misdemeanor punishable by a fifty-dollar fine.

But a few cities tried for cycle paths. In Minneapolis there was a great deal of newspaper talk about such roads. The city engineer recommended that they be built with wooden surfaces, which he maintained would be cheaper to construct and would last longer. He probably had one eye fixed on the vast forests of pine in northern Minnesota, enormous stands of virgin timber that were shortly to disappear into the sawmills of the Midwest. A wooden bicycle path was never constructed in Minneapolis, but by 1898 a considerable amount of work had been done to connect the parks of the city with the nearby lakes.

St. Paul, Minneapolis' neighbor and rival, was not to be outdone in constructing bicycle paths. In 1898 five thousand dollars was expended on such roads, about 40 per cent of which came from private individuals who sometimes built stretches of path by themselves. At a cost of approximately one hundred dollars a mile for cycle paths four feet wide, this expenditure gave St. Paul a respectable fifty miles of paths reserved for cyclists. Elsewhere in the state there were cycle-path associations, almost all rural, and there was some talk about building cycleways between various towns and villages.

Cycling in the far Western states was never as popular as in the East, but a rising city like Seattle could make a good showing in 1899, with more than twenty miles of paths reserved for bicycles. All this was to accommodate a phenomenal incrase from two hundred bicycles in 1896 to nearly four thousand in 1899. Southward in California there were two systems of bikeways, one in the Bay area and the other connecting Sacramento and Stockton, some fifty miles apart. But in Southern California, the future home of the freeway, there was little to cheer the heart of cyclists. In 1895, Santa Monica wheelmen paid five hundred dollars out of pocket to improve the Santa Monica Road and construct cycle paths around the worst stretches. Two years later, the *Los Angeles Times* charged that "property owners and supervisors took extra pains to destroy"[8] the path and that it had lapsed into disuse. Some people contended that the way to handle the competition for space was to construct cycle paths where teamsters and streetcars and pedestrians could not get at them—up in the air! In 1896 New York City took a look at its crowded and inadequate trasnportation system and decided something had to be done. One suggestion was that the elevated railways be rearranged to provide for a double-decked, eight-track system. Originally this had nothing to do with bicycles, but riders were quick to seize any opportunity to find more and better roadways for the machine. Although traction magnate Jay Gould had reputedly originated the idea, its expression came from Lawson Fuller, who recommended that the upper deck of the renovated system be roofed over and converted into a two-lane elevated cycle road.

The concept had an immediate attraction for cycling buffs, who grabbed eagerly at anything that offered relief from the crowded streets and would get them beyond the wheels of the hated teamsters.

When it came to visualizing the future of such a roadway, the cyclomaniac became downright lyrical. A writer for the *New York Journal* imagined the great elevated roadway on a balmy summer's night, lighted by electric lights and "Japanese lanterns."

> A steadily moving throng of wheelmen in natty costumes especially designed for evening wear, and fair wheelwomen in the most modish of cycling garbs whirl rapidly over the smooth path. At the soda fountains, cafes, and smoking bazaars corresponding in dimensions with the "L" depots below, other cyclists and throngs of interested spectators recline in easy chairs upon the verandas to enjoy the entrancing, exhilerating scene.
>
> Under a myriad of lights the scene is of fairyland. The men all seem brave and women fair. The sounds of cheerful chatter and gay laughter are heard above the soft rustle made by the rubber tires as they skim over the perfect surface. In the distance can be heard the strains of an orchestra—for there will be music by the band at regular distances. . . . Silver mounted and

pearl-inlaid wheels will be so common as to invite but casual comment, the wheel deluxe having already made its appearance in New York.

What a delightful tour it will be on a balmy midsummer night, spinning over the Ninth Avenue line from Harlem to the Battery, catching glimpses of the Hudson at the cross streets, until the moonlit bay bursts upon the view in all its silvery glory![9]

It was characteristic of cycling enthusiasts never to stop to wonder how one might hear the "cheerful chatter," the "gay laughter," or the "soft rustle" above the clanging of the elevated trains on the levels below. Surely the "balmy midsummer" air would be rendered toxic by the smoke and carbon monoxide from the locomotives, and one would spin from one end of Manhattan to the other in a dense cloud of smoke and soot. But what did all that matter—a cyclist could dream, couldn't he?

Chicago, as usual, was not to be outdone when it came to such speculating. Its citizens talked constantly about a plan for an elevated cycleway that would not be connected with the elevated train system. As projected, it would stand sixteen feet above the ground, sufficiently high to allow wagons and streetcars to pass under it. There would be two traffic lanes protected by a separating fence. The cyclists who whirled along the smooth pine roadbed would pay a toll of ten cents for the eight miles of cycleway. The icing on this cycling cake would be electric lights located every two hundred feet, a system that would enable fans to cycle at night in the cool breezes off Lake Michigan. In spite of the rumor that a million dollars had been raised to construct not just this system but also one that would go all the way to Milwaukee, nothing came of it but talk.

However, out in Southern California they did more than just discuss the desirability of such an elevated system, they went to work on it. The result was the Pasadena Cycleway, conceived by a local entrepreneur, Horace Dobbins, who broke ground on the project in 1898. Like the other plans, the Pasadena Cycleway was grand in its conception. The entire road was to be constructed of Oregon pine. From its Moorish-style depot on Daytone Street in downtown Pasadena it would run south along the Arroyo Seco, terminating at the Plaza in Los Angeles, nine miles away. Because of the uneven nature of the terrain and the necessity of maintaining a level gradient for cyclers, the pathway was to be entirely elevated, in some places fifty feet above the ground. To prevent cyclers from going over the sides, the road would be fenced with woven wire painted an attractive green. The entire roadway would be illuminated every hundred yards by electric lights.

The road was to have other attractions. For example, a ten-cent ticket would enable the cycler to ride all day long, and repair stations were to be located at the terminals. Furthermore, one would be able to rent a bicycle in Pasadena, then pedal to Los Angeles and leave the machine there. It was estimated by the management that the road would bring in a profit of ten thousand dollars a year.

Construction was begun on the cycleway on March 4, 1898, and in two years approximately two miles of road were finished southward to Columbia Street, where the cycleway joined the arroyo. However, at that point the organized fans of cycling ran afoul of a major obstacle, the powerful Southern Pacific Railroad. Fearing that the cycleway might cut into profits from passenger traffic between Pasadena and Los Angeles, the company got an injunction against the continuation of the cycle path. These legal difficulties coincided with the decline in cycling enthusiasm, and the scheme was allowed to collapse. Finally the city of Pasadena pulled down the cycleway.

One of the consequences of this sustained agitation for cycleways and improved roads was the rise of the so-called "sidepath" movement near the end of the century, a movement to build cycle roads linking the cities of the United States. While some cities had small cycle-path systems around them, there was not much of an intercity system. One exception was a continuous sidepath that ran along the shore of Lake Erie from western New York through Ohio. Called the Lake Shore Route, it offered excellent touring, both because it was unbroken and because the terrain was good.

A particularly grandiose proposal was the Great Sidepath, which was to run from Chicago to Minneapolis and to be a joint undertaking of the states of Illinois, Wisconsin, and Minnesota. This road, which would be exclusively for bicycles, would be approximately 530 miles long, the longest completely paved stretch in the nation. Part of the route was already in hand, since Chicago had extended a cycleway along Sheridan Drive toward Milwaukee, and the remaining distance was filled with scattered stretches that merely had to be connected. As proposed, the road would run westward from Milwaukee, through the resort district of the Dells, to La Crosse on the Mississippi River. From La Crosse the sidepath would cross the river and follow the west bank through Winona, Minnesota, then Red Wing, and on to Minneapolis. Approximately half of the last hundred miles of this route had already been constructed. It was a cyclist's dream. Further, if a proposed Manhattan-Buffalo-Ohio route could be connected with the Chicago-Minneapolis sidepath, and if these systems were then hooked onto a proposed Minneapolis-Omaha route, Americans would have one of the longest stretches of paved highway in the world. Unfortunately, none of the schemes came to fruition. It remained for the automobile to be the prime mover in the realization of such a network, but cyclists would be recognized for having first proposed such an idea.

Wheelmen were interested in more than smooth cycling; they also introduced other ideas that have become firmly grafted to the massive business of traveling in the United States. Cyclists were the first large group to make numerous short trips into the country, and they needed help to keep from getting lost. Being city folk, they might never have been more than four blocks from a trolley line before. And they were frequently at the mercy of rural people who were not above deliberately giving wrong directions to city dudes.

The confusion, fatigue, and exasperation that sometimes resulted moved the LAW to recommend that its members keep accurate logs of their trips, noting both distance and direction exactly. It is probable that the cyclometer was developed partly for this purpose. These logs, which were called road books, at first were the exclusive property of the local clubs, but they eventually became the imposing road maps of the league, usually published by the state divisions.

These prototypes of modern road maps even used some of the same symbols. For example, a heavy red line marked a good road for cycling, and a lighter red line stood for one that was not so suitable. Distances between points were shown on the maps, which ultimately outlined the best and shortest routes through major towns and cities along the way. Because cyclists needed special information, the maps carried other notations of a surprisingly exact nature. The maps sited hills, stated whether or not they were ridable, and indicated the length and direction of the grade. Altogether, they were a remarkable set of publications, and it is no wonder that each edition was grabbed up almost as quickly as it was printed. Touring cyclists were particularly anxious to get the special maps mounted on muslin, a backing that made it possible to fold them without creasing them badly and so destroying their usefulness.

By 1897 most of the LAW divisions were distributing maps of their own states, free to members but also available to nonmembers by purchase. The road-reporting service of the larger and richer divisions published even more precise information. For instance, the New York division printed a weekly road report listing the state of repair and the condition of the roads within its jurisdiction. And when the league addressed itself to the state of the roads it spoke with authority; its Committee on Road Improvement knew more about the subject than any other group in the nation.

For those cyclists who were not members of the LAW or did not have the money to buy the maps, road information was provided by local newspapers, especially in the metropolitan areas. The *New York Times* printed reasonably detailed maps of the roads within a radius of sixty miles of the city, as well as some roads running toward the eastern end of Long Island. Subsequent newspaper maps showed the improved city streets, the best routes to the ferry slips, and where each ferry went.

The LAW's desire to make traveling more comfortable and pleasant for its members led to another innovation. The league pioneered in the use of the road signs that are today found along every highway in the nation and on most of the streets.

The signs were simple, consisting only of a circle enclosing the initials "LAW" and some arrows. A stenciling set could be obtained from the league, along with instructions for their use. To prevent trouble and to cement friendly relations, members were warned to obtain the consent of local authorities as well as private persons before stenciling the symbols on posts or fences, and to be neat, even to the extent of laying on a coat of varnish to improve the appearance of the signs.

Only three symbols were authorized, although others could be used at the discretion of individual clubs. A circle with an arrow pointing to the right or to the left indicated the best direction for cyclers to take. The same circle with the arrow pointed down at forty-five degrees was cautionary and warned the cycler to proceed with care; if the symbol appeared at the top of a hill, it meant dangerous coasting. The sign for "danger" was the circle with the arrow pointed straight down, an admonition to the cyclist to dismount. If it occurred at the top of a hill, it meant that no coasting should be attempted.

Other combinations of arrows and circles meant different things. In the days before the quarrel over who could use the sidewalks, there was one sign advising cyclists to take to the walk instead of using the road. Another, the forerunner of more modern bits of advice to travelers, called attention to a nearby inn or hotel that gave special preference to members of the league. One combination of symbols alerted the cyclist that he was near an attractive vista; another showed the location of a "post office" where cyclers might leave messages.

One of the more vexing problems cyclists faced was the transportation of their machines. At first they never worried about getting their bicycles anywhere except through their own power. Then, as the cycle became more popular, people began to think of taking their wheels with them when they went on vacations. Naturally most did not want to ride there but only wanted a bicycle for pleasure when they arrived. Further, it seems that many bicyclers hopped on trains on weekends, took their cycles fifty or more miles out into the country, and then pedaled back. Others simply wanted to take short rural excursions without the bother of riding out through the crowded streets of the cities.

The difficulty arose because the streetcar companies and especially the railroads were reluctant to allow a bicycle to take up space unless that space had been paid for. When cycling was in its infancy, the railroads had gladly transported the machines free, apparently to attract the passenger traffic. However, as the bicycle became more popular, the railroads abolished this policy, most likely because it would cost too much to transport half a car of passengers and half a car of nonpaying cycles. In doing so, the railroads aroused the wrath of cycledom and caused a massive outburst of political opposition.

In February, 1896, a bill requiring the railroads to carry all bicycles free as personal baggage was put before the New York State legislature. The cyclists swung behind the proposition with a petition containing thirty thousand signatures, with more promised as the session continued. The pressure in behalf of the Armstrong Bill, as the measure was called, was strong enough to cause the *Chicago Tribune* to remark that in comparison with the cycle lobby, the railroad lobby was but a "puling infant."[10] Another paper said that "there was doubtless a silent recognition of the fact that it would not be well to antagonize the vast army that pedals its way about the empire state."[11]

Apparently the legislature saw things the same way. Only one member of the Assembly and four state senators voted against the measure. Chauncey Depew, *bon vivant* and president of the Vanderbilt railroads, rushed up from New York City and did his best to persuade Governor Levi Morton to veto the bill, but the governor could count votes as well as the next man. Altogether, the passage of the Armstrong Bill was a striking example of what organized cyclists could do.

Not every railroad capitulated to such pressure, nor did all states. In California the powerful Southern Pacific Railroad, hard at work building the reputation that produced Frank Norris's *The Octopus*, turned its grim countenance on the fifty thousand cyclists of the state and continued to charge twenty-five cents for every machine it transported. There was a great deal of grumbling by the cycling fans and some dark talk about boycotting the road and electing senators who would pass a law like the Armstrong Law, but there was no indication that the Southern Pacific was much frightened at the prospect. In any case, the road knew more about electing senators and controlling legislatures than the cyclists ever would know.

The campaign for the free transportation of bicycles continued through the year 1897. New Jersey proposed a fine of ten dollars to be paid by any railroad that refused to carry a bicycle as personal baggage. Interestingly enough, the fine was to be paid to the offended cycler. Faced with such a threat and mindful of the legislative history of the Armstrong Law, the railroads capitulated. In the Midwest the going was harder. Illinois and Wisconsin legislators sat tight, a stubborn resistance that caused a LAW official to say that the time had come to "show up" such people at the polls. He hinted that at least seventeen Wisconsin lawmakers had been marked for political execution.

Early in 1897 the Passenger Committee of the Trunk Line Association, a management group, announced that its members would transport bicycles free. This victory for cycling was extensive but not complete, since some railroads did not belong to the association. New York, Pennsylvania, New Jersey, Ohio, Michigan, Indiana, parts of Illinois, California, and Colorado were affected. But Wisconsin, northern Illinois, Minnesota, and the New England states were not. In Kentucky, where cyclers constituted no very important segment of the voting public, the governor vetoed such a bill. Nevertheless, all in all the cyclers had done very well.

Like a tame animal developing a taste for raw meat, the cyclists next turned on other forms of transportation. New York City's inhabitants were dependent on ferries to transport them to the Coney Island Path, the glades of Sabury Park, or north to the pleasures of Westchester County. It was of little use to get the railroads to carry cycles free if the savings were eaten up by ferry charges. Running on the momentum supplied by the capitulation of the Trunk Line Association, the cyclists sniped away at the ferry companies throughout the summer of 1897, arguing that ten cents for the passenger fare and another dime for the cycle was too much money. However, the ferry companies were in a stronger position than the railroads because they monopolized the major means of transportation across the rivers. When they held firm, the cyclists spun around and concentrated on tolls for using the Brooklyn Bridge. This time they won. Bicycles were not charged for crossing.

The plain fact was that any agency, public or private, that tried to infringe on either the rights or the pocketbooks of bicycle riders was in for trouble. For example, in 1895 Pennsylvania cyclists tried to overturn the right of private toll roads to charge for bicycles. The Supreme Court of the state held for the companies, much to the anger of the cycling fraternity, who said that bicycles ought to be allowed to use the toll roads free because such use was a positive good. The bicycles, they argued, packed the roadway to an even firmness and neither damaged the road nor necessitated rapairs, the last the prime reason for charging tolls in the first place.

Other arguments were equally interesting. New Jersey cyclists argued that they should not be forced to pay tolls on private roads because the charters under which the highways were originally incorporated did not specify that bicycles should be charged. No doubt this was because the charters were given before the bicycling craze came into existence.

Toll charges on private roads eventually were dropped, not so much as a result of the pressure applied by cyclists as from the threat of damage suits rising from injuries. As an official of a Maryland toll road described it, the company was allowed to charge only half a cent a mile for a bicycle, and accepting the toll implied that the company guaranteed a "good, if not perfect, road" for the wheelmen to ride on. The spokesman pointed out that the company could not "go over the pike on our knees every day and pick up the sharp stones and splintered rock"[12] in the effort to avoid damage suits for puntured bicycle tires. Certainly it could not do so on the meager profits derived from tolls of half a cent a mile.

If there was anything that really aroused the wrath of cyclists it was the idea of taxing their machines. Elkhart, Indiana, put a tax of two dollars on each bicycle as early as 1893 without precipitating any sort of cyclists' revolt, but when Chicago tried it in 1897 things were different.

In July, 1897, Chicago's Mayor Carter Harrison signed an ordinance calling for a tax of seventy-five cents a year. Cycles would be tagged, and a description of each machine would be kept at police headquarters. The LAW and the Associated Cycling Clubs supported the taxation, since it was earmarked for road improvements. *Wheel Magazine* also arrived at the conclusion that licensing would be a good thing. Not only would it make for better roads, it would even deter bicycle thieves, because each machine would bear a number that would make it easier to trace. "Think of the benefit," *Wheel* suggested, "to the morals of those who seem to have an irresistible tendency to gather in other people's wheels."[13]

But the cyclist-on-the-street didn't agree. A former judge, Lorin C. Collins, filed suit to enjoin the collection of the tax. He charged that the bicycle tax would open up a vast field for exploitation by "venal and corrupt legislative bodies." Then Judge Collins warned a complacent public that the next step would be to tax a man's shoes because they helped wear out the streets, then his walking stick for the same reason, and then his baby carriage! Let the municipal tax on bicycles remain, he warned, and "soon everything a man ate or wore would be submitted to a petty municipal tax."[14] The judge got his injunction, but ultimately the licensing of cycles was allowed to stand.

It was no easier to get a licensing ordinance put through in New York City than in Chicago. In 1896, with the cycling fad about to peak, the fathers of Gotham entertained the idea of a license fee of a dollar a year, a proposition that failed of passage. The following year the body considered raising a tax on cycles to two dollars, a proposition that made cyclers indignant. A spokesman took up Judge Collins' argument and said it would be just as fair to tax boots and shoes. By contrast, the cyclists of Tacoma, Washington, petitioned their city council to impose a tax of a dollar a year on all bicycles and then to use the funds to construct a cycle path. The council agreed to do so.

Much of this agitation for improved roads and better surfaces, extra favor, and preferential treatment subsided under the mounting enthusiasm for war. The United States and Spain had worked themselves into an impasse during 1897, and by the spring of 1898 the two nations were on a collision course. Cyclists turned their attention to the use of their favorite machine in what seems to be one of mankind's favorite occupations.

CHAPTER 12

"The Elusive Bicycle Corps"

THE MILITARY ROLE OF THE BICYCLE

BICYCLE INSTITUTE OF AMERICA

LEG OVER HANDLE

No matter how versatile the bicycle had proven, to some people the ultimate test would not be passed until the birotate chariot had been tried in the crucible of war. From the very moment the ordinary appeared, disciples prophesied that the bicycle would play a significant military role. At first, however, the debate over the appropriate military employment of the machine occupied foreign enthusiasts rather than Americans. England's G. Lacey Hillier, for instance, called attention to the fact that cyclists were less conspicuous and more silent than cavalrymen and in most cases could travel faster and farther than hussars.

In the United States, serious consideration of the application of cycles to war did not come until the appearance of the safety bicycle. And the first moves were made by the state militia, not by the regular Army. In 1891 the Connecticut militia formed a cycling unit under the guidance of Captain Howard A. Giddings, a signal officer. The unit was used in summer maneuvers, a fact that *Outing* pointed out to the War Department, along with the recommendation that it begin experimenting immediately with the cycle. The Connecticut unit was followed shortly by the creation of a bicycle detachment in the Second Company of the District of Columbia National Guard and similar units in Illinois and Colorado. Generally speaking, these troops were composed of men who furnished their own machines and were used only in times of civil disturbances, in most cases strikes.

The District of Columbia unit was put on the alert when Washington was invaded in 1893 by Jacob Coxey's "army," a band of five hundred jobless men who had come to petition Congress for relief. However, the unit spent its call-up sitting in the armory waiting for orders. Possibly the men filled the vacant hours rereading pages 50 and 51 in General Albert Ordway's *Cycle-Infantry Drill Regulations.*

General Ordway, who had served during the Civil War, wrote his drill manual in 1892. It was published by no less a person than Albert Pope, who seldom missed a chance for publicity. For the most part, the book merely outlined drill procedures with sets of diagrams. But the nineties came at the end of the Era of Upheaval, a thirty-year period during which the state militias had been used extensively in labor disputes. Consequently, Ordway included a section entitled "Street Riot Duty."

> Riots may be prevented by breaking up mobs before they can formulate plans of action and organize to carry them into effect. Consequently cycle-infantry would be invaluable in cases of local disturbance of the peace, for the reason that they can be moved to the points of incipient trouble with great rapidity.[1]

The general went on to say that such troops should always dismount in the presence of the mob and immediately go on the offensive. In those cases where the crowd was too large, the cyclist-soldiers should adopt a defensive posture and wait for help.

> To assume a defensive position against attack in one direction, form the company into line, facing that direction, and ground, invert, or stack cycles. The cycles will form a troublesome barricade against assault by the mob.[2]

On the last page of the manual Colonel Pope got in a bit of advertising. There, under the caption "The Soldier's Standard Bicycle," was displayed the newest model of the Columbia Light Roadster, complete with dispatch case and a rifle. Pope proudly announced that it was the only cycle used in the regular military service in the Army—an inaccurate statement, since the regular Army had no such machines.

Militia units of cyclemen were used in the Cripple Creek Strike in Colorado in 1894 and against Illinois coal miners in 1895. Most of this service consisted of carrying messages, and the cyclists seem to have been kept busy. Possibly they followed the recommendation later laid down by Captain Giddings of the Connecticut unit that "couriers serving in cities during riots can perform their duties in citizen's dress."[3] Considering the temper of the American workingman in the nineties, it was just as well not to call attention to one's self when both hands had to be on the handlebars.

In 1894 there was a meeting in Denver attended by national-guard representatives from several states. Delegates predicted confidently that there would soon be an army of fifty thousand cycling soldiers scattered through the nation, men who were well drilled and "practically invincible." This was anticipated because no less a person than General Nelson Miles, the ranking officer of the Army, was a strong proponent of the use of the bicycle in war.

A year later the commander of the signal services of the United States Army, General A. W. Greeley, was saying that the value of the bicycle in military communications could not be overestimated, although he cautioned that the movement of large bicycle units over great distances had not been tested. This last was certainly true, because the regular Army still had taken no official notice of the bicycle. As a result of this lack of interest, the guardsmen carried out their own experiments.

On June 9, 1895, Lt. George Wise and Pvt. Arthur Weed rode out of Madison Barracks at Sackets Harbor on Lake Ontario with messages to be delivered to Governors Island in New York Harbor. Eighty-eight hours later they presented themselves to the officer commanding, having covered approximately 397 miles at a respectable speed of nearly five miles an hour, total elapsed time. It is unlikely they pedaled more than fourteen or fifteen hours a day, so the real speed for the trip was nearer eight miles an hour, or about the same rate attained by cavalry at a gallop. Of course, no cavalryman would gallop the same horse nearly four hundred miles in less than four days.

The experiment was not over. Private Weed then got back on his trusty iron steed and pedaled back to Madison Barracks. But he must have been fatigued, because the return trip took him almost eight hours longer. No wonder General Miles was quoted as saying that the bicycle was the answer for small bodies of men who had to cover long distances.

No doubt some of this experimentation, and much of the interest shown by Miles, came from watching European nations making extensive tests of the bicycle as a troop mover. Germany, France, Belgium, Britain, and Russia were hard at work adapting the cycle to military use, even to the perfection of a thirty-pound folding bicycle. Taking due note of such developments, *Scientific American* reported in 1895 that military men believed there were few parts of any civilized country where wheelmen could not cover twice the maximum distance ordinarily allotted to the cavalry.

So America's military brass continued to be interested. Even before Weed's ride, Miles had tested the sending of messages by bicycle, using relays of riders provided by the League of American Wheelmen. One such group covered 975 miles in four days and a half despite adverse weather. In 1894, a message from General Greeley in Washington to the commanding officer in Denver, a distance of over two thousand miles, was delivered by cycle in six and a half days. Regrettably neither of these rides was carried out under the official aegis of the regular Army.

There were other indications of public interest. During October, 1895, a newly organized association calling itself the United States Military Wheelmen held a convention in New York City and solemnly listened to papers covering such subjects as the role of the bicycle in the next war, the proper weight for a military bicycle, the proper weight for the uniform for bicycle troops, and whether military cyclists should avoid military titles. Not to be outdone by such masculine doings, Mrs. Belva Lockwood told the Atlanta Women's Press Association that in the war to come, women correspondents should be sent to the front on bicycles. Mrs. Lockwood's motives were pacific rather than warlike; she contended, for some reason, that the presence of women would prevent "entangling alliances or foreign complications." Mrs. Lockwood was not a woman to be lightly regarded. She was the most prominent female lawyer in the country, had been instrumental in getting a law passed enabling women to practice before the U.S. Supreme Court, and in 1888 had run for the Presidency as the candidate of the Equal Rights Party. However, this formidable reputation did not overawe the *Minneapolis Tribune*, which sourly commented that women at the forefront of battle would only add to the horrors of war.

Some Americans were prepared to put their money where their mouths were. At the height of the so-called Venezuelan Crisis, when President Grover Cleveland was rattling the saber at England, the Liberty Athletic Club Wheelmen of New York debated their proper role in the impending collision. Some members contended that they should offer their services to the Government in the event the quarrel culminated in war. However, the peace group won the day, and the club refused by fifteen to ten to offer their help. Cleveland probably sighed in relief.

In the meantime a steady flow of military hardware for the bicycle poured from the fertile minds of American inventors. A Brooklyn crowd watching a cycle parade in the summer of 1895 saw a military duplex—two safety bicycles mounted side by side—with a small mountain cannon fastened to a bracket connecting the common rear axle. The *New York World* greeted this latest example of American ingenuity with breathless praise but never once raised the question of whether it was possible to pedal cycles in the mountains or why two bicycles could go where one mule could not. The newspaper illustrations leave one with the impression that the gun, about a one-pounder in caliber, was designed to be fired from the cycles; but in the absence of a trail spade or some kind of recoil mechanism, one assumes that the first shot would send the whole contrivance racing off down the mountainside.

The mountain gun was only the beginning. The same carriage was shown in *Harper's Weekly* with a forward-firing machine gun mounted on it, and a single bicycle was shown with a Colt automatic gun fastened to the front fork. The latter machine had a firing handle just about where the cyclist's groin would be when pedaling, so one supposes the bicycle was stopped before the gun was fired. One inventor patented a similar machine except that the weapon was connected to a device on the rear wheel that fired the gun automatically until it was disconnected or ran out of ammunition. Given the tendency for quick-firing weapons to spray their shot all around the countryside, one can envision the bicycle charging down the highway, raining death so long as the wheel was in motion—but on whom?

After the election of 1896, American sentiment became distinctly more warlike as the Cuban rebels fought against the Spanish government. In December General Miles recommended to the House Committee on Military Affairs that the bicycle be adopted for infantry organizations, and that each garrison have a cycle squadron of at least ten men. He also proposed that the Federal Government manufacture its own bicycles, a hard blow to Pope and Spaulding. Well . . . to Albert Pope, anyway, since Spaulding gleefully announced that *his* bicycles had gone to equip an experimental unit based at Ft. Missoula, Montana, out on the Great Plains. The Government did not go into the business of making its own cycles, nor did it adopt Miles's recommendations. But the Ft. Missoula experiment turned out to be a dramatic demonstration of what cyclists could accomplish and seemed to bear out Giddings' prediction that cyclists could outmarch cavalry.

In June, 1897, a cycling unit from the Twenty-fifth Infantry Regiment left Ft. Missoula in the rain. The soldiers were members of a Negro outfit, only one of several then doing garrison duty on the plains. The cyclists included Lieutenant James Moss, an attending physician, an official reporter, and nineteen enlisted men. Forty days later they wheeled past the sentries at Jefferson Barracks in St. Louis, Missouri. The men had traveled two thousand difficult miles, across open country for the most part, at a respectable rate of fifty miles a day. After this demonstration it is no wonder that, as the hostility toward Spain mounted, there was an increase in the talk about cycle troops.

Would the American cycle troops be prepared? Well, they should have been, because they had before them Captain Giddings' *Manual for Cyclists, For the Use of the Regular Army, Organized Militia, and Volunteer Troops of the United States.*[4] At the beginning the author included definitions, such as "CYCLIST. A soldier using a bicycle as a means of locomotion." After discussing visual signals to control cycling units, Giddings then turned to the "School of the Cyclist," which subject comprises most of the book and makes for quaint and sometimes humorous reading. Commands were obviously derived from those used by the cavalry, although some of them reflect the specialties of the new mount. Whatever the task, it was to be done in a military manner, as the following example will illustrate.

INSPECTION CYCLES

1. *Inspection;* 2. CYCLES. At the first command, grasp the left grip with the left hand and the upper bar of the frame at the balance with the right hand. At the command *CYCLES* run the cycle forward on the rear wheel, at the same time raising the front wheel in the air, take one step to the right, bring the saddle against the legs and grasp the right hand grip with the right hand.

As the inspector approaches, draw the handlebar toward the body, lifting the rear wheel from the ground. After the cycle is inspected, lower the rear wheel to the ground, grasp the upper bar at the balance with the right hand, take one step to the left, run the cycle backwards, bringing the front wheel to the ground, resume the position of stand to cycle.[5]

Giddings devoted some space to mounted pistol drill, although what cyclists might be expected to hit with a pistol while pedaling is more than one can imagine. He also gave instructions on how to carry out

wall-scaling operations and fording maneuvers, including recommendations on how to hide the bicycles *under* water to prevent the enemy from
finding them! Giddings stoutly maintained that burying the machines
in water would be less harmful than concealing them in the brush, where
alternating dew and hot sun would cause them to rust. Taking a leaf
from artillery traditions, the captain preached that a cycle should never
be allowed to fall intact into the hands of the enemy. Instead, a soldier
should disable it by smashing the spokes with the rifle, buckling the
frame by jumping on it, or cutting the tires.

Giddings described how bicycles could be maneuvered in companies
and battalions—the last a monumental case of wishful thinking—and
then turned to a description of the military cycle. This was a heavy safety
bicycle, equipped with hand-operated brakes and a frame case suspended
from the center bar, which constituted the cycle soldier's knapsack. The
gears and chain of the machine were enclosed to protect them from dust,
grease, and moisture, and the regulation rifle was hung, muzzle to the
front, on two leather-lined hooks mounted to the crossbar. The cyclist
straddled the weapon just as the cavalryman straddled his carbine in
the boot.

Giddings recommended that the cyclist-soldier training to take the
field should begin by cycling ten miles a day and end two weeks later
by cycling fifty miles a day fully equipped. He warned that the stomach
was the organ most affected by bicycle marches and that one should
take special care that it did not become "deranged." The manual did
not say exactly what "deranged" meant.

As for the military employment of cyclists, Giddings pointed out that
they were especially adapted to courier service, as signalmen, and for
reconnaissance work. He believed they could be used to good effect in
combat by seizing distant points and holding them until the infantry
came up. Conversely, they could be utilized in delaying operations where
it was necessary to be able to retreat fast. Cyclists could be used during
civil disturbances where it was necessary to move quickly to disperse
mobs or to defend property.

Giddings concluded his manual with a list of trumpet calls, allegedly
"abbreviated" to include only those "most useful in the field," but actually containing no fewer than fifty-one separate signals, beginning with
"First Call" and ending with "Lie Down." One thing was certain, if the
United States went to war there would be no problem in training the
bicycle troops.

The chance came to put the cyclists' dreams into operation. On

April 11, 1898, President William McKinley reviewed the Government's involvement in the Cuban imbroglio, Congress responded, and our "splendid little war" with Spain was on. Isaac Potter of the League of American Wheelmen told reporters that a small group of cyclists would demand more attention from the enemy than a regiment of ordinary soldiers. According to Potter, the rapid appearance and disappearance of cycle troops behind the enemy's lines would befuddle any general and create panic in the rear echelons. Then while the Spanish troops were wandering around in a "bewildered state trying to keep track of the elusive bycycle corps," the regular Army could sneak up from the rear and take them all as prisoners. All that was needed to make this confusion and terror possible was to put the roads of Cuba into good condition.[6]

However, no bicycle corps was destined to "bewilder" the Spaniards, and cyclomaniacs ultimately had to concede that the jungle thickets around Santiago were closed to the wheel. Some newspapers did try to maintain enthusiasm in the states. One paper showed a squad of bicycle troopers standing ready behind a barricade of their machines, just like cavalry set to repel an Indian attack. The caption was appropriate to the American mood. "Come on, Mr. Spaniard. We rather fancy Mauser bullets ourselves, but, please, don't puncture our tires."[7]

The war quickly came and went and the bicycle failed to get the opportunity to show its mettle in combat, although its friends did not forget it and continued to practice. Twenty-eight men of the New York National Guard conducted their own maneuvers on Long Island. The star performer was one Private Dixon, who rode one hundred miles in seven hours to deliver a message. According to one newspaper, these maneuvers amply proved that the bicycle could be an important factor in war—but it forgot to add, only in those areas where there were good roads, and provided, of course, that combat remained fluid and open.

Otherwise, things looked bad for the military cycle. The United States turned its back on the machine, although European nations continued to develop new cycles and to train troops. The early stages of the First World War, before it settled down to the stalemate of trench warfare, saw battalions of cycle troops rolling silently along the roads of Belgium and France. But that, too, ended, and the money and the time spent on bicycle troops was mostly wasted. Despite the ardor of the advocates of the military uses of the bicycle, there were no Billy Mitchells among them. The possibilities were foreclosed.

Real and Fanciful Uses

RIDING HIGH, BY ARTHUR PALMER, E. P. DUTTON, INC., 1956

Cartoons of 1896 showing the bicycle "applied." Some of the suggestions were more imaginative than practical.

Real and Fanciful Uses

Top: from saddle to bicycle seat—a new way of enforcing the law
Bottom: a new bicycle sleigh shown in *Scientific American,* 1897

BOTH: CULVER PICTURES, INC.

Real and Fanciful Uses

TOP, LEFT, MIDDLE, LEFT, AND BOTTOM BICYCLE INSTITUTE OF AMERICA

Real and Fanciful Uses

Top: from saddle to bicycle seat—a new way of enforcing the law
Bottom: A new bicycle sleigh shown in *Scientific American,* 1897

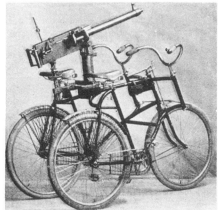

The bicycle prepared for war—it never got there.

BOTTOM: NEW YORK PUBLIC LIBRARY PICTURE COLLECTION

CHAPTER 13

"Goodbye and Hello"

THE ECLIPSE AND RESTORATION
OF THE BICYCLE

BALANCED
ON PEDAL

BICYCLE INSTITUTE OF AMERICA

The failure of the bicycle to live up to the glowing military predictions made by its fans seems to have been the signal that the craze was at an end. True, bicycle clubs continued to announce Sunday tours, and no fewer than fifty-three were out from New York City on June 4, 1899, but the bloom was off the rose. The portents were everywhere.

In the summer of 1899 the owners of electric automobiles were clamoring that they, too, should be admitted to Central Park and were threatening to go to court to force the issue. Furthermore, talk of organizing an American automobile club had reached the point where owners were meeting at the Waldorf-Astoria to draw up their plans. At their first gathering the group took two firm stands, one against the park commissioners and the second against automobile manufacturers who took orders for more vehicles than they could supply.

There were other little signs. In 1896 Miss Dunbar had made her reputation by posing for portraits of the "bicycle girl," but in 1899 pictures of the bicyclienne were giving way before those of the "automobile girl." The latter was said to have had a distinct advantage over her predecessor, because the girl in the electric runabout was always at ease and never flushed of face or disordered in dress, unlike her sister on the birotate chariot.

An equally ominous story came from Newport, where it was said that Miss Daisy Post, formerly a cyclist, was eliciting praise for the skill with which she handled her electric automobile. Running close competition with Miss Post was the wealthy and influential Mrs. Herman Oelrichs, and both were setting the style for the famous summer resort. As if all this were not enough, the newspapers began to print cartoons that showed warfare conducted from "horseless carriages" and polo being played from the same. And *Wheel Magazine* called the attention of cycling fans to the fact that the horseless carriage would supply the one

> desideratum which has even been lacking in the bicycle to make it an abso-
> lute success. The love-making possibilities that are shadowed forth in the
> horseless carriage will cause it to be the vehicle more favored by those
> sentimentally inclined than the bicycle can ever hope to be, since the
> riders' attention on the wheel has to be divided between love-making and
> speed-making.[1]

There were other shadows. *Outing* had begun its career as a publicity organ for cycling, but in 1900 it swallowed a long, hard swallow and declared that the future would belong to the automobile. Not that the bicycle was gone forever; it was simply that the craze had passed into "meritted eclipse," following which the machine could take its proper place as a part of the development of a great system of transportation.

The publication reported other visible evidence of decay. The fight to control racing had crippled the League of American Wheelmen and caused its membership to decline rapidly, while at the same time the cycling clubs had decreased both in numbers and activity. Newspapers and magazines reflected this diminished interest. The *New York Herald* of July 30, 1899, ran its bicycle news on a back page, along with notices of ship sailings.

By 1900 the bicycle was moribund. Four years later, in June, 1904, Abbott Bassett, perennial secretary of the LAW, conducted the post-mortem for *Harper's Weekly* and spoke the eulogy. Bassett reminisced about the coming of the ordinary and the safety bicycle, the advent of the pneumatic tire, and the first LAW-sponsored races in 1890. The veteran cyclist had memories, some not so old, of the 7,600 salesmen who had scoured the country "talking up the wheel," and the eighty-five journals devoted to cycling news. He remembered the fight for better roads and the struggle to force public carriers to transport cycles as personal baggage. Those were the happy memories.

Then came less happy ones. The expanding interurban railway system delivered people to rural areas with less effort than cycling and required no special costume for participation. Also, high society, ever fickle, had turned to other sports and thus deprived cycling of the attraction that comes from being able to emulate the wealthy.

But Bassett laid most of the blame for the bicycle's decline on the bicycle trust. Prior to the organization of the American Bicycle Company, there had been at least ninety-five bona fide bicycle makers whose salesmen were engaged in selling and publicizing the machines. Bicycle agencies were opened in almost every village, and lights sparkled at night along "bicycle rows" in the big cities. But after the trust was organized, emphasis shifted from sales to management. After all, a near-monopoly needed no emphasis on selling. The formation of the trust was followed, said Bassett, by the dismissal of salesmen and the curbing of advertising in the cycling journals and papers. This in turn led to the collapse of cycling papers and magazines, since they had been deprived of the financial support of advertisers. Newspapers, left with partially empty tills, decreased their coverage of cycling events. The League of American Wheelmen stopped publishing its own journal, thus depriving the cycling fraternity of its rallying point and further eroding the spirit of comradeship. With that gone, membership declined and the cycling boom subsided. Of course, Bassett failed to explain why cycling continued to thrive in Europe, without cycling papers and magazines and rallying points.

Whatever the causes, the great craze ebbed, and "My Merry Oldsmobile" replaced "A Bicycle Built for Two" on the sheet-music shelves in the department stores. It was easy to get on the automobile bandwagon. General Greeley, that powerful and vocal advocate of the military bicycle, was just as zealous a publicist for the automobile, although he admitted that most experiments in this country with the military car had been failures. Postmasters tried the new machine for collecting the mail, and it was predicted that the horseless carriage would double the range of rural mail delivery. It was alleged that the auto would speed ambulance service and expedite commercial deliveries. Waldon Fawcett told the readers of *Woman's Home Companion* that the electric runabout would become an immediate hit with the ladies. Even he could not anticipate that the internal combustion engine would drive the electrics from the streets and deprive women of the social equality the bicycle had given them.

History was almost repeating itself. Dr. William Howard became alarmed over the "speed mania" that had affected motorists by 1905 and condemned the fact that children were "literally whirled through the world at an age when their nervous systems need quiet and normal development."[2] He went on to say that women, who he said could not tolerate rivalry, had begun to provoke their husbands into senseless speed and recklessness, something that could not be said for the bicycle. He also contended that the "constant use of auto-machines" by schoolboys would destroy their ability to concentrate.

And as if coming a full circle, Professor Frederic Sutton, a fan of the steam-driven automobile, announced that he had driven two thousand miles and had never stampeded a horse. However, he admitted that whenever he encountered one of the beasts, he subjected the animal to the closest scrutiny, and if "he seems nervous and shy, I stop at the side of the road and speak to him. . . . For women and children I usually get out and help by leading the horse."[3]

Yet although the big bicycle boom slowly died, the list of advances, technological and otherwise, laid at the feet of the cycle industry is long. It was the first industry of any size to resort to assembly-line techniques for mass-producing vehicles. Further, the cycle makers were pioneers in testing their products and their improvements in metallurgy were described as "little short of revolutionary."

The industry was the primary developer of machines to carry out small operations. Bicycle makers were the first to experiment with variable-speed gears, the shaft-driven wheel, improved ball bearings, and the extensive use of lightweight steel tubing. The cycle industry was the first maker of vehicles to develop satisfactory brakes. The bicycle was the first machine to be equipped with dynamos to provide electric lights at night. And last but by no means least, the industry was responsible for the invention and perfection of the tubeless pneumatic tire.

Albert Pope, the Spaulding brothers, A. H. Overman, and their colleagues were pioneers in the initiation of new sales techniques that were destined to be seized upon and exploited by other manufacturers. The bicycle industry was the first to establish an extensive sales force and to set up an equalized freight rate for the nation as a whole, and it was among the earliest to offer guarantees for their machines. In addition, the cycle makers created the system of planned obsolescence to stimulate sales, the idea of concealing models until they could be unveiled at the cycle shows, and the ballyhoo and the hard sell that were later a part of the automobile business.

It was in the area of publicity for improved roads that cyclists made one of their greatest contributions. Financed and encouraged by the makers, the fans of the wheel were chiefly responsible in the nineties for the drive to upgrade both city streets and country highways. One is tempted to suggest that if they had made no other, this would have been a sufficient bequest to the nation. Indeed, the LAW changed its name after 1900 to the American Road Makers and then to the American Road Builders Association and kept up the good fight. It hoped that automobile owners would espouse the cause, and they did. However, the motorcar was a thoroughly aristocratic vehicle in its infancy, a rich man's toy, and improving highways for the wealthy was not as attractive a proposition as it was in the days when thousands praised the bicycle as an engine of democracy. Nevertheless, the road-improvement program would continue to roll on the impetus given it by the cyclists.

Cycle touring produced other contributions to the present. The cyclists first made and used road maps, first issued regular reports on road conditions, first listed approved hotels and taverns for travelers, and first developed road signs and traffic signals. Furthermore, the very numbers of cyclists were responsible for forcing a drastic overhaul of the traffic-control systems of American cities and bringing some order out of the chaos that reigned in the nation's streets.

The sociological consequences of the bicycle boom are more difficult to trace than its technological contributions, and like all residual effects of the mania, they have a tendency to be obscured by the rise of the automobile. Nonetheless, the bicycle was the first machine to prove a serious threat to the American practice of regular Sunday church attendance. To be sure, the expanding interurban system did its share, but ministers of the Gospel during the nineties did not attack the streetcar; instead they aimed their choicest strictures and their heaviest condemnation at the cyclists. Not until the 1900's, after the motorcar underwent its own production revolution to become a mass-consumed vehicle, did that vehicle encounter the anathemas formerly hurled at the wheel.

In all probability the most lasting social consequence of the bicycle craze was the effect it had on American women. Most of them did not ride bicycles during the nineties, but those who did were outspoken advocates for what they called the "new woman," who wanted to dress as she pleased, to take a position of equality with men, and not to be treated as a hothouse plant. The drive to wear "rational dress" in the 1890's might be considered quite innocuous in light of the sometimes silly costumes the bicyclettes affected, but to discard the bustle, eliminate multiple petticoats, and get rid of yard upon heavy yard of heavy blue serge material was a much greater blow in behalf of the emancipation of women than taking off a brassière.

Yet despite these advances, the bicycle was rapidly reduced to the level of a child's toy as Americans rushed headlong into their love affair with the automobile. Twenty years slipped by, the doughboys marched down Fifth Avenue to the strains of "Over There," and only the professional six-day riders were left to remind the public that the cycle was still a sporting machine.

During the Roaring Twenties the bicycle made little noise. There was a modest upswing in production in the middle of the period, but it amounted to less than a third of the output of 1899. Even then the cycle did not return to its former urban strongholds but found most acceptance in the new suburbs, where children and women constituted the most important members of the cycling caste. For that matter, the strongest centers of cycling were the women's colleges, and Smith and Wellesley became famous for their cycling students.

Without question the twenties belonged to the Model T, the Marmon, the Hupmobile, the Willys-Knight, and the other automobiles that rolled out of the factories of Detroit. Consequently, when Miss Margaret Fish called for cycle paths so those with "nervous depression" brought on by lack of exercise would have someplace to ride, she was largely ignored. Mrs. Sherman Woodward anticipated the future by pleading that Central Park be opened to cyclists and closed to automobiles after the rush hours. Such a regulation would create a "heavenly oasis of quiet and peace, free from carbon monoxide."[4] She too was ignored. And in 1930 the Newburgh Wheelmen's Club disbanded after a continuous existence of forty-four years. Its members had given up hope that a revival of cycling would come in their lifetimes.

And with good reason, for there were few to bewail the passing of the bicycle. The country was too involved with the price of Atwater-Kent Radio stock, not to mention the thousands of others whose value had climbed to astronomical heights on the call boards of the Stock Exchange. Then came those bleak, shattering days of October, 1929, followed by the dark months during which it was alleged that one could not walk down Wall Street without being struck by a falling banker.

And then there was a bicycle revival. The next several years were grim for the automobile, but not for its erstwhile competitor. The wheel was returning to public favor. E. L. Yordan, writing for *The New York Times*, reported in 1935 that ten cycle factories were busier than they had been in the previous twenty-five years and had manufactured over 600,000 bicycles that year. Chicago was said to be the center for the revival, with 250,000 cyclists, give or take a few thousand, and Los Angeles and Minneapolis were already registering bicycles in the vain effort to halt the renascence of the bicycle thief. Yordan estimated that approximately 3,000,000 cyclists were abroad in the nation.

One newspaper reporter, L. H. Robbins, said that Americans had taken once again to the cycle because it was the most convenient means at hand to express their biological and spiritual dissatisfaction with the machine age. In 1936 over a million bicycles were sold. The bicycle appeared on New York's Fifth Avenue for the first time since the Gay Nineties. Ominously, the number of bicycle-related accidents climbed also, transcending five hundred a year in fatalities and fourteen thousand injured.

Other ghosts of the past crept back. Robert B. Morrison, a Jersey City architect and former captain of the Harlem Wheelmen, rode his high-wheeler across the George Washington Bridge in December, 1932. The hale and robust Mr. Morrison, dressed in knickerbockers and other garments appropriate to the olden days, was "gaped at" by the passing motorists. Bob Morrison did not mind, and his time of eighteen minutes was good for a sixty-three-year-old man. Two years later two bicycle relay teams crossed the country from San Francisco to New York City, one from each direction. One of the teams sped across the country in seven days, two hours, and fifty-one minutes, almost 430 miles a day on the average! However, one must keep in mind that the roads had improved considerably in the decades that separated the nineties from the thirties.

Then came the attack on Pearl Harbor and World War II. The bicycle was immediately seen as a partial solution to the problem of gasoline rationing, and the government encouraged bicycle makers to produce more. But it is significant that the production of all children's machines was halted, and these had accounted for 85 per cent of those produced in 1941. All of which suggests that the cycling revival in the thirties was a phenomenon confined predominantly to youngsters; in no way did it resemble the intoxication of the Gay-Nineties adult with the machine.

When the war was over, bicycle manufacturers went back to full production. An upswing in cycling was predicted on the assumption that war brides, especially those who came from Britain, would want to continue their cycling when they came to the United States. Production did go up, and by 1948 it was estimated that over twelve million bicycles were in use in the country, an increase of over 30 per cent from 1941. Two years later this estimate had jumped to nineteen million.

During the fifties cycling remained primarily an avocation of youth, although here and there an adult fan wrote to express his disgust with cities that catered only to the automobile and to complain over the lack of facilities for cycling. Foreign makers rushed into the competition for the American market, Dr. Paul Dudley White became the evangelist of health-through-cycling, and mail carriers in Kansas City experimented with the machine while beset by dogs and jeered at by little boys.

Then in the 1960's Americans, aroused by the congestion of automobiles in their cities, once again began to clamor for the expansion of restricted bicycle paths.

In 1966 the old League of American Wheelmen got a new lease on life, and the *Bulletin* was once more made available to cyclists. Furthermore, the great boost given cycling by health experts contributed to the increased attention that was lavished on the birotate chariot. And the growing awareness that the internal combusion engine was one of the prime sources of air pollution led ecologically oriented Americans to join health fans in an army of cyclers that by 1970 had become a vocal force in the country.

But to review the present program of organized cycling is to take a walk through the past. For example, there has been an enormous increase in demands for special paths for cyclists, just as there was at the height of the Gay Nineties craze. To assist in this work, the Bicycle Institute of America published a "how-to-do-it" kit for those who wanted help in organizing support and applying pressure to get bicycle paths for commuters. The kit, entitled "Pedal Power," instructed cyclists on how to set up commuter bicycle rides for publicity; gave sample comments from editorials and newspapers; contained a "Commuters Bill of Rights," and provided sample form letters to be sent to mayors and editors. In short, it was a most complete little packet of instructions on how to apply political and social pressure. The LAW could not have done it better at the peak of its power.

On the whole, this pressure has paid off handsomely. In 1966 the Federal Government took notice of the rebirth of the cycling phenomenon, and the Bureau of Outdoor Recreation granted over $367,000 to a dozen cities to be used in developing bicycle paths and trails. By 1970 the bureau was recommending fifty miles of cycle paths for every 100,000 city dwellers, and calling for the construction of another 100,000 miles of cycle paths in the ten years after 1970. However, most of the bicycle tracks seem to be products of state or local planning.

Presumably the drive for special roads for cyclists started in 1961 in Homestead, Florida, when Mr. and Mrs. George Fletcher began agitating for a special safety route for cyclists. One year later they realized their objective, and Dr. Paul Dudley White was on hand to dedicate the path, or bikeway, to use the term now generally applied throughout the nation.

By the late 1960's the new bike-path boom was on. Ohio has nearly five hundred miles of bikeways, and in May, 1970, over one thousand cyclists made the 210-mile trip through the Scioto River Valley between Columbus and Portsmouth. Wisconsin is especially proud of its 320-mile bikeway—the modern realization of an old dream—which passes through the rolling dairylands between Milwaukee and the Mississippi River. Or there is the "Mississippi Meander," a hundred and seventy miles along the Mississippi River south of St. Paul. For the hardier cyclist there is the "Gold Rush Ride" through the mother-lode country of California. Virginia has opened a multiple-use freeway with bicycle paths along the fringe. As yet, nobody has seriously broached the subject of a transcontinental system.

Somewhat the same thing is happening in the cities. That freewheeling city planner, Robert Moses, began laying out bicycle paths in New York City in the thirties, but his success was limited. In 1961 the metropolis had only half a hundred miles of such roads scattered among five boroughs. Then in the late 1960's the automobile was excluded from Central Park two evenings a week and from sunrise to sunset on the weekend. Not to be outdone, Chicago's Mayor Richard Daley called for an additional two hundred miles of bicycle routes to aid commuters.

The first working urban bikeway was planned and put into operation at Davis, California, home of a branch of that state's university. Visitors are amazed at the streams of bicycles that flow along special lanes. The campus itself is closed to automobile traffic during most of the day, and parking racks for bicycles are found everywhere. At one time the community had more bicycles than year-round residents.

The revival of cycling followed the past in other ways. During the late sixties it became chic to cycle. According to the *New York Times*, the "third annual cycling season" (!) got under way in May, 1969, with a champagne party, followed by a jet-set "bike Bash" in Central Park at a later date. After riding a while, the cyclists settled down to a picnic lunch of smoked scallops and lamp chops washed down with Bloody Marys and a good white wine. The curious who came to gape saw Gucci shoes and bicycle costumes by Yves Saint Laurent. It reminds one of the long-dead Michaux Club.

And all sorts of celebrities were seen awheel, just like in the good old days. Mrs. John F. Kennedy rode in the park before her remarriage. Mayor John Lindsay, Senator Jacob Javits, and many screen and television stars were all seen cycling at one time or another. Even David Dubinsky, that silver-haired elder statesman of the American labor movement, got back on a two-wheeler in memory of the days when he used a bicycle to court his wife. In fact, so many New Yorkers showed up in Central Park that the old bicycle patrol had to be revived. The volunteers, who wore red armbands, supervised cyclists and helped control traffic.

Cyclists now, as well as then, were sometimes scofflaws. An indignant pedestrian complained that he was "dicing with death at every corner on weekends" because of wheelmen who ran red stoplights and rode against traffic on one-way streets. He was not alone in protesting, but it also worked the other way around. One Boston cyclist suggested that in any collision between an automobile and a bicycle in a cycle lane, the driver of the car should automatically be held at fault. He pointed out that the likeliest offenders would be cab drivers, who should lose their licenses.

Coinciding with the new bicycle boom was a national upswing in bicycle thefts. A New Yorker who ran a rental business said that 60 per cent of his machines would be stolen in the course of a single year. He said weekends were a prime time for such thievery and that gangs of young men roamed Central Park, mugging the unwary for their bicycles. As if that were not enough, sixty-thousand-dollar truckload of cycles was stolen from a New York pier. These were ultimately traced to a warehouse, but 90 per cent of the machines so lost are never recovered.

One thing is new in the revived interest in cycling, and that, of course, is the ecological orientation. One *New York Times* reporter called for the creation of urban centers that were 80 per cent automobile-free. He contended that the problems of converting from autos to bicycles could be solved with a lightweight enclosure for cyclists to use in cold weather, better obedience of the traffic laws, and a more stringent enforcement of the laws against bicycle theft. The alternative, according to the reporter, was simple suffocation. With this in mind, demonstrations and parades in behalf of the bicycle as a nonpolluter have occurred in communities as far apart as Boston and Los Angeles, Portland and Miami.

Cycling Californians, remembering the oil slick stemming from a leak in an offshore oil well, argued that shifting to cycling would reduce the use of automobiles, thus making oil wells unnecessary, thus reducing the chances of having beaches covered with oil and dead birds and dead fish. Former Secretary of the Interior Stewart Udall told Chicagoans, "Putting the bicycle back in the city is 10 times more important than building the SST (supersonic transport.)"[5]

The well-wisher is tempted to see in the back-to-the-bicycle movement a total re-enactment of the past, history repeating itself. However, it appears that one important ingredient is missing in the cycling renaissance, the wide-eyed wonderment at the technological miracle. Automobiles go faster and farther, airplanes travel at a speed that exceeds that of sound, and rockets probe the inner reaches of the universe. Nevertheless, the thrill of controlling one's own machine has not disappeared. And today's cyclist, like his earlier counterpart, is still able

To skim the ground
Til the pulses bound
And the heart bursts into song![6]

NOTES

CHAPTER 1

1. *Minneapolis Tribune*, Jan. 11, 1896.
2. Eleventh Census of the United States, 1900, Vol. X, Pt. 1, p. 325.
3. *Harper's Weekly*, Aug. 23, 1890, p. 669.
4. Charles E. Pratt, *The American Bicycler* (n.d.), p. 20.
5. *Ibid.*, p. 30.
6. *Wheelman*, June, 1883, p. 194.
7. Edward Howland, "The Era of the Bicycle," *Harper's Monthly*, June, 1881, p. 283.

CHAPTER 2

1. *Scientific American*, May 2, 1891, p. 304.
2. *New York Journal*, Jan. 2, 1897.
3. *Minneapolis Tribune*, Oct. 26, 1890.
4. *Outing*, June, 1892, p. 56.
5. *Harper's Weekly*, Apr. 11, 1896, p. 358.
6. *Chicago Tribune*, June 21, 1896.
7. *Riverside Daily Enterprise*, Aug. 25, 1896.
8. *Scientific American*, Dec. 1, 1894, p. 346.
9. *Minneapolis Tribune*, Nov. 9, 1895.
10. *Ibid.*, June 12, 1896.
11. *Scientific American*, Jan. 12, 1895, p. 31.
12. *New York Herald*, June 30, 1897.
13. *Harper's Weekly*, July 24, 1897, pp. 747–48.
14. *Ibid.*, Oct. 2, 1897, p. 985.
15. *Outing*, Mar., 1900, p. 461.

CHAPTER 3

1. Quoted in *Minneapolis Tribune*, May 1, 1896.
2. *Ibid.*, Oct. 12, 1895.
3. *Ibid.*, Mar. 21, 1896. Italics added.
4. *Scientific American*, July 20, 1895, p. 43.
5. *New York Times*, Aug. 1, 1897.
6. *Minneapolis Tribune*, Sept. 7, 1895.
7. Quoted in *New York Times*, June 7, 1896.
8. *Riverside Daily Enterprise*, June 6, 1896.
9. Quoted in *Minneapolis Tribune*, Apr. 25, 1896.
10. *Ibid.*, Dec. 7, 1895.

CHAPTER 4

1. *Scientific American*, Jan. 12, 1895, p. 25.
2. *Chicago Tribune*, May 19, 1895.
3. *New York Herald*, June 13, 1897; June 27, 1897.
4. A. L. Benedict, "Dangers and Benefits of the Bicycle," *Century Magazine*, July, 1897, pp. 471–73.
5. *Scientific American*, July 1, 1893, p. 10.
6. *Riverside Daily Enterprise*, Aug. 16, 1896.
7. *Outing*, Aug., 1892, p. 98.
8. *Riverside Daily Enterprise*, Aug. 16, 1896.
9. *Minneapolis Tribune*, July 20, 1895.
10. *Boston Globe*, May 9, 1896.
11. *Minneapolis Tribune*, July 20, 1895.
12. J. B. Bishop, "Social and Economic Influence of the Bicycle," *Forum*, Aug., 1896, pp. 680–89.
13. *Ibid.*, p. 689.
14. *Chicago Tribune*, June 17, 1895.
15. *Ibid.*, July 17, 1896.
16. *New York Herald*, June 24, 1895.
17. *Chicago Tribune*, June 24, 1895.
18. *New York Herald*, June 17, 1895.
19. *Ibid.*, June 17, 1895.
20. *New York Tribune*, July 28, 1895.
21. *New York Herald*, Aug. 3, 1897.
22. *Chicago Tribune*, July 5, 1896.
23. *Ibid.*

24. *Outing*, Sept., 1893, p. 460.
25. *Minneapolis Tribune*, Aug. 17, 1895.
26. *Ibid.*, Mar. 12, 1894.
27. *Harper's Weekly*, Oct. 3, 1896, p. 937.
28. *Minneapolis Tribune*, June 6, 1896; May 29, 1897.
29. *Wheelman*, Dec., 1883, p. 192.
30. *Minneapolis Tribune*, Aug. 17, 1895.
31. *Boston Globe*, June 13, 1897.
32. Quoted in *Riverside Daily Enterprise*, July 26, 1896.

CHAPTER 5

1. Pratt, *loc. cit.*, pp. 182–83.
2. *Ibid.*, p. 110.
3. *Overland Magazine*, Aug., 1895, p. 128.
4. *New York Herald*, June 2, 1895.
5. *Outing*, Aug., 1891, p. 104.
6. *Ibid.*, Feb., 1892, p. 96.
7. *Ibid.*, June, 1892, p. 59.
8. *Ibid.*
9. *Minneapolis Tribune*, May 27, 1894.
10. *Ibid.*, Dec. 16, 1894.
11. *Ibid.*, June 1, 1895.
12. *Ibid.*, April 21, 1895.
13. *New York Times*, June 15, 1895.
14. *Minneapolis Tribune*, Dec. 16, 1894.
15. *New York Herald*, June 28, 1896.
16. *New York Times*, July 12, 1895.
17. *Minneapolis Tribune*, Sept. 21, 1895.
18. *Chicago Tribune*, July 31, 1895; June 8, 1895.
19. *Atlanta Constitution*, July 14, 1895.
20. *Minneapolis Tribune*, Aug. 10, 1895.
21. *Ibid.*, Dec. 7, 1895.
22. *Ibid.*, Aug. 31, 1895.
23. *Riverside Daily Enterprise*, Aug. 14, 1896.
24. *Harper's Weekly*, Oct. 3, 1896, p. 937.

CHAPTER 6

1. *Minneapolis Tribune*, Sept. 14, 1895.
2. *Scientific American*, June 27, 1896, p. 391.
3. Bishop, *op. cit.*, p. 685.
4. *Outing*, June, 1884, p. 223.
5. *New York Journal*, July 28, 1897.
6. *Riverside Daily Enterprise*, June 12, 1896.

CHAPTER 7

1. *New York Herald*, July 21, 1893.
2. *Outing*, May, 1892, p. 35.

CHAPTER 8

1. *New York Times*, Aug. 28, 1898.
2. *Harper's Weekly*, Apr. 11, 1896, p. 375.
3. *Outing*, Apr., 1891, p. 11.
4. *Minneapolis Tribune*, Aug. 18, 1894.
5. *Harper's Weekly*, Mar. 23, 1895, p. 286.
6. *Boston Globe*, May 2, 1895.
7. *Harper's Weekly*, Mar. 23, 1895, p. 286.
8. *Minneapolis Tribune*, Aug. 18, 1894.
9. *Ibid.*, Aug. 26, 1894.
10. *Ibid.*, Sept. 16, 1894.

CHAPTER 9

1. *Minneapolis Tribune*, Sept. 7, 1895.
2. Quoted in *ibid.*, Mar. 4, 1894.
3. *Ibid.*
4. *New York Times*, Oct. 3, 1897.
5. Quoted in Marshall W. Taylor, *The Fastest Bicycle Rider in the World* (1928), pp. 20–22.
6. *Minneapolis Tribune*, June 18, 1898.

CHAPTER 10

1. *Outing*, Dec., 1899, p. 326.
2. *Minneapolis Tribune*, May 11, 1895.
3. Stephen Crane, *Maggie* (1960), pp. 26–28.
4. *New York Journal*, June 5, 1897.
5. Pratt, *op. cit.*, p. 125.
6. *Minneapolis Tribune*, Sept. 8, 1895.
7. *New York Herald*, May 11, 1896.
8. *Ibid.*, June 9, 1897.
9. *Riverside Daily Enterprise*, July 10, 1896.
10. *Scientific American*, Aug. 3, 1895, p. 67.
11. *Chicago Tribune*, Aug. 1, 1897.
12. *Minneapolis Tribune*, June 3, 1894.
13. *Chicago Tribune*, Aug. 1, 1897.
14. *New York Herald*, May 23, 1895.
15. *New York Journal*, July 19, 1897.

CHAPTER 11

1. *Outing*, Apr., 1891, p. 12.
2. Archer Hulbert, *Pioneer Roads and Travelers*, Vol. II (1904), p. 181.
3. *Ibid.*
4. *Minneapolis Tribune*, Oct. 5, 1895.
5. *Outing*, Oct., 1892, pp. 7–10.
6. *New York Herald*, Apr. 21, 1895.
7. *Outing*, May, 1892, p. 37.
8. *Los Angeles Times*, July 19, 1897.
9. Quoted in *Minneapolis Tribune*, Feb. 29, 1896.
10. *Chicago Tribune*, June 14, 1896.
11. *Minneapolis Tribune*, Apr. 20, 1896.
12. *Ibid.*, May 30, 1896.
13. *Ibid.*, May 28, 1893.
14. *Chicago Tribune*, Aug. 5, 1897.

CHAPTER 12

1. Albert Ordway, *Cycle-Infantry Drill Regulations* (1892), pp. 50–51.
2. *Ibid.*
3. Howard A. Giddings, *Manual for Cyclists* (1898), p. 98.
4. *Ibid.*, passim.
5. *Ibid.*, p. 43.
6. *Minneapolis Tribune*, Apr. 17, 1898.
7. *Ibid.*, July 14, 1898.

CHAPTER 13

1. Quoted in *Minneapolis Tribune*, Oct. 5, 1895.
2. William L. Howard, "Speed Mania," *Saturday Evening Post*, Sept. 30, 1905, as quoted in R. Brosseau and R. Andrist (eds.), *Looking Forward* (1970), p. 156.
3. Brosseau and Andrist, p. 159.
4. *New York Times*, May 12, 1928.
5. *Bicycle Institute of America*, "Boom in Bikeways," Vol. 5, No. 3, p. 3.
6. *Minneapolis Tribune*, Apr. 25, 1896.

BIBLIOGRAPHY

BOOKS

Beebe, Lucius, *The Big Spenders*. Doubleday, 1966.
Brosseau, Ray, and Andrist, Ralph, eds., *Looking Forward*. American Heritage Press, 1970.
Clementson, George B., *The Road Rights and Liabilities of Wheelmen*. Callaghan and Co., 1895.
Crane, Stephen, *Maggie*. Premier Books, 1960.
Giddings, Howard A., *Manual for Cyclists*. Pope Manufacturing Co., 1898.
Hulbert, Archer, *Pioneer Roads and Travelers*, Vol. II. A. H. Clark, 1904.
Maxim, Hiram, *Horseless Carriage Days*. Harper and Brothers, 1937.
Nevins, Allan, and Ford, Frank E., *Ford*. Scribner's, 1963.
Ordway, Albert, *Cycle-Infantry Drill Regulations*. Pope Manufacturing Co., 1892.
Pierce, Bessie, *As Others See Chicago*. University of Chicago, 1933.
Post, Emily, *By Motor to the Golden Gate*. D. Appleton and Co., 1916.
Pratt, Charles E., *The American Bicycler*, n.d.
Sears, Roebuck and Co., *Consumers Guide for 1897*. 1968 Edition.
Still, Bayrd, *Mirror for Gotham*. New York University, 1956.
Taylor, Marshall W., *The Fastest Bicycle Rider in the World*. Wormless Publishing Co., 1928.
United States Government, *Eleventh Census of the United States*, Vol. X, Pt. 1.
———, *Foreign Relations of the United States*, Pt. 2., 1895

PERIODICALS

In addition to the general files of *Harper's Weekly Magazine*, *Harper's Monthly Magazine*, *Wheel-man Magazine*, *Wheelman and Outing Magazine*, *Outing Magazine*, *Scribner's Magazine*, *Century Magazine*, *Overland Magazine*, *Forum Magazine* and *Scientific American Maga-zine*, the following special articles were used.
Allen, T. G., and W. L. Sachtleben, "Across Asia on a Bicycle." *Century Magazine*, Vol. 26, (May–October, 1894), pp. 83–98, 181–196, 389–400, 521–538, 685–701, 915–925.
"Annual Bicycle Exhibition at Madison Square Garden." *Scientific American*, Feb. 1, 1896, p. 66.
"Annual Bicycle Show at Madison Square Garden." *Scientific American*, Jan. 26, 1901, p. 57.
"Annual Cycle and Automobile Exhibition." *Scientific American*, Feb. 11, 1899, pp. 89–90.
"Annual Bicycle Exhibition at the Grand Central Palace." *Scientific American*, Feb. 20, 1898, pp. 122–123; Feb. 27, 1898, pp. 138–139.
Barton, S. M., "Evolution of the Wheel—Velocipede to Motorcycle." *Sewanee Review*, Jan., 1897, pp. 48–62.
Bassett, Abbott, "Outdoor Season—Revival of Cycling." *Harper's Weekly Magazine*, June 11, 1904, pp. 906–907.
Baxter, Sylvester, "Economic and Social Influences of the Bicycle." *Arena*, Oct., 1892, pp. 578–583.
Benedict, A. L., "Dangers and Benefits of the Bicycle." *Century Magazine*, July, 1897, pp. 471–473.
"Bicycle Artillery." *Scientific American*, Dec. 28, 1901, p. 21735.
"Bicycle Brakes." *Scientific American*, May 3, 1902, pp. 22016–22017.
"Bicycle Relay Race Across the Continent." *Scientific American*, Sept. 19, 1896, pp. 680–689.
"Brooklyn's Big Bicycle Parade." *Harper's Weekly Magazine*, June 29, 1895, p. 604.
Bruce, R., "Bicycle Side-path Building in 1900." *Outing Magazine*, May, 1900, pp. 182–184.
"Charm of the Bicycle." *Scientific American*, May 13, 1899, p. 292.
"Chicago Bicycle Show." *Scientific American*, Feb. 6, 1897, p. 83.
"Club-run Luncheon." *Harper's Weekly Magazine*, June 15, 1895, p. 568.

Cushing, H. A., "Moderns Awheel." *Harper's Weekly Magazine*, Apr. 11, 1896, p. 353.

Desgranges, Henri, "The Safety Bicycle as It Now Is and Its Probable Future." *Scientific American*, Jan. 12, 1895, p. 22.

Dickinson, R. L., "Bicycling for Women: The Puzzling Question of Costume." *Outlook*, Apr. 25, 1896, pp. 751–752.

———, "Bicycling for Women: Some Hygenic Aspects of Wheeling." *Outlook*, Mar. 28, 1896, pp. 550–553.

"Effects of Bicycle Boom on Trade." *Scientific American*, June 27, 1896, p. 407.

"Etiquette of the Road." *Harper's Weekly Magazine*, Oct. 3, 1896, p. 973.

Garrigues, Henry J., "Woman and the Bicycle." *Forum*, Jan., 1896, pp. 576–587.

Gideon, George D., "Defence of the Two-class System in Bicycle Racing." *Harper's Weekly Magazine*, Mar. 23, 1895, p. 286.

Goullet, Alfred T., and McGuirk, Charles J., "The Infernal Grind." *Saturday Evening Post*, May 29, 1926, pp. 18–19, 174–180.

"Grotesque Forms of Cycles." *Scientific American*, Dec. 30, 1899, pp. 421–422.

"Half a Century in the Development of the Bicycle." *Scientific American*, Feb. 10, 1900, pp. 88–89.

Hillier, G. Lacey, "Use of the Cycle for Military Purposes." *Longmans*, Vol. X, pp. 268–275.

"History of the Bicycle." *Scientific American*, May 13, 1899, p. 298.

Holder, C. F., "California Cycleway." *Scientific American*, July 14, 1900, p. 27.

Howland, Edward, "A Bicycle Era." *Harper's Monthly Magazine*, Vol. 63, pp. 281–286.

Hubert, P. G., "Bicycle; The Wheel of Today." *Scribner's Magazine*, June, 1895, pp. 692–702.

Jacobsen, P. N., "The Detroit Wheelmen." *Outing Magazine*, Vol. XVIII, p. 35.

"Kyphosis Bicyclistarum, A Deformation Caused by Bicycling." *Scientific American*, July 1, 1893, p. 10.

"Lenz's World Tour Awheel." *Outing Magazine*, Vol. XXIV, pp. 284, 360, 342; Vol. XXV, pp. 35, 152; Vol. XXVI, pp. 224–467; Vol. XXVII, pp. 51–467; Vol. XXVIII, pp. 47–456; Vol. XXIX, pp. 57–267.

"Michaux Bicycling Club." *Harper's Weekly Magazine*, Jan. 19, 1895, pp. 63–64.

"Mile in Less than a Minute on a Bicycle." *Scientific American*, July 15, 1899, pp. 41–42.

"Monument to the Inventors of the Bicycle Pedal." *Scientific American*, Nov. 10, 1894, p. 317.

Mott, Alfred, "Racing Side of Bicycling." *Harper's Weekly Magazine*, Apr. 11, 1896, p. 366.

"National Cycle Show in Madison Square Garden." *Scientific American*, Feb. 2, 1895, pp. 66–67; Feb. 9, 1895, p. 81.

"New Army Bicycles." *Scientific American*, Feb. 8, 1896, p. 91.

"New Military Folding Bicycle." *Scientific American*, Oct. 20, 1900, p. 244.

Parker, George F., "American Bicycles in England." *North American*, Dec., 1896, pp. 688–695.

Potter, Isaac, "Bicycle Outlook." *Century Magazine*, Sept., 1896, pp. 785–790.

———, "Bicycle's Relation to Good Roads." *Harper's Weekly Magazine*, Apr. 11, 1896, p. 362.

Pratt, Charles E., "American Cycling and Its Founder." *Outing Magazine*, Vol. XVIII, p. 342.

———, "Legislation on Cycling on Highways." *Outing Magazine*, Vol. X, p. 157.

———, "A Sketch of American Bicycling." *Outing Magazine*, Vol. I, pp. 343–347.

Prial, F. P., "Cycling in the United States." *Harper's Weekly Magazine*, Aug. 30, 1890, p. 72.

"Rail Fence Bicycle Railway." *Scientific American*, Apr. 16, 1892, p. 247.

"Ravages of the Bicycle Craze." *Scientific American*, June 20, 1896, p. 391.

Richardson, B. W., "How Cycling Injures Health." *Review of Reviews*, Apr., 1890, pp. 287–288.

———, "What to Avoid in Cycling." *North American*, Aug., 1895, pp. 177–186.

Roosevelt, J. W., "A Doctor's View of Bicycling." *Scribner's Magazine*, June, 1895, pp. 708–713.

"Round the World on Bicycles." *Harper's Weekly Magazine*, Jan., 1893, p. 46.

Townsend, J. B., "Cycle Touring." *Harper's Weekly Magazine*, Apr. 11, 1896, p. 354.

———, "The Social Side of Cycling." *Scribner's Magazine*, June, 1895, pp. 704–708.

Wells, H. G., "The Cyclist Soldier." *Fortnightly*, Dec., 1900, pp. 914–928.

Wheeler, Christopher, "Meet of the Keystone Wheelmen, 1890." *Outing Magazine*, May, 1891, pp. 137–141.

Williams, H. S., "The Bicycle in Relation to Health." *Harper's Weekly Magazine*, Apr. 11, 1896, p. 370.

NEWSPAPERS

Atlanta Constitution
Boston Globe
Chicago Tribune
Los Angeles Times
Minneapolis Tribune

New York Herald
New York Journal
New York Times
Riverside (Cal.) *Daily Enterprise.*

INDEX